Return

Date | D

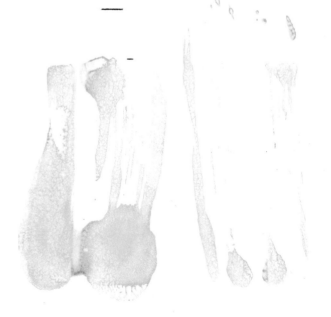

PERSONALITY, POWER, AND POLITICS

PERSONALITY, POWER, AND POLITICS

*A
Social Psychological Analysis
of the
Italian Deputy
and His
Parliamentary System*

GORDON J. DiRENZO

UNIVERSITY OF NOTRE DAME PRESS

NOTRE DAME — LONDON

Table of Contents

v

APPENDICES

List of Tables

List of Charts

Acknowledgments

THIS STUDY WAS realized with the co-operation and assistance of a host of people. It is a pleasant duty to record here—unfortunately, all too inadequately—my debt of gratitude to these associates and friends.

The Italian Government, through the Institute of International Education, provided a research grant for me to spend the academic year 1960–1961 in Italy. Hospitality at the University of Rome was extended graciously by Professor Vittorio Castellano, director of the Research Center of Empirical Sociology, the facilities of which were placed at my disposal. The faculty and staff of the Center tendered many kindnesses. I wish to acknowledge particularly, in this respect, the helpful discussions and suggestions offered by my American colleague, Professor Alfred McClung Lee of Brooklyn College, who at the time was serving as visiting Fulbright professor of sociology at the University.

Professor Franco Ferrarotti of the Institute of Sociology of the University of Rome, and former member of Parliament, generously devoted much of his time to advise about the design of the study and to assist in numerous ways throughout the field-work phases of the research process. Assistance in the translation of the research instruments was given graciously by Professor Pier Giovanni Grasso, director of the Institute of Psychology of the Salesian University in Rome.

Professor Milton Rokeach of Michigan State University was most co-operative in advising about the administration of his Dogmatism Scale as the personality inventory which is employed in this study. Acknowledgment in this regard is due also to Dr. Rolf Schulze for his development of an abbreviated version of the Rokeach Dogmatism Scale. Valuable assistance in the standardization and the validation of the personality instrument was given by Professor Luigi Meschieri, director of the Institute of Psychology of the Italian National Research Council. Doctors Bruno Celli and Eraldo De Grada of the Institute assisted in other preliminary phases of the research.

Several other professional colleagues provided, through correspondence, information and materials that were of significant use in this study. In particular these are Professors Theodore W. Adorno, Gordon W. Allport, Flavia Zaccone Derossi, Alex Inkeles, Joseph LaPalombara, Daniel J. Levinson, Leonard W. Moss, Richard Christie, and Arnold M. Rose. Mr. Alex Fanelli, formerly regional director of the United States Information Service in Rome, performed several personal courtesies and made available the use of his sociological library.

The following American journalists serving as correspondents in Rome receptively briefed me on the nature of the current political situation in Italy: Mr. Jack Casserly, formerly of the Hearst papers; Mr. Barrett McGurn of the *New York Herald-Tribune;* and Mr. Leo Wollemborg of the *Washington Post.*

Assistance for the interviewing phase of the research proc-

ess was given most generously by the following: Caterina
De Grandes Bartoli, Pasquale Calcagni, Massimo Ceccotti,
Romania De Franceschi, Giancarlo Porsi, Flavio Russino, and
Antonio Vasto. Grateful acknowledgment is given similarly to
the several student pollsters from the University of Rome who
gathered the data for the control group.

Special appreciation is due to the staff of the Notre Dame
Center of Rome, and most especially to its director, Mr.
Vincent G. McAloon, for the innumerable contributions of
resourceful assistance to this study, as well as for the cordial
hospitality throughout my stay in Rome. My two secretarial
assistants, Mrs. Luciana Hankin and Miss M. Stella Avarello,
skillfully performed their duties, and their personal ingenuity
added much to the project.

The Tektronix Corporation of Portland, Oregon, kindly
awarded, through the University of Portland Foundation, a
small research grant to make possible the tabulation and statistical elaboration of the research data, and provided as well
the use of its data processing and computing facilities. My
appreciation in this regard goes particularly to Mr. Bjorn Heg-
lie of the Corporation for the technical assistance which he
rendered so enthusiastically; and to Rev. William A. Botzum,
C.S.C., assistant dean of the Graduate School, University of
Notre Dame, for his suggestions and assistance with the statistical analysis.

A most particular debt of gratitude is recorded to the many
members of the Chamber of Deputies of the Italian Parliament who participated as subjects in this study. Each freely
devoted his time, not only to be interviewed but also to be
helpful in many other ways. It is regretted that they must
remain anonymous in this acknowledgment of their cordial
reception and co-operation. I am grateful also to the personnel
of the Chamber, and to the secretariats of the political parties
represented in Parliament, for their friendly assistance and

kindnesses in arranging interviews with the political subjects.

One man has been very closely associated with this project throughout its entire course. To Professor William V. D'Antonio, chairman of the Department of Sociology of the University of Notre Dame, a singular expression of appreciation is offered for his wise guidance, patient support at every turn, and many personal kindnesses.

For assistance in the presentation of this volume, I am grateful to the staff of the University of Notre Dame Press, and especially to Mr. John Ehmann, editor, for his very kind and patient efforts.

A special word of gratitude is recorded for Miss Mary K. Ryan, who contributed in many personal ways to this project, and in particular for her assistance in the preparation of the index.

To all these people, and to the many others whose contributions regretfully have not been acknowledged specifically, I express my most sincere appreciation for their gracious co-operation and assistance.

G. J. D.

Notre Dame, Indiana
April, 1967

This book is dedicated
with affection and gratitude
to my grandparents
SANTO AND JULIA DIRENZO
who, in so many ways, made it possible,
and through whom I learned to love Italy and its people.

CHAPTER I

Personality and Politics

THE STUDY of social behavior must confront the study of the human person. No analysis of a social system can be complete without an examination of the person who participates in and maintains that social system. As Fromm tells us, "To understand the dynamics of the social process we must understand the dynamics of the psychological processes operating within the individual, just as to understand the individual we must see him in the context of the culture which molds him."[1] This is no less true for the study of political behavior. Any analysis of politics and political behavior ultimately must face the question of political man—his nature and his functional relationship to such behavior.

Within the past several years, social research has suggested an intimate relationship between personality and political behavior—in fact, that to an extent political behavior is a function of personality. Considerable evidence has also been offered that ideologies and beliefs—both aspects of personality

1

—influence the type of political structure, organization, and government that one may prefer. The work of Adorno and his associates[2] was one of the first studies to show that personality and psychological dynamics are related intimately with concrete political attitudes. Several later studies have reported personality relationships with participation and interest in political behavior[3] as well as with ideological preferences[4] and voting patterns.[5]

The relationship between politics and human character has been recognized as a major problem since classical Greek thought.[6] As Lane points out:

> Plato (*Republic*) dealt with the problem of instilling in youth the qualities of character necessary for effective citizenship; Aristotle (*Politics*) remarked on the necessity of fitting the constitution of a city to the character of the people; Hobbes (*Leviathan*) dealt with the question of national character and personality, under the heading "the interiour beginnings of voluntary motions commonly called the passions; and the speeches by which they are expressed"; and John Stuart Mill wrote: ". . . political machinery does not act of itself. As it is first made, so it has to be worked by men, and even by ordinary men. It needs not their simple acquiescence, but their active participation; and must be adjusted to the capacities and qualities of such men as are available."[7]

Sociological studies of political man up to this time have been confined mainly to research into the social backgrounds of decision-makers.[8] Even these studies have tended generally to be very limited in scope by considering only a few variables, such as age, sex, education, occupation, religion, experience, and ethnic backgrounds.[9]

The principal reason for this interest in social backgrounds, of course, has been to obtain a better understanding of the behavior of decision-makers in office and a greater insight into their decisions.[10] On the basis of this kind of research the political decision-makers have been located in the social structure, and the association of social background characteristics with the acceptance of political ideology and political party affiliation has been demonstrated.[11] Moreover, studies of this nature have been used to gain an understanding of the *cursus honorum* of the politician under the assumption that social backgrounds reveal much about social development and orientations, as well as the facilities and opportunities that have been instrumental in acquiring political office. It is known from these studies that social backgrounds influence both opportunities and political skills, and thus the degree of political success.

PERSONALITY AND POLITICAL MAN

It is necessary, of course, to specify the social backgrounds of those holding the power for decision-making and the routes to such positions. The utility of these studies is not questioned, but to confine sociological research to this area is to make political man and political behavior the epiphenomena of social backgrounds and social characteristics. Much interest has been devoted to determining *who* these people are, but little has been given to determining *what* they do.[12] Moreover, very little is known about *why* people seek and hold positions of power, and *how* they use these positions. Knowledge about social characteristics and social backgrounds is not in itself sufficiently enlightening for these questions. As Bendix and Lipset state, all such studies subscribe to an "elite theory" of politics:

> To know who these power wielding individuals are is thought to be sufficient; it is a secondary matter to inquire into how they use their power. That they will do so in their own interests is self-evident, and the nature of that interest is inferred from the status which they occupy. Hence, social and economic status rather than the competing strategies of the political struggle are regarded as the sufficient causes of political decisions.[13]

In this view, social characteristics become the main variables that determine political behavior, and the political decision-makers are guided by the values and the interests of their social backgrounds. This approach may be too simple. Missing is the consideration of individual interest and personal motives; about this Lane offers the following comment:

> Explanations of political decisions which rely wholly upon analyses of the social environment, while they may have high predictive value, neglect a vital link: they never explain why an individual responds to the environment the way he does. Such purely external analysis tends to presume that the two individuals behaving in the same way in a given situation are responding identically. But as seen from inside out, from the point of view of the individuals, the forces to which they respond may be quite dissimilar. For example, our analysis shows that persons rated as authoritarians according to one attitude scale, vote in about the same proportions as those rated as equalitarians. But the equalitarians respond to a sense of civic duty, to conscience, while the authoritarians respond to the pressure of their social groups to act conventionally, and possibly also to a desire to exercise a small degree of political power.[14]

Another criticism of the social backgrounds approach has been made by Rossi. His following statement perhaps best reaches the point which we are trying to make here:

> But the consideration of how an issue, or even issues, are viewed by decision-makers, has not been given much attention in the studies of the decision-making process within the community context. The decision-maker is almost regarded as having no "internal" dynamics of his own but is "ruled by his own group affiliations and interaction patterns."[15]

Only minor attention has been given to the personality of the professional politician. While some limited study has been done relating to personality traits of politicians,[16] this research has focused primarily on those traits, capacities, and skills thought to be suitable or ideal for effective leadership—regardless of specific types of leadership or its particular domain. That is to say, the concern has centered on psychological qualities and personality for leadership in general rather than on political leadership as a more specific type. The basic assumption in much of this research is that the same personality qualities are required and are suitable for a leader in whatever situation.

The general problem is that in nearly all research on the relationship of personality and occupations, the stress has been placed on personality traits, capacities, and skills. This research, therefore, has been restricted in that it is based upon a faulty conception of personality. Personality is not merely the sum of the individual's personality traits; rather it is a complex entity with its own unique structure and organization that must be seen essentially as a system. As with any kind of system there is necessarily content (beliefs, ideologies, values, attitudes, motives, drives, psychodynamics, emotions, temperament, abilities, capacities, and so forth), but the neglected and the more important aspect which gives the personality system its uniqueness is the element of *structure*. No concern has been given to the general personality type or over-all personality structure that characterizes the professional politician (the political decision-maker). Matthews comments as follows on this matter:

> But the principal weakness of this type of research is that it is based on a misleading conception of human personality. Personality is not the sum of the traits of which it is made. To assume this is ". . . to ignore one of the fundamental properties of personality, its possession of *organization*. The same 'trait' will function differently in personalities which are organized differently . . . It is only when attention is paid to arrangement or position that organization, as such, can be brought into account." The trait approach completely ignores this important fact.[17]

Research with this kind of orientation has been especially lacking in the sphere of political behavior. Perhaps little doubt exists that personality influences the way roles are performed, but many social scientists seem reluctant "to entertain the hypothesis that personality factors enter *systematically* as significant influences in the performance of whole sets of roles such as those of the occupational realm, the kinship system, or the political order."[18] Social scientists have described many of the roles involved in political participation, but as Lasswell states, "The study of political roles has not been planned or extended to the consideration of the total personality structure of the politician, or its developmental history."[19] Apparently political scientists in particular usually evince a considerable degree of skepticism about the possibility of arriving at a useful conception of the impact of personality on politics.[20]

We are fundamentally concerned in this study with distinguishing a general personality type that characterizes the professional politician. And in this context we intend to ask what significance this has for the functioning of political systems. We accept as a general proposition the position that any profession[a] is apt to be marked by a relative concentration of certain kinds of personalities.[21] This assertion is based upon the hypothesis that certain personality types tend to be attracted and/or recruited to particular professions in a differential rather than in a random or unsystematic fashion, and to be so disproportionately present as to constitute modal personality types for these occupations. There is some empirical evidence to substantiate this position.[22] The tentatively plausible explanation for this situation is that there is a congruent relationship between the personality and the profession which is functional for the social system and psychologically gratifying for the individual.

This hypothetical principle suggests that personality would be a potent factor in the choice of politics as a profession. It would follow that political activity could have nonpolitical functions for those individuals who are involved actively in

[a] The term "profession" is used generically for such designations as occupation, vocation, career, job, work, and so forth.

politics. That is to say, there may be a nonpolitical nature to political motives and political behavior. Political activity, as with any other form of human activity, may be used to serve a variety of purposes and wants—physical as well as psychological. We may ask, then, what are the psychological motives underlying the desire for a political career. Does politics offer a particular appeal to certain individuals because of any psychological qualities that it may have? Thus, we propose to determine whether or not there can be distinguished a political man in the sense of a distinct personality type. As Lane states, "The idea of a distinctive type of person, political man, is attractive in many ways: if there were such a type, it would do much to clarify the problems of leadership selection, circulation of elites, and so forth."[23]

POWER AND POLITICS

Dahl has made the most recent conceptual statement on this question by producing a dichotomy of *homo civicus* (civic man) and *homo politicus* (political man). It is an error to confuse civic man with political man. *Homo politicus* is created out of the apolitical *homo civicus*, who is not by nature a political animal.[24] All people do—and must—live in social systems, but many do not actively participate, nor are they interested, in the political life of society. Only a minority of any general population comprises its active political stratum. This is a situation which seems to be nearly universal, at least in democratic societies. Why is it so? Dahl asserts that with all the insightful speculation throughout man's history, not much can be said confidently about the factors that create *homo politicus* out of *homo civicus*. He ventures that presumably political activity is discovered as a powerful source of gratifications. Therefore, political man seeks to gain and to maintain control over government policies, and thus necessarily over government officials, and consequently over voters wherever officials are elected.[25]

More particularly, however, several statements have been made in which political man is presented essentially as a power-oriented and power-seeking individual. This view dates back to Spranger, who contended that every personality is characterized by the dominance of a cultural value, of which he distinguished six: science, wealth, art, love, power, and religion.[26] This arrangement yielded a classification of six basic types of men. Power became the dominant or supreme value for the "political type" of man, of whom Spranger wrote, "The purely political type makes all value regions of life serve his will to power."[27] Accordingly, in this perspective the political type of man is also Machiavellian.

The most extensive writings on the concept of *homo politicus* in this personality perspective are those of Lasswell, who similarly conceives of the political man as one who is distinctive by virtue of his pursuit of power and adds that the motive for this is to overcome feelings of personal deprivations and subordinations.[28] Lasswell's early work, *Psychopathology and Politics*, was concerned with the application of a psychoanalytic approach to biographical analyses of psychopathological politicians. His intentions were to establish tentative hypotheses about the personality development of politicians and the bearing of this on political behavior in general. From this work Lasswell offered a formula for the psychological development of the politician, which is a repetition of the nucleus of Spranger's thinking: "The *homo politicus* is characterized by the following relationship between desire, method, and success: desire to control the motives of others; methods varying from violence to wheedling; and success in securing communal recognition."[29]

Lasswell's thesis of the power-oriented *homo politicus* is presented more thoroughly in a later statement in which he contends that "in a political type in this sense, the basic char-acteristic will be the accentuation of power in relation to other values within the personality when compared with other per-sons."[30] Such an accentuation of power, nevertheless, must be seen in its cultural context. In a particular culture, power may be a dominant or central value which as such would be mani-fested in a more modal fashion in the national character of that society. Says Lasswell, "anyone who accentuates power in such a setting closely approximates the most drastic popular and scientific idea of what constitutes the *homo politicus*."[31] His theoretical model of political man is as follows:

> Our political man: 1) accentuates power, 2) demands power (and other values) for the self (the primary ego plus incorporated symbols of other egos), 3) accentuates expectations concerning power, 4) acquires at least a minimum proficiency in the skills of power. The man who ac-centuates power is doing so *relative* to others, and therefore power personalities can be detected, by comparing them with standard expec-tancies for a culture, a social layer, a crisis or some other specified frame of reference.[32]

The general thesis of power-orientation as the distinctive mark of the politician has been stated to a lesser extent by several others. Michels, in his view that there is a universal power drive in human nature, says that there is a "natural greed for power" in leaders,[33] and Gottfried contends that most politicians are formed by the "love of power."[34] Heberle de-scribes the professional politician as the man who lives not *for*, but *off*, politics,[35] while Matthews states that the desire for power and prestige may be one incentive for political activity.[36] And Lane similarly suggests that political activity can be used for the pursuit of power, that is, the enjoyment of power as a value or a satisfaction in itself.[37]

In the same vein Schumpeter maintains that the competitive struggle for power is primary in political behavior and that the social function of legislating is fulfilled incidentally as somewhat of a latent consequence.[38] This thesis of the power-centered political personality has been stated more recently by Downs. For his model of an economic theory of democracy Downs accepts the self-interest axiom as the basis of human behavior: private ambitions are the ends of human actions; social functions are usually the by-products.[39] In this conception he presents the view that politicians are motivated solely by the desire for power, prestige, and income which come from being in office: "Thus politicians in our model never seek office as a means of carrying out particular policies; their only goal is to reap the rewards of holding office *per se*. They treat policies purely as means to the attainment of their private ends, which they can reach only by being elected."[40] All of this is related to the fundamental hypothesis of Downs' model of an economic theory of democracy: "political parties formulate policies in order to win elections, rather than win elections in order to formulate policies."[41]

No society, of course, can exist without power. All political activity is a struggle for power; whatever the ultimate goal of politics, power is always the immediate need. Thus, as Weber rightly states, the "power instinct" is a normal quality of the politician, since the striving for power is one of the driving forces of all politics.[42] Power, then, is an unavoidable means in this occupation. But the more pertinent question concerns the significance which such means have for the political man, that is, what are the value-conception and the orientation of the particular individual toward power? Certainly these may vary, but the implication in the several relevant statements presented above is that the politician has a basically authoritarian orientation toward power. In these many evaluations political man, or, more specifically, the professional politician, is presented as a fundamentally authoritarian personality. Empirical evidence, however, that the personally power-motivated individual is attracted to politics is almost totally lacking.

Only four pieces of research are more or less directly rele-

vant to this question. McConaughy administered the Edwards
Unlabelled Fascist Attitudes Test to eighteen state legislators
in South Carolina and to a control group. He found no statistical significance either way, but concludes that politicians are
less fascist than the control group.[43] Hennessy, as a result of an
exploratory study of party workers, officials, and candidates in
Arizona, claims that politicians as a whole have stronger orientations toward power than nonpoliticians and have stronger
desires for direct influence over persons and things.[44] None of
the differences between these two categories, however, meet
conventional standards of statistical significance. Harned, in
a study of ward committee chairmen in the city of New Haven,
found no evidence that people of high rather than low authoritarian tendencies are more likely to work for political parties.[45]
Her assumption was that activity in political parties may have
special appeals to those with authoritarian traits both because
of the hierarchical structure of the parties and the relationship of their members to the agencies of political power in the
community. Using projective techniques on samples of unsuccessful candidates, of former appointed and elected political
officials at the local level, and of politically inactive business-
men, Browning and Jacob reportedly found no differences in
power, affiliation, or achievement motives between politicians
and nonpoliticians.[46] Other research which shows that authoritarian personalities vote no more nor less than others,[47] that
they are less likely to join political groups,[48] and that they are
more apt to be politically apathetic,[49] has cast further doubt
upon the positive relationship of a power value and political
activity.[50] The question, nevertheless, remains unanswered.
Aside from the theoretical bias of the instruments[b] as well as
the restricted samples that were used in these studies, the

[b] With the exception of McConaughy, and the work by Browning and Jacob,
these studies used the F-scale as a personality measure, which taps only one
kind of authoritarianism, namely, the fascist variety. We shall discuss this point
more fully in Chapter II.

more important fact is that actual professional politicians (or, as Lasswell says, the active elite of government or political parties) have not been studied.

OBJECTIVES OF THE STUDY

By utilizing a sample of active professional politicians holding office in the national legislative branch of a democratic political system, we shall attempt to discern a general personality type that distinguishes the political man. As Meynaud has suggested, "The question is whether elected members of Parliament—and also, within certain limits, those who aspire to this position—reveal any special psychological predisposition or, in other words, may be identified outright by certain behavioural features."[51] There is an almost total lack of research on this subject. More specifically, we shall test empirically the hypothesis of power-orientation in the political personality. This study is the first of its kind to employ actual politicians (particularly at an uppermost echelon) in the test of this hypothesis.

Those few studies which have given attention to the more politically relevant realms of personality have failed to gather data on the political party affiliation of the subjects.[52] Consequently, the use of these studies is limited. Another major objective of this study, then, will be to relate more specifically the concept of political personality to individual political parties and to diverse ideological positions. Little research, if any, has been done on political parties with the social psychological orientations suggested here.[53] Sociological research in this regard too has focused primarily on the social bases of political parties.

One of the tasks of political sociology is to explain why individuals make the selections that they do from the available political alternatives. We may ask, then, whether or not personality is instrumental in this respect. Very little is known about the conditions under which the role of personality in political participation is maximized or minimized.[54] This study will consider certain political issues—such as government coalitions, political recruitment, party factions, and changes in political ideology—in relation to this question. The multiparty system which we will study lends itself ideally to these and many other theoretical questions, which in such a setting can be approached with greater precision.

There are many areas of theoretical applications for this study. A few of the more significant ones may be mentioned briefly. The primary relevance of the general theoretical approach is to offer a more thorough analysis of personality, social organization, and social behavior. In this regard the foremost question is that of congruity between social systems and personality systems. What are the functional consequences of the relationship between these two elements in a given situation? More specific to this study is the question of whether or not the institutions of government in a particular society are related dependently to its modal personality type, or at least to that modal personality type which may be recruited into the political subsystems. As Inkeles points out, "Almost all the modern students of national character are convinced that the answer to this question is in the affirmative. Systematic empirical evidence for this faith is unfortunately lacking."[55]

In the following chapter we shall specify the hypotheses which will be the focus of this study, as well as describe the design of the research and its methodology. Chapters III and IV will be devoted respectively to descriptions of the political system which constitutes the context of our study and its national character setting. These will be followed by two chapters in which we shall elaborate on the empirical evidence and offer interpretations for these data. Chapter V will treat the question of distinguishing the politician and the nonpolitician in terms of personality structure and power-orientations, while Chapter VI will relate the concept of the political personality to individual political parties and diverse political ideologies. Then the significance of the relationship between personality structure and political ideology for the decision-making process will be considered in regard to the general questions of political consensus and political cleavage. In this respect Chapter VII will illustrate specific political issues relating to political alliances and changes in political party affiliation. Consideration of the influence of social backgrounds on personality will be given in Chapter VIII. The final chapter will discuss the theoretical relevance of the findings, particularly the question of the relationship of personality systems to social systems, and the problems of congruity in this respect.

NOTES

[1] Erich Fromm, *Escape From Freedom* (New York: Holt, Rinehart & Winston, 1941), p. viii.

[2] T. W. Adorno, Else Frenkel-Brunswik, Daniel J. Levinson, and R. Nevitt Sanford, *The Authoritarian Personality* (New York: Harper & Row, 1950).

[3] Raymond B. Cattell, *Personality: A Systematic, Theoretical, and Factual Study* (New York: McGraw-Hill, 1950); Paul H. Mussen and Anne B. Wyszynski, "Personality and Political Participation," *Human Relations,* V (1952), 65–82; Morris Janowitz and Dwaine Marvick, "Authoritarianism and Political Behavior," *Public Opinion Quarterly,* XVII (1953), 185–201; and Henry L. Manheim, "Personality Differences of Members of Two Political Parties," *Journal of Social Psychology,* L (1959), 261–268.

[4] Henry V. Dicks, "Personality Traits and National Socialist Ideology," *Human Relations,* III (1950), 111–153; and Herbert McClosky, "Conservatism and Personality," *American Political Science Review,* LII (1958), 27–45.

[5] Janowitz and Marvick, *op. cit.;* Ohmer Milton, "Presidential Choice and Performance on a Scale of Authoritarianism," *The American Psychologist,* VII (1952), 597–598; P. V. Gump, "Anti-Democratic Trends and Student Reaction to President Truman's Dismissal of General MacArthur," *Journal of Social*

Psychology, XXXVIII (1953), 131–135; and Lawrence S. Wrightman, Jr., Roland W. Radloff, David L. Horton, and Michael Mecherikoff, "Authoritarian Attitudes and Presidential Voting Preference," *Psychological Reports*, VIII (1961), 43–46.

[6] Harold D. Lasswell, "The Selective Effect of Personality on Political Participation" in Richard Christie and Marie Jahoda (eds.), *Studies in the Scope and Method of "The Authoritarian Personality"* (Glencoe: The Free Press, 1954), pp. 197–198.

[7] Robert E. Lane, *Political Life* (Glencoe: The Free Press, 1959), p. 97.

[8] For a review of this question see Donald R. Matthews, *The Social Backgrounds of Political Decision-Makers* (New York: Randon House, 1954).

[9] One recent exception is Donald R. Mathews' study, *U. S. Senators and Their World* (Chapel Hill: University of North Carolina Press, 1960).

[10] Matthews, *Social Backgrounds*, p. 60.

[11] On this latter point see, for example, Seymour M. Lipset, *Political Man* (London: William Heineman, 1960).

[12] Dwaine Marvick, "Political Decision-Makers in Contrasting Milieus" in Dwaine Marvick (ed.), *Political Decision-Makers: Recruitment and Performance* (Glencoe: The Free Press, 1961), p. 13.

[13] Reinhard Bendix and Seymour M. Lipset, "Political Sociology: An Essay and Bibliography," *Current Sociology*, VI (1957), 81–85.

[14] Robert E. Lane, *Political Life*, p. 98.

[15] Peter Rossi, "Community Decision-Making" in Roland Young (ed.), *The Study of Politics* (Evanston: Northwestern University Press, 1958), pp. 378–379.

[16] For reference see Matthews, *Social Backgrounds*.

[17] *Ibid.*, pp. 35–36.

[18] Alex Inkeles and Daniel J. Levinson, "The Personal System and Social Structure in Large-Scale Organizations," *Sociometry*, XXVI (1963), 217–230.

[19] Harold D. Lasswell, "The Selective Effect of Personality on Political Participation" in Richard Christie and Marie Jahoda (eds.), *Studies in the Scope and Method of "The Authoritarian Personality"* (Glencoe: The Free Press, 1954), p. 202.

[20] *Ibid.*, p. 203.

[21] The significance of this issue perhaps was captured initially by Hughes, who posed the question: "To what extent do persons of a given occupation 'live together' and develop a culture which has its subjective aspects in personality?" Everett C. Hughes, "Personality Types and the Division of Labor," *American Journal of Sociology*, XXXIII (1928), 768.

[22] See Alex Inkeles, "Personality and Social Structure" in Robert K. Merton, *et al.* (eds.), *Sociology Today* (New York: Basic Books, 1959).

[23] Lane, *Political Life*, p. 124.

[24] Robert A. Dahl, *Who Governs?* (New Haven: Yale University Press, 1961), pp. 223–226. Some of the ideas expressed here are taken from an earlier draft of Dahl's book.

[25] *Ibid.*

[26] Eduard Spranger, *Types of Men* (Halle: Max Niemeyer, 1928), p. 104. It should be pointed out that these psychological types are intended as ideal types. Spranger was fully aware that the pure type seldom, if ever, exists.

[27] *Ibid.*, p. 190.

[28] Harold D. Lasswell, *Psychopathology and Politics* (New York: The Viking Press, 1960), p. 52 (original edition: Chicago: University of Chicago Press, 1930).

[29] *Ibid.*

[30] Harold D. Lasswell, *Power and Personality* (New York: W. W. Norton, 1948), p. 22.

[31] *Ibid.*, p. 33.

[32] *Ibid.*, pp. 57–58.

[33] Robert Michels, *Political Parties* (New York: Collier Books, 1962), p. 205.

[34] Alex Gottfried, "The Use of Socio-Psychological Categories in a Study of Political Personality," *Western Political Quarterly*, VIII (1955), 234–247.

[35] Rudolf Heberle, "Changing Social Stratification of the South," *Sociology and Social Research*, XXXVIII (1959), 481.

[36] Donald R. Matthews, *Social Backgrounds of Political Decision-Makers*, p. 57; and *U. S. Senators and Their World*, p. 48.

[37] Lane, *Political Life*, pp. 123–124.

[38] Joseph A. Schumpeter, *Capitalism, Socialism, and Democracy* (New York: Harper & Row, 1950), p. 282.

[39] Anthony Downs, *An Economic Theory of Democracy* (New York: Harper & Row, 1957), p. 29.

[40] *Ibid.*, pp. 28–30.

[41] *Ibid.*

[42] Max Weber, *From Max Weber: Essays in Sociology*, trans. H. H. Gerth and C. W. Mills (New York: Oxford University Press, 1958), p. 116.

[43] John B. McConaughy, "Certain Personality Factors of State Legislators in South Carolina," *American Political Science Review*, XLIV (1950), 897–903.

[44] Bernard Hennessy, "Politicals and Apoliticals: Some Measurements of Personality Traits," *Midwest Journal of Political Science*, III (1959), 336–355.

[45] Louise Harned, "Authoritarian Attitudes and Party Activity," *Public Opinion Quarterly*, XXV (1961), 393–399. The validity of the statistical procedures used in this study, however, are questionable.

[46] Rufus P. Browning and Herbert Jacob, "Power Motivation and the Political Personality," *Public Opinion Quarterly*, XXVIII (1964), 75–90.

[47] Robert E. Lane, "Political Personality and Electoral Choice," *American Political Science Review*, XLIX (1955), 173–190.

[48] Fillmore H. Sanford, "Public Orientation to Roosevelt," *Public Opinion Quarterly*, XV (1951), 189–216.

[49] Paul H. Mussen and Anne B. Wyszynski, "Personality and Political Participation," *Human Relations*, V (1952), 65–82; and L. W. Milbrath and W. W. Klein, *op. cit.*, pp. 52–66.

[50] Lane, *Political Life*, pp. 126–127.

[51] Jean Meynaud, "General Study of Parliamentarians," *International Social Science Journal*, XIII (1961), 513–543.

[52] See Alex Inkeles, "National Character and Modern Political Systems" in Francis L. K. Hsu (ed.), *Psychological Anthropology* (Homewood: The Dorsey Press, 1961).

[53] One attempt along these lines is that of Henry L. Manheim, "Personality Differences of Members of Two Political Parties," *Journal of Social Psychology*, L (1959), 261–268.

[54] Daniel J. Levinson, "The Relevance of Personality for Political Participation," *Public Opinion Quarterly*, XXIII (1958), 9–10.

[55] Alex Inkeles, "National Character and Modern Political Systems," *op. cit.*, p. 194.

CHAPTER II

The Study of Personality

ONE OF THE PRINCIPAL difficulties in this kind of research is the variety of political circumstances which undoubtedly create divergences in the character of the leaders who have to deal with them.[1] The concept of political man as used in the preceding chapter may have a myriad of definitions. We wish to speak of one type of political man—the professional politician. Who is the "professional politician"?[2] The answer is that there are different types of professional politicians. The term "professional politician" is usually used to denote both the career man and the full-time noncareer decision-maker, that is, one who devotes himself completely, and usually permanently, to political activity. Yet professional politicians also include those who have avocational careers or who are part-time or temporary political decision-makers. Our use of the concept *professional politician* may include all of these, since we simply want to discern between the elected (self-recruited) politician and the appointed (recruited) politician. The concern here is with

18

the former type of professional politician—the political man who freely seeks elective political office as an opportunity to be a political decision-maker.

The focal variable in this research is personality. The word "personality" has been used for many diverse denotations—to include or to exclude more or less of what often are referred to as the aspects, elements, and levels of personality. Personality may be defined as the acquired, and relatively enduring, dynamic configuration of one's predispositions to behavior. Personality, as we have suggested, must be seen essentially as a systematic entity which has its own structure and organization; however, it is not behavior or response, but rather willingness or predisposition to or for behavior and response. Yet we wish to confine ourselves to only one aspect of personality, namely, *personality structure,* since it is this element that accounts for the uniqueness that characterizes every personality.

As we intimated before, basic to any study of political behavior is the concept of power. For us it is central. This term also has a host of meanings and conceptualizations, even as used within the sphere of politics. It is not necessary to review the nature of power, but we shall state an operating conception of it for the purpose of this research: "Power in its most general sense refers to a capacity or ability to control others and, in this context, to control the decision-making process (which implies the control of others)."[3] As such, power resides in the very essence of the social process. It is the influence or control that one has or may exercise on the behavior of another because of the relationships involved. Power, then, is essentially sociological in nature. Orientations to power, however, are a psychological matter. As such, power may become part of everyone's personality. For our purpose, power is considered a value in the sense that it is something desired. Moreover, the possession of power is part of an individual's personality—it is one of his qualities.

THE RESEARCH HYPOTHESES

The following hypotheses constitute the focus of this research. Further justification for them will be given in the chapters that follow.

Hypothesis I

The political personality is characterized by a structural syndrome of authoritarianism or dogmatism to a relatively strong degree.

Hypothesis II

There is a significant difference in the dogmatic personality structure between politicians and nonpoliticians such that the former are more closed-minded than the latter.

Hypothesis III

The political personality is characterized by an authoritarian orientation toward power.

Hypothesis IV

The dogmatic political personality varies along the political continuum such that significant differences in personality structure may be discerned among political parties.

Hypothesis V

Politicians maintaining extremist ideologies tend to be more dogmatic than those maintaining moderate ideologies.

Hypothesis VI

Politicians of the extreme political left and those of the extreme political right differ significantly from each other in terms of dogmatism.

THE SELECTION OF THE PERSONALITY INSTRUMENT

The merits of this study will be strongly contingent upon the personality measure that shall be used. It will be well, therefore, to justify our selection with considerable elaboration. Concerning the theoretical orientation of over-all personality type we needed an instrument that would discern the relatively more enduring, consistent, and basic aspects of one's personality that would account for the generality of behavior in seemingly diverse contexts and situations. We particularly needed—because of the type of subjects—a tool that was concise and seemingly relevant politically, as well as one having theoretical foundations in line with their research problem.

The Conceptual Orientation

There has been considerable preoccupation with the concept of the "authoritarian personality" in the behavioral sciences during the past twenty years. The theoretical implications of this concept relate to our hypotheses concerning power-orientation in the political personality.

The concept of the "authoritarian character" was originated by Fromm in his psychoanalytic attempt to describe those factors that predispose people to accept the ideologies of Fascism and Nazism.[4] The "authoritarian character" may be characterized essentially by his particular attitude toward authority. This attitude is manifested in the authoritarian individual's sado-masochistic nature that designates his simultaneous admiration for and submission to authority, and his desire to be an

authority and to have others submit to him.[a] The most important feature of the authoritarian character is his attitude
toward power: "For the authoritarian character activity is
rooted in a basic feeling of powerlessness which it tends to
overcome."[5]

With the exception of clinical consideration by Maslow,[6] the
concept of the authoritarian character received little attention
until it was utilized by Adorno and associates.[7] This California
study started out as part of a series on the psychology of prejudice. Originally the Adorno group was not concerned directly
with authoritarianism but rather with the attempt to show that
those individuals high in ethnic prejudice differed in personality structure from those low in ethnic prejudice. The delineated syndrome was found to be true not only of people who
are prejudiced and ethnocentric but also of those who may be
described as authoritarian or antidemocratic. Thus, because of
the nature of the syndrome of authoritarianism, other concepts
to which it refers are used interchangeably and synonymously,
such as ethnocentrism, prejudice, and antidemocracy. The
various attitudes of these elements are closely interrelated.[8]

On the basis of traits and characteristics which were found
to be associated with this syndrome, an attempt was made to
construct the F[b]-scale as a measure for the potentially antidemocratic personality, that is, more specifically as an estimate
of fascist receptivity. Its developers feel that the scale includes
a fair sample of the ways in which this pattern characteristically expresses itself.[9] The development of the F-scale focused

[a] Note here that Fromm is speaking, not of the neurotic individual, but
rather of the "normal" person. Erich Fromm, *Escape From Freedom* (New
York: Holt, Rinehart & Winston, 1941), pp. 141–164.

[b] For fascism: the name derives from the dominant world of authority in the
social and political structures of fascist systems. The "authoritarian character"
is meant to represent the personality structure which is the human basis of
fascism. Hence, the term "fascist" is often used synonymously for the "authoritarian personality."

on nine cluster-variables: conventionalism, authoritarian submission, authoritarian aggression, anti-intraception, stereotypy,
power, cynicism, projectivity, and sex.[c] These variables form
a single syndrome that constitutes a relatively enduring personality structure which allegedly renders one susceptible to
antidemocratic propaganda. To repeat, the central variable in
the authoritarian personality is his general orientation toward
power and authority, specifically his admiration and motivation for them. This major element is manifested in two expressions: authoritarian aggression and authoritarian submission.
Since these variables are central in fascist ideology, they are
thought to be crucial for distinguishing the antidemocratic or
fascist individual from the democratic one.

What is to be noted about authoritarianism, however, is that
it is not a discrete, but continuous, variable. Accordingly, the
"authoritarian personality" is an ideal-type concept found at
one end of a continuum. Its antithesis, the "democratic personality," is hypothesized at the opposite end. Ideal descriptions
of the authoritarian personality may be found in Fromm,[10]
Maslow,[11] Adorno,[12] and Saenger.[13]

Perhaps no single study in the behavioral sciences has
brought about as much research activity as has *The Authoritarian Personality*.[14] The F-scale has been used extensively in
an array of research studies, particularly those focusing on this
major theme of antidemocratic proclivities. Nevertheless, although the Adorno group did succeed in showing that there
exists a determined relationship between concrete social and
political attitudes and one's personality, psychodynamics, and
psychological dispositions, much criticism has been directed
toward the methodology of this now classic study, and more
especially toward the validity of its F-scale.[15]

[c] A description of each of these cluster-variables may be found in T. W.
Adorno, Else Frenkel-Brunswik, Daniel J. Levinson, and R. Nevitt Sanford,
The Authoritarian Personality (New York: Harper & Row, 1950), p. 228 ff.

The conception of the "authoritarian character" as presented by Fromm may be manifested in a variety of ways. Critics contend that the F-scale[d] was designed, not to disclose the authoritarian personality as such, but rather to measure only authoritarianism of the extreme political right. Shils claims that *The Authoritarian Personality* had a restricted range of interest in "the proposition that political opinions are distributed on a unilineal scale and that the Left being at the other end of the scale from the Right was of necessity its opposite in every respect. . . . the investigators have failed to observe that at the Left pole of their continuum, there is to be found an authoritarianism impressively like the Authoritarianism of the Right."[16] Others have made the same claim, which has been substantiated in independent research.[17] Moreover, the F-scale admittedly is based heavily on Nazism, which, as one specific kind of ideology, differs concretely in content to some extent from other authoritarian ideologies with which it may share a basically similar ideological structure. The California group acknowledges that it stressed the fascist variety of authoritarianism under the influence of the times and the nature of its specific research.[18] Accordingly, we can admit Christie's charge that the F-scale is content-laden in that the specific references of its items are based on real experiences for certain people.[19]

This particular charge has been substantiated for our purposes by Rose. Conducting social research in Italy a few years ago, Rose administered five items of the F-scale (translated directly from the American version) and found them to be very inadequate.[20] Only two people in a sample of 251 cases answered negatively to each of the five items.[21] The mean response was 3.2 out of a possible +5. These findings contrast with those obtained by Srole, who, in using the same five items

[d] One of the major difficulties in discussing the F-scale is the multitude of different versions, ranging from four to sixty-six items, which have been used under the title "F-scale."

with an American sample, obtained a mean of 2.23, with eighteen percent of the cases achieving a neutral score.[22] In the light of this situation Rose concludes that Italians are no more authoritarian than Americans. He contends that the results obtained are due to the fact that these scale items are culture-bound and thus were not tapping "pure" authoritarianism in the personality, but rather were influenced strongly by the structure of the Italian culture and its recent history.

Rose's observations, however, are an *ex post facto* analysis, and as such neither prove nor disprove that the Italian people are more authoritarian than Americans. The Italian may have scored high on these items because the Italian society is structurally authoritarian. Or, on the other hand, even if the Italian society is authoritarian in structure, the individuals in this sample may not possess an authoritarian personality. Nevertheless, we concur with Rose's contention that the five items in question are culture-bound—at least for the Italian culture, since they relate directly to specific contents or real elements of Italian culture, society, and history.

This position is substantiated in research done by Derossi, who, in an administration of an F-scale to another Italian sample consisting of ninety-one subjects of various social backgrounds and ages, obtained a mean score of 4.53, which she felt was very high compared to American samples.[23] She explains that at the base of this there certainly are cultural factors, and asserts that the structure of social organizations in Italy—family, school, church, government, industry, military, and so forth—are fundamentally authoritarian. Other Italian psychologists support this position. Thus the F-scale, as Rose contends, does not lend itself very well as a valid international measure of authoritarianism.[24]

In the light of all this evidence we could not accept the F-scale as our personality instrument, primarily on theoretical and methodological grounds. We seemed to be headed, how-

ever, in the proper conceptual direction with the F-scale. All
that needed to be done was to alleviate the critical factors of
culture-boundness and especially the content of an unilineal
emphasis on authoritarianism. This seems to have been accomplished in a more recent conceptual approach devised by
Rokeach that focuses upon modes of cognitive functioning
rather than dealing primarily with those psychodynamics that
traditionally comprise the psychoanalytic orientation. *The Open
and Closed Mind*[25] (the concept of *dogmatism*) has been presented as an alternative approach to that of *The Authoritarian
Personality*.

The Dogmatic Personality

Rokeach argues that the major criterion distinguishing the
authoritarian personality is not specific or substantive ideological content, nor even a formal content of ideology which
may be shared in common with others (for example, that all
people believe in God), but rather the psychological structure
of one's ideologies.[26] As Rokeach maintains, "It is not so much
what you believe that counts, but *how* you believe."[27]

> To study the organization of belief systems, we find it necessary to
> concern ourselves with the *structure* rather than the *content* of beliefs.
> The relative openness or closedness of a mind cuts across specific con-
> tent; that is, it is not uniquely restricted to any one particular ideology,
> or religion, or philosophy, or scientific viewpoint. A person may adhere
> to communism, existentialism, Freudianism, or the "new conservatism"
> in a relatively open or in a relatively closed manner. Thus, a basic
> requirement is that the concepts to be employed in the description of
> belief systems must not be tied to any one particular belief system;
> they must be constructed to apply equally to all belief systems.[28]

Rokeach prefers to conceive of authoritarianism in an ahis-
torical way so that it will be equally applicable to all periods
of history and to alternative forms of authoritarianism within
a given historical period. His attempt is a refinement of the
conception of intolerance and prejudice, such that the meas-

urement of these may be identical to authoritarians of the political left, center, and right. As Rokeach explains:

> Authoritarianism and intolerance in belief and interpersonal relations are surely not a monopoly of Fascists, anti-Semites, Ku Klux Klanners, and conservatives. We have observed these phenomena, as no doubt has the reader, among persons adhering to various positions along the total range of the political spectrum from left to right. We have observed them in religious circles and in antireligious circles; in the academic world where the main business at hand is the advancement of knowledge; and in the fields of art and music, and so on.

> . . . .

> Authoritarianism can be observed at any one time in history in a variety of human activities, and we should think that it would have similar properties regardless of whether it is exhibited under Caesar, Napoleon, Hitler, Stalin, Khrushchev, Roosevelt, or Eisenhower. What is needed is therefore a deliberate turning away from a concern with the one or two kinds of authoritarianism that may happen to be predominant at a given time. Instead, we should pursue a more theoretical, ahistorical analysis of the properties held in common by all forms of authoritarianism regardless of specific ideologies, theological, philosophical, or scientific content. We would then be in a position to apply more powerfully the fruits of such analysis to any specific authoritarianism we might happen to be interested in now or in the future.[29]

Rokeach's conceptual distinction allows for different kinds of authoritarianism by avoiding reference to the specific or substantive content of authoritarian ideologies, by concentrating on formal content, or what they share in common, and even more particularly by concentrating on the structural properties common to various authoritarian ideologies. By means of the concept of dogmatism Rokeach is concerned essentially with the organization of belief systems[e] and more specifically with what he calls the openness and closedness of belief systems.

[e] According to Rokeach, "The belief system is conceived to represent all the beliefs that a person at a given time accepts as true of the world in which he lives." Milton Rokeach, *The Open and Closed Mind* (New York: Basic Books, 1960), p. 33.

Dogmatism as a concept is defined as a "relatively closed cognitive organization of beliefs and disbeliefs about reality, organized around a central set of beliefs about absolute authority which, in turn, provides a framework for patterns of intolerance and qualified tolerance toward others."[30] The intention, therefore, is to delineate that personality structure which is associated with opened and closed belief systems respectively.[31] Rokeach defines the closed-minded individual as one who has a closed or dogmatic way of thinking about any ideology regardless of its content, is rigid in regard to opinions and beliefs, makes an uncritical acceptance of authority, rejects those who disagree with him, and makes a qualified acceptance of those who do agree.[32] Thus the closed-minded person may be described as an authoritarian and intolerant person. He has, consequently, an authoritarian outlook on life and manifests intolerance toward those with opposing beliefs and sufferance under those with similar beliefs.[33]

The underlying structural orientations of the dogmatic personality may be applied to three kinds of acceptance-rejection situations, namely, those of ideas, people, and authority. The structural hypothesis established by Rokeach implies that the manner in which these three factors are accepted or rejected is essentially the same. Consequently, to know something of the way one relates himself to ideology may serve as an indication of the way one relates to people and authority.[34] Moreover, in regard to our particular concern, the structure of one's belief system—that is, the extent to which one's belief system is structurally open or closed—may serve as an indication of the manner in which one is apt to orient himself to such things as politics and religion.[35]

This closed-mind/open-mind dichotomy is not to be thought of as a discrete classification of personality types. Rather, these are defined as ideal types that occupy respective poles of a continuum. Thus dogmatism is a continuous variable. Individuals are more or less dogmatic, approximating in terms of measurement either the closed-minded pole or the open-minded pole respectively.

The closed-minded/open-minded dimension is in conformity with the F-scale tradition and the authoritarian character concept as suggested by Fromm. As Rokeach states, "In attempting to formulate the basic defining characteristic of openness-closedness, we could have let the whole matter go by simply saying that the fundamental basis is the extent to which there is a reliance on absolute authority."[36] The operational measurement for dogmatism is the Dogmatism Scale which has been constructed on these theoretical orientations. This instrument is the first and foremost measure of the extent to which the *total* mind is an open or closed one.[37]

The following psychological dynamics have been found to be associated with dogmatism or closed-mindedness: authoritarianism, bigotry, prejudice, ethnocentrism, conservatism, and intolerance.[38] Research shows that on the whole the attempt to formulate and measure general authoritarianism and intolerance has been successful. Rokeach validated his scale by correlating dogmatism scores and F-scale scores against Opinionation Scales measuring liberal and conservative political attitudes.[39] That the Dogmatism Scale is actually measuring general authoritarianism has been substantiated independently by Barker, who in his attempt to discern a general syndrome of authoritarianism has shown that the Dogmatism Scale correlates with the following measures: tolerance, anti-intraception, F-scale, Opinionation, and stereotypy—all at the .01 level of statistical significance.[40]

Examining the variables upon which the F-scale was constructed, we can see a near identity with the elements involved in Rokeach's approach. Accordingly, the authoritarian personality and the dogmatic personality[f] are nearly equivalent struc-

[f] The term "dogmatic personality" has never been used by Rokeach in any of his writings. It should be understood, therefore, as an innovation of the present author.

tures. As Rokeach states, "All we can say, then, is that we have demonstrated thus far that our scales perform essentially the same diagnostic function as those performed by the comparable Berkeley scales."[41] By administering both the Dogmatism Scale and the F-scale to the same subjects Rokeach obtained results to substantiate his assertion. Statistically significant correlations between the Dogmatism Scale, the F-scale, the Opinionation Scale, and the Ethnocentrism Scale were found for these test samples.[42] Thus, although not completely identical, the following concepts are often used interchangeably: authoritarianism, dogmatism, closed-mindedness, and power-orientation.

One of the major criticisms of the F-scale has been the influence which the factor of education is alleged to have upon an individual's score. Hyman and Sheatsley suspect that reports of differences in F-scores often were due not to personality but to simple variations in the language of different social classes.[43] Similarly, Christie contends that F-scores vary inversely with cultural sophistication and education.[44] The Dogmatism Scale has revealed no bias for educational level or other indicators of social class.[45]

Thus, from all the evidence we see that the Dogmatism Scale performs the same functions as the F-scale but in a more refined and precise manner. Conceptually speaking, the Rokeach instrument is theoretically superior to any other instrument that has been developed thus far for its clinical purpose as a measure of general authoritarianism. Furthermore, its structure—rather than content—orientation makes it a more suitable tool for international research on authoritarianism. The Dogmatism Scale, moreover, has even more theoretical relevance for our particular purposes of obtaining a scale which would delineate over-all personality structure rather than merely personality elements or variables. It is possible with the Dogmatism Scale to investigate many spheres of mental activity—such as, the ideological, conceptual, perceptual, and esthetic—through the common structural bond that unites them all in the individual belief system.[46] Rokeach claims that his conceptual approach yields a simple, yet more powerful, procedure to a unified analysis of personality, ideology, and cognitive behavior which is just as appropriate as the typically different concepts or methods which have been employed to study personality organization, ideological organization, and cognitive organization, since personality is seen essentially as an organization of ideological and cognitive behavior.[47] Thus, this instrument is actually a general personality measure that stresses much "more" of personality than heretofore possible with the F-scale and, more especially, with the trait scales as referred to in the preceding chapter. Accordingly, on the basis of all these considerations, we accepted the Dogmatism Scale as our personality instrument.

Since we felt that the length of a personality inventory would be a crucial consideration with political subjects, we adopted an abbreviated version of the Dogmatism Scale, known as the D-10 Scale. This shortened form was developed by Schulze, who utilized Guttman's scalogram analysis to select those items from the Dogmatism Scale which best meet the various criteria of unidimensionality, item consistency, and reproducibility and which are most representative of the single factor of dogmatism.[48]

The D-10 Scale was tested for validity with two samples. The coefficients of correlation between the final forty-item version of the Dogmatism Scale (D-40) and the D-10 Scale were + .76 and + .73 respectively.[g] Coefficients of correlation similar to those of the parent scale were obtained when the shortened version was associated with instruments measuring other elements in the dogmatism syndrome. Its coefficient of reproduci-

---

[g] These correlations, of course, are somewhat inflated since identical items appear in both scales.

bility is .83 in the scalogram analysis. Despite the question which this creates about the unidimensionality of this instrument, these consistent results have suggested that it is reasonable to accept the ten-item scale as a sufficiently reliable and valid substitute for the full-size Dogmatism Scale in research where brevity is desired.

Standardization of Instrument

The D-10 Scale had to be standardized for Italian usage through translation and further validation. The translation was done by the author with the assistance of Italian psychologists. Literal translations were made in order to preserve the essential validity of the instrument as well as to facilitate comparisons with the American versions. Nevertheless, it was necessary in some instances, for the sake of style and rhetoric, to "Italianize" to an extent those items which would not translate directly into the Italian language. This procedure was necessarily true of idiomatic phrases. In the standardization all proper caution was exercised to introduce neither content nor cultural bias. Three working versions of the translation were used over a period of several weeks. Both the second and third versions were pretested with Italian samples to ascertain comprehension and to determine that the scale was neither culture-bound nor content-laden for Italian use—either in its original or translated form.

Validation for the discriminatory power of the instrument was performed by using a modification of the Method of Known Groups. The D-10 scale, under the title of "Scale of Opinions," was administered to a sample of nineteen *carabinieri sottufficiali* (noncommissioned carabineers of the Italian national gendarmes), who as part of their training were being subjected to a series of psychological examinations. Results showed that ten scored positively, seven negatively, and two obtained zero scores within a possible range of − 20 to + 20.

During another series of psychological tests the same subjects were asked to nominate from among themselves five individuals whom they thought to be most endowed with specified dogmatic characteristics[h] and the five individuals who in their opinion least manifested these characteristics. On the basis of these two sets of nominations the sample of nineteen men was placed into two corresponding hierarchies according to the number of nominations received. These two hierarchies were then tested for rank correlation. A *rho* value of $-.748$ was derived, which indicates a statistically significant correlation: $p < .01$. In order to analyze these data on the basis of dogmatism scores, we applied the Mann-Whitney U test[i] for difference between two independent samples; only the first nine positions (about one-half) of each hierarchy were used.[j] This application yielded a U-value of 18, which is statistically significant[k] at the .05 level on the basis of a one-tailed probability.[l]

It is interesting to note that seven out of nine subjects nominated in the upper one-half of the dogmatic hierarchy achieved positive scores, whereas in the upper one-half of the nondogmatic hierarchy there were three negative scores, two neutral scores, and four positive scores. This validation procedure in slightly modified form was repeated with nine platoons of

[h] These were the following: obstinately adhere to their opinions, intolerant of others, show remarkable self-confidence, have rapid and hasty mannerisms, and manifest a strong esprit de corp.

[i] This nonparametric statistical technique was utilized in the light of the small N's, in which cases it did not seem appropriate to make an assumption of normal distribution. See Sidney Siegel, *Non-Parametric Statistics for the Behavioral Sciences* (New York: McGraw-Hill Company, 1956), pp. 116–127.

[j] The mean dogmatism score for the nominated dogmatic hierarchy was $+3$; that for the nominated nondogmatic hierarchy was $+.66$.

[k] Statistical significance refers to the probability of obtaining a given value as the result of chance alone. Probabilities of five percent or less are conventionally regarded as significant.

[l] The one-tailed test of significance is employed here since the direction of the difference was predicted in advance.

Italian soldiers, ranging in size from twenty-two to thirty-four men. On the basis of the Mann-Whitney U test statistically significant differences (one-tailed probabilities) were obtained in three cases at the .05 level or beyond, and two others were nearly significant. Thus, we can take all this evidence to indicate sufficient validity of the instrument for our purposes.[m]

It should be pointed out that military personnel[n] are not apt to be the best kind of judges for dogmatism. Military environments are structured in a tightly authoritarian manner which as such tend to "tone down" the dogmatic and authoritarian individual. Theoretically speaking, an authoritarian individual in this type of setting is more apt to express the authoritarian submission dimension of this personality structure rather than that of authoritarian aggression unless, of course, he occupies a position of superior authority within the group structure. Likewise, even the more open-minded individual is apt to become more closed-minded or submissive within such an authoritarian structure. Then, too, the perception of the individual within his group role is apt to distort the appraisal of his fundamental personality structure. Thus the very use of authoritarian structures in this type of experiment is more likely to yield somewhat negative results. Seen in this light, the results obtained here are all the more significant.

A few minor changes in three or four sentence structures were made in the final version of the scale selected for our use. Since these changes were in the style rather than in the content of the items, there was no alteration in their intention or meaning. The final version then was retranslated literally into English to determine the amount of objective deviation in this respect. The reconverted version was sent to the author

[m] This pretesting and validation work was done at the *Istituto di Psicologia del Consiglio Nazionale delle Richerche* (Institute of Psychology of the National Council of Research).

[n] We were limited in the choice of groups available to us that were sufficiently acquainted with one another to make possible this type of experiment.

of the Dogmatism Scale, who found the items to be perfectly acceptable, with no modification having been made in the structure-orientation of the instrument. This scale, then, became our personality measure. It may be inspected in Appendix A.

The Political Sample

The subjects for this research are the members of the Chamber of Deputies of the Third Republican Parliament.

Selection Procedures

The Chamber consisted of 596 members representing eight major political parties and several independents. The disparity in size of the parliamentary representation of these parties did not make it feasible to use a single technique for selecting a sample. Accordingly, the entire membership of the smaller parties was included in the selected sample: *Partito Socialista Democratico Italiano, Partito Liberale Italiano, Partito Democratico Italiano, Movimento Sociale Italiano,* and *Misto.*° These parties range in size from seventeen to twenty-four members. For the three larger parties—*Partito Socialista Italiano, Partito Comunista Italiano,* and *Democrazia Cristiana,* ranging from 87 to 203 members—a twenty percent sample was taken. Selections for these subsamples were made by means of a table of random numbers. The roster of deputies published in the *Annuario Parlamentare 1960* was used for this purpose.[49] For each of the three parties the deputies were numbered consecutively in the alphabetical order of the entries. Actually, two samples were drawn for each of these three parties. The first sample constituted a twenty percent representation of the party universe. However, since we had anticipated difficulty in ob-

---

° The *Misto* is a parliamentary grouping which constitutes a collection of independent deputies representing various political parties that have a membership of less than ten in the Chamber.

taining interviews with this entire sample, another sample of approximately equal size was drawn.

We attempted in this approach to derive as homogeneous a sample as possible so as to reduce any bias for uncontrolled variables. Since the number of women in the Chamber was twenty-two, only a few could be expected in our sample, and the smaller parties have no female representatives. Accordingly, our study thus was confined to only the male membership. Also the factor of parliamentary experience, in terms of service and political positions, could be influential. The same would seem to be true for currently held positions, such as party leaders, Chamber officers, and governmental officials. Yet to have controls for these elements would have meant the loss of a sizeable number of subjects. Moreover, if these elements were ruled out in the smaller parties, very few—if anyone—would be left to sample. Random sampling, in any event, allows for these variables to be present in the proper proportion. Furthermore, it will be possible to cross-tabulate in some instances. Our universe, therefore, may be defined as the male membership of the Chamber of Deputies for the year 1961.

Table 1 contains the relevant data for the universe and sample selections. The total number of selections for the potential sample was 193 out of 596 members, or thirty-two percent of the Chamber membership. Of the original ninety-nine randomly selected subjects forty-one percent entered into the sample. The remaining thirty-three individuals (twenty-five percent of the 132 names drawn) were taken from the second wave. Thus fifty-five percent of the seventy-four randomly selected subjects[p] were taken from the first wave, and forty-five percent from the second wave. In each wave the subjects were contacted simultaneously for participation in this study.

---

[p] Christian Democracy included three subjects that were not randomly selected. This accounts for the total number of seventy-seven subjects for these three parties.

TABLE 1

DISTRIBUTION OF POLITICAL PARTIES
IN UNIVERSE AND SAMPLE

Party	Universe		Sample		
	Number	Percent	Number	Percent Universe	Percent Sample
Christian Democracy (DC)	273	45.8	31	11.3	24.0
Italian Communist Party (PCI)	141	23.6	25	17.7	19.3
Italian Democratic Party (PDI)	19	3.1	3[a]	15.7	2.3
Italian Liberal Party (PLI)	18	3.0	11	61.1	8.5
Italian Social Democratic Party (PSDI)	17	2.8	8	47.0	6.2
Italian Social Movement (MSI)	24	4.0	18	75.0	13.9
Italian Socialist Party (PSI)	87	14.5	21	24.1	16.2
Misto[b]	17	2.8	12	70.5	9.1
Totals	596	99.6	129	21.6	99.5

[a] Five defected members (Independent Monarchists) are classified as Misto. Thus, this subsample actually constitutes 42 percent of the PDI.

[b] Includes five of the six deputies of the Italian Republican Party (PRI).

When the first wave was exhausted after a period of a few weeks, the procedure was repeated with the second wave. The final number of subjects that entered into the study is 129, which constitutes sixty-four percent of our current samples and about twenty-two percent of the universe for Chamber membership. While our sample constitutes about one-fifth of the membership of the Chamber, the percentage of the individual parties represented in the sample is much higher in many cases.

Representativeness of the Sample

The political sample is adequately representative of the membership of the Chamber of Deputies. Approximate fre-

quency distributions have been obtained for the following factors: age, education, occupations, parliamentary experience,
and regional constituencies represented. The mean age for the
sample is forty-nine, which compares favorably to that of forty-
eight for the entire chamber.[50] The largest professional categories represented are lawyers, journalists or publicists, and
teachers. About two-thirds of the sample is Catholic, and the
remaining one-third has no religious affiliation. Descriptive
data for all of these social background characteristics are given
in Tables 16 to 23 which may be found in Appendix B.[51]

The Collection of the Data

The major phases of this research were conducted in Rome
during the academic year 1960–1961. Preliminary preparations
over a period of five months included a general orientation to
the Italian society and culture. In particular this consisted of
a familiarization with the Italian political structure; the form
of government; the electoral system; the strengths and followings of the political parties; their ideologies, platforms, and
factions; and the major political figures and issues. Techniques
in this regard primarily consisted of interviews with American
journalists in Rome, university professors, lower echelon politicians, and, of course, the "man in the street." Some limited
observational travel also was helpful.

The Interviewing Process

The data for this study were gathered by means of an interview schedule, which incorporated the personality inventory;
the instrument was pretested with Italian subjects.

The total sample consists of 129 deputies. All but twenty-
nine of these were interviewed by the author. Of this latter
number, eleven self-administered the instrument, and the
remaining eighteen were interviewed by a team of seven

assistants, of whom four were university students and the other three professional social workers.

The duration of the simple[q] interview ranged from 15 to 195 minutes. The mean time was forty-four minutes, the median time thirty-seven minutes. Approximately forty percent of the subjects decided to chat beyond the regular interview on various political and social topics. This extra time ranged from five to seventy-five minutes, so that the mean time for the complete interview was fifty-one minutes, the median time forty-one minutes.

The majority of the interviews (ninety-one percent) were conducted during the months of June and July, 1961 (fifty in June and sixty-seven in July). Seven were conducted in the last week of May and three during the first week of August, and another two were mailed in during the month of September. Thus, all the data were collected in a span of about ten weeks.

Forty-four of the interviews took place at the Chamber of Deputies, and another twenty-five were held in party offices located in the Chamber complex, five in party offices located elsewhere, fifteen in private offices, ten in homes or hotels, and eighteen in miscellaneous locations. The remaining eleven were self-administered.

Every expedient means was used to arrange interviews with the sample. Several political parties cooperated by furnishing local addresses and telephone numbers of their parliamentary representatives. An assistant called to explain the nature of the research and to request an appointment. With the cooperation of the Chamber personnel, messages were delivered to those who could not be contacted. These individuals were asked to contact the researcher's office. When this was done, the nature of the research was explained and an appointment was requested. In a few cases, particularly for individuals maintain-

[q] To cover just the material in the schedule.

ing major positions, letters with the necessary information and request were sent. The party secretariats graciously cooperated in several cases by personally contacting their deputies, and occasionally some of the deputies consented to solicit the cooperation of their colleagues. In other instances mutual friends were utilized as intermediaries. This reassurance of the legitimacy of the study was most helpful.

On the whole it was not very difficult to arrange appointments with the subjects. Nor were they uncooperative; on the contrary, for the most part they were very cordial and hospitable. The length of the interviews attest to the receptive attitude. In fact, the author was the recipient of several gifts (mostly books and political speeches) and numerous personal invitations for cocktails, dinner, and visits to constituencies throughout Italy—many of which were accepted. Several deputies took a personal interest in the research and asked to be kept informed of its results. Our success in this respect was undoubtedly facilitated by the author's being a *professore,* by the status this title connotes in Italian society, and by being an *Americano,* particularly one of Italian descent.

The only difficulty in obtaining interviews concerned members of the Christian Democracy who held government (Third Fanfani Government) posts, such as the ministers and undersecretaries. These men felt that any comments that they might make would be taken as official statements of the current government. There were no refusals from these people, but they were dropped from the study sample for the sake of expediency rather than to contend with a complicated bureaucracy to obtain appointments. Several of our interviewees, however, were members of previous governments. Moreover, since the completion of our field work, some of our respondents have assumed government posts as ministers and undersecretaries.

Our failure to achieve in some instances the established sample quotas was not due to interview refusals. Of all the subjects that were contacted personally, only three openly refused to be interviewed. Seven men accepted schedules (four by mail and three personally) but failed to return them. Interviews were obtained with six others (thus, an actual total sample of 135), but these had to be deleted from the sample since only partial answers were obtained, particularly on key questions. While it is true that some of these parliamentarians undoubtedly ignored our request and others may have been too busy to contact us, most of these deputies were never in a position to accept or reject our request for an interview. Some were ill, others were absent from the country, and still others were in the executive branch of the government. Moreover, nearly all of these deputies with whom we were never in direct contact lived a considerable distance from Rome, particularly at the northern or southern extremes of the nation or on the islands. Many of these deputies seldom came to Rome, and when they did so it was only for a short time. We could have drawn another wave of subjects, but parliament adjourned during our interviewing period, and this curtailed our field work.

The interviewing process was initiated by a short statement of introduction designed to cover the researcher's university affiliation, the general nature of the research study, its sponsorship, the selection of subjects, and a guarantee of anonymity. The interview commenced immediately with open-ended questions about social problems and political events of a general nature. This procedure gave the respondent an opportunity at the outset to offer brief discourses about the social and the political scene. In addition to providing a smooth introduction, this method yielded an excellent fund of unsolicited background information. Questions about personal backgrounds were confined to the conclusion of the interview.

The usual interviewing procedures and techniques were followed. Although the majority of the questions were precoded, in all cases the respondents were encouraged to talk at length. A supportive approach was used.

About one-fifth of the sample raised preliminary questions

about the study, that is, its purpose, sponsorship, and future publication. A few were curious to know how they were selected. The major criticism (and this apparently explained some rejections) came from a few not favoring the empirical procedures or scientific methods which were being used in the research process. Three stated that they did not like the rigid "Anglo-Saxon mentality" and the methodical "American mentality" as manifested in the precoded questions. Many did not appreciate giving categorical answers and contended that this simplified matters too much and as a consequence reflected neither the real Italian situation nor their actual comments.

Several respondents, as expected, withheld comment occasionally on a specific question. There was no particular pattern to this except for one question[r] to which the Communists and Socialists in particular preferred not to answer. This reaction was true for thirty-six percent of the Communist deputies and sixty percent of the Socialists—twenty-two out of forty-six respondents. One Communist subject commented that he had been told by his colleagues about "the famous question," and another felt that the question was a bit embarrassing but amusing. Some respondents evaded certain questions, such as those regarding the relationship between politics and labor, with "do not know" answers that seemed most unlikely. Others commented that they thought some questions were delicate, personal, or loaded. Further comments were made to specific questions. All of these were recorded and analyzed. They will be mentioned where appropriate in the following chapters.

Administration of the Personality Inventory

One serious obstacle to this kind of research in the field has been the difficulty of inducing professional politicians to submit

[r] "Which of the world political personalities represents best, in your opinion, the type of political leader most suitable for Italy at the present (independently of his political ideology)?"

to the research techniques involved.[52] We were apprehensive about submitting the personality inventory to men of such political stature, not so much because it was a psychological tool, but rather for the fear and suspicion that might be aroused by its obviously projective nature, and thus for the potential jeopardy to the validity of the responses. At face value these scale items would not be at all in conformity with the general sociological tone of other questions tapping social and political attitudes. One or two of these items, moreover, were openly quite personal. We had thought of interspersing the scale throughout the schedule. This procedure was not very feasible since it would need the tedious repetition of directions, which undoubtedly would have aroused more suspicions. Ultimately the scale was "disguised" by positioning it well into the interview—practically toward the conclusion—after sufficient rapport had been established. Two neutral items were included to give the scale a somewhat political tone. These items do not form part of the scale, and thus were not admitted in a derivation of the subject's dogmatism score. Moreover, the logical sequence of the items was arranged so that those seemingly more germane to the total interview appeared initially. We moved into the scale without any introductory statement (except for the answering directions), for we thought that any kind of an explanation might arouse suspicions.

The directions for answering the D-10 Scale were basically the same as those used by Rokeach in his original work with the exception of one modification. The usual six alternative answers for each item (I agree a little, on the whole, very much; I disagree a little, on the whole, very much) were modified to the following four: partly agree, completely agree; partly disagree, completely disagree. While it would not have been difficult to translate literally into Italian the six answers of the English version, these would have been rhetorically poor and would have made the whole thing sound non-Italian. Furthermore, these four alternative answers are more standard in Italian psychological terminology and usage. This modification appears to be valid. No "neutral attitude" response was used in order to force a selection.

Very little difficulty was encountered in the administration of the personality inventory. Only one subject absolutely refused, without reason, to answer the scale, even though he was extremely cooperative for the remainder of the schedule. About twelve other subjects made particular comments: two respondents wanted to know why these questions were so different from the preceding ones; another two thought they were "strange"; four subjects criticized the questions as being "too formal," "too scholastic," "too categorical," and "too stereotyped"; and one subject wanted to know the difference between "partial agreement" and "partial disagreement." One subject commented, "I never took an exam like this"; another said that he had "an acquaintance with these tests"; and still another stated that he liked the indirect method of getting to the "character" of the deputy: "Nobody would say openly if he were egotistical, but your questions may get at those psychological elements"; and another exclaimed: "But this is a confession!"

Those concerned about the seeming strangeness of these questions were told that we were seeking their personal opinion on the nature of society and certain social issues. Coming from a sociologist, this answer seemed plausible, legitimate, and acceptable. No other difficulty was encountered.

Validity of the Data

The inevitable questions certainly must be in the mind of the reader: Do politicians mean what they say? Is there a discrepancy between their verbal and nonverbal behavior? Did they tell the truth? In regard to the validity of the data our major concern is of course with the personality instrument. We have reason to believe that these data are both valid and reliable. As the party responses to the individual items in the D-10 Scale are surveyed (see Appendix D), we find that for nearly all parties there is a distribution of answers in all four response categories for every item. Moreover, from an evaluation of the comments that the deputies made while answering the scale items, it is our conviction that these respondents were giving truthful answers. The validity of this belief appears to be reflected in their unsolicited, original, and varied comments which we shall mention where appropriate.

Analysis of the Data

The Dogmatism Scale in conjunction with selected items of other data from the schedule will be used to test the research hypotheses. Specific analytical procedures will be discussed in the following chapters.

The Control Group

In order to relate our findings for the political sample to nonpoliticians, a control group was drawn from the Italian population. We established a simple quota sample of about 500 individuals who were administered a brief questionnaire consisting of the D-10 Scale and several questions relating to social and political backgrounds.

Each of twenty-five freshmen students at the University of Rome who were taking courses in public opinion was asked to select twenty respondents. Specific directives were given to approximate the proportional distributions of the political sample in terms of sex, age, education, and professional backgrounds. Beyond these requirements the choice of individuals was left to the student pollsters. Some difficulty was experienced in obtaining respondents because of questions on religious affiliation and especially political party preference.[s] Nevertheless, well over 500 responses were obtained. From this number was extracted a usable sample of 436 "nonpolitical" individuals who neither have been elected to political office nor have been political candidates.

Since professional politicians at the parliamentary level are seldom representative of the total general population which they represent, the nonpolitical sample as selected should not be expected to be a precisely matched control in terms of a frequency distribution for political party affiliation and social background factors, such as religion, occupation, and education. The control group is, in fact, considerably skewed in terms of religion toward Catholicism, and in terms of education toward the upper levels. Moreover, supporters of Christian Democracy are disproportionately represented.

The control group in some respects is apt to be more representative of the general Italian population. In drawing this control, however, we were confined to the geographic locality of metropolitan Rome. Regional and provincial residence in Italy seems to be a social and psychological variable of considerable importance. Perhaps, in this respect, the control is not truly representative of the Italian people and is apt to be predominantly Southern in mentality. Nevertheless, in spite of these handicaps the nonpolitical sample, which we use as suggestive rather than probative, appears to be a suitable control for our purposes, particularly since the critical variables are more likely to be skewed antithetically to the hypothetical directions. Data on the social characteristics of this control sample are given in Tables 24 to 28, which may be found in Appendix C.

---

[s] This is apparently rather common. Almond and Verba report that 32 percent of Italians in their studies of the political culture of democracy refused to reveal voting decisions to their interviewers. This contrasts to a figure of 2 percent for people in the United States. See Gabriel A. Almond and Sidney Verba, *The Civic Culture* (Princeton: Princeton University Press, 1963), pp. 117–118.

The Statistical Analysis

The statistical analysis which will be applied to the data consists principally of the *analysis of variance* and *Student's t* techniques for testing the difference between categorical means of dogmatism scores, and the *chi-square* (X^2) technique will be used limitedly in appropriate cases to test for differences in classified frequencies. All F-ratios and t-values, unless otherwise specified, are determined on the basis of a two-tailed probability. Statistical significance is established at the .05 level. Other standard procedures are used as necessary.

NOTES

[1] Jean Meynaud, "General Study of Parliamentarians," *International Social Science Journal*, XIII (1961), 513–543.

[2] See *ibid.*, 526–531, for a treatment of this question.

[3] William V. D'Antonio and Howard J. Ehrlich, "Democracy in America: Retrospect and Prospect" in William V. D'Antonio and Howard J. Ehrlich (eds.), *Power and Democracy in America* (Notre Dame: University of Notre Dame Press, 1961), p. 132.

[4] Erich Fromm, *Escape From Freedom* (New York: Holt, Rinehart & Winston, 1941). A similar conceptual attempt was made by Wilhelm Reich, *The Mass Psychology of Fascism* (New York: Orgone Institute Press, 1946).

[5] Fromm, *op. cit.*, p. 172.

[6] A. H. Maslow, "The Authoritarian Character Structure," *Journal of Social Psychology*, XVIII (1943), 401–411. One of the first treatments to delineate clinically the authoritarian syndrome in which Maslow sets forth his general disagreements with Fromm.

[7] T. W. Adorno, Else Frenkel-Brunswik, Daniel J. Levinson, and R. Nevitt Sanford, *The Authoritarian Personality* (New York: Harper & Row, 1950).

[8] See Else Frenkel-Brunswik, "Interaction of Psychological and Sociological Factors in Political Behavior," *American Political Science Review*, XLVI (1952), 44–65.

[9] Adorno, *et al.*, *op. cit.*, p. 228.

[10] Fromm, *op. cit.*

[11] Maslow, *op. cit.*

[12] Adorno, *et al.*, *op. cit.*

[13] Gerhart Saenger, *The Social Psychology of Prejudice* (New York: Harper & Row, 1953).

[14] See, for example, H. Edwin Titus and E. P. Hollander, "The California

F-scale in Psychological Research, 1950–1955," *Psychological Bulletin,* LIV (1957), 47–64; and Richard Christie and Peggy Cook, "A Guide to Published Literature Relating to the Authoritarian Personality Through 1956," *Journal of Psychology,* XLV (1958), 171–199.

[15] See, for example, Herbert H. Hyman and Paul B. Sheatsley, "The Authoritarian Personality—A Methodological Critique" and Edward A Shils, "Authoritarianism: 'Right' and 'Left' " in Richard Christie and Marie Jahoda (eds.), *Studies in the Scope and Method of "The Authoritarian Personality"* (Glencoe: The Free Press, 1954).

[16] Shils, *op. cit.,* p. 38.

[17] See Edwin N. Barker, "Authoritarianism of the Political Right, Center, and Left," *Journal of Social Issues,* XIX (1963), 63–74.

[18] Else Frenkel-Brunswik, "Interaction of Psychological and Sociological Factors in Political Behavior," *American Political Science Review,* XLVI (1952), 44–65.

[19] Richard Christie, "Authoritarianism Re-examined" in Richard Christie and Marie Jahoda (eds.), *Studies in the Scope and Method of "The Authoritarian Personality"* (Glencoe: The Free Press, 1954), p. 175.

[20] Personal correspondence.

[21] Arnold M. Rose, *Indagine sull'Integrazione Sociale in Due Quartieri di Roma* (Rome: Università di Roma, Centro Richerche di Sociologia Empirica, 1959), p. 21; and also "Prejudice, Anomie, and the Authoritarian Personality," *Sociology and Social Research,* L (1966), 141–147.

[22] Leo Srole, "Social Integrations and Some Corollaries," *American Sociological Review,* XXI (1956), 707–716.

[23] Personal correspondence.

[24] T. W. Adorno, in a personal letter, maintains that the F-scale items must not be simply translated for use in different cultures.

[25] Milton Rokeach, *The Open and Closed Mind* (New York: Basic Books, 1960).

[26] Milton Rokeach, "Political and Religious Dogmatism: An Alternative to the Authoritarian Personality," *Psychological Monographs,* LXX (1956), No. 18, Whole No. 425.

[27] Milton Rokeach, *The Open and Closed Mind,* p. 6.

[28] *Ibid.*

[29] *Ibid.,* pp. 13–14.

[30] Milton Rokeach, "The Nature and Meaning of Dogmatism," *Psychological Review,* LXI (1954), 195.

[31] Rokeach, *The Open and Closed Mind,* p. 19.

[32] *Ibid.,* p. 102.

[33] *Ibid.,* pp. 4–5. A more detailed description of open and closed systems may be found on pages 55–57 of the same volume.

[34] *Ibid.,* p. 8.

[35] *Ibid.,* pp. 7–8.

[36] *Ibid.*, p. 60.

[37] *Ibid.*, p. 397.

[38] *Ibid.*, pp. 121–125.

[39] *Ibid.*, p. 121.

[40] Barker, *op. cit.*

[41] Rokeach, *The Open and Closed Mind*, p. 107.

[42] *Ibid.*, pp. 102–108.

[43] Herbert H. Hyman and Paul B. Sheatsley, "The Authoritarian Personality —A Methodological Critique" in Richard Christie and Marie Jahoda (eds.), *Studies in the Scope and Method of "The Authoritarian Personality"* (Glencoe: The Free Press, 1954), p. 96.

[44] Richard Christie, "Authoritarianism Re-examined" in Richard Christie and Maria Jahoda (eds.), *Studies in the Scope and Method of "The Authoritarian Personality"* (Glencoe: The Free Press, 1954), pp. 169–172.

[45] Rokeach, *The Open and Closed Mind*, p. 111.

[46] *Ibid.*, p. 398.

[47] *Ibid.*, pp. 6–7.

[48] Rolf Schulze, "A Shortened Version of the Rokeach Dogmatism Scale," *Journal of Psychological Studies*, XIII (1962), 93–97.

[49] *Annuario Parlamentare* (Rome: Segretariato Generale della Camera dei Deputati, 1960), pp. 21–59.

[50] *I Deputati e Senatori del Terzo Parlamento Repubblicano* (Rome: La Navicella, 1960), p. xxxi.

[51] For a more complete treatment of the social backgrounds of Italian deputies see a recent study of 1358 members of the Chamber of Deputies since the establishment of the Republic: Giovanni Sartori, *Il Parlamento Italiano, 1946–1963* (Naples: Edizioni Scientifiche Italiane, 1963).

[52] Jean Meynaud, "General Study of Parliamentarians," *International Social Science Journal*, XIII (1961), 518.

CHAPTER III

The Italian Political System

IF EVER THERE WERE a political maze to fathom, Italy is not only typical, it is a classic example. The confusions of Italian political life often baffle even the native. Upon learning of the writer's intentions to study their political system, Italian friends remarked that to grapple with such a curious complexity would require much determination and perseverance. Several situations account for this quandary. Two of the more important seem to be the turbulent political history of the nation and its particular national character. It is difficult to determine which in this context has the more dominant influence. Each appears to be both agent and product of the other. We shall discuss in this chapter the historical and contemporary nature of the Italian political system, and the topic of national character will be considered in the one to follow.

THE HISTORICAL PERSPECTIVE

Within the past forty years alone, Italy has known three

major forms of political rule—constitutional monarchy, dictatorship of totalitarian fascism, and democratic republicanism —and has experienced ninety-eight different governments.[a] Nonetheless, all of this, as with the current political situation, should be seen in its historical context. As one of the oldest civilizations in continuous existence, few can offer a more striking political history than Italy.

A little over a century ago there was no Italy—politically speaking. The Italian nation was composed then of a number of independent states, most important among which were the Bourbon Kingdom of Naples and Sicily, the Papal States in central Italy, the Grand Duchy of Tuscany, the duchies of Modena and Parma, the provinces of Lombardy and Venetia under Austrian administration, and the states of Piedmont and Sardinia of the House of Savoy. Although the ties among these separate states were tenuous, there was nevertheless an "Italy" in a strong sentiment of nationalism and an intense desire for unity.

About 1858 several patriotic personages began to work actively for the political unification of Italy. Among the more important of these people were Giuseppe Mazzini, Camillo di Cavour, and Giuseppe Garibaldi. There was considerable difference of opinion concerning the form of government which a new united state should take.[1] Young idealists supported Mazzini's desire for the establishment of a republic. Religious-minded patriots believed that the most practical solution would be a federation of the Italian states under the presidency of the Pope. The majority of the moderate nationalists advocated a constitutional monarchy that would be built upon the foundation of the Kingdom of Piedmont-Sardinia. The aims of this third group were gradually crystallized and effected under

[a] From March 1848 (Balbo ministry) until the end of 1922 (Mussolini ministry) there were seventy-one governments, each lasting about one year except for the twenty-year reign of Mussolini. Since 1943 there have been twenty-seven governments, each with an average duration of ten months.

the leadership of Cavour, who served as minister and prime minister for the Piedmont-Sardinian governments. When the *Risorgimento* was accomplished in 1870, the title of King of Italy was conferred upon Victor Emmanuel II and his successors of the House of Savoy. The capital was transferred to Rome in 1871, and thus was born the modern state of Italy.

There were twenty-three constitutions or fundamental statutes within the various Italian states between 1797 and 1849. The most important of these documents was the *Statuto Fondamentale del Regno* (Fundamental Statute of the Kingdom), published in and for the Kingdom of Piedmont-Sardinia by King Charles Albert in March 1848. The *Statuto* was extended by successive decrees to the new territories that were annexed to the Kingdom. Until the formation of the democratic Republic in 1946, it served as the constitution or fundamental statute of the Italian state, even though it underwent extensive modification during the intervening reign of the Fascist dictator Benito Mussolini.

The Italian political system after 1870 was modeled upon that of England. Article Two of the Fundamental Statute defined the form of government as a "representative Monarchical government." The executive power belonged exclusively to the Crown, which governed through a ministry that was responsible to Parliament. This Parliament consisted of two houses: the Senate (without fixed size) of hereditary and life members appointed by the Crown, and the Chamber of Deputies elected by the propertied and educated classes for five-year terms. Effective power, however, was left to the Chamber, since the Senate only rarely exercised its legislative authority. There were two parties, *Sinistra* and *Destra,* marked by no essential differences. Constructive debate or the alternation of power was less than a hope. The major activity of Parliament during this period was devoted to keeping its members in office.[2] Great stress was placed on avoiding a clear-cut division of opinion; little was done to face the pressing socioeconomic problems of the times.

Beginning about the turn of the century, however, a host of parties developed: the Socialist party as an extreme on the left, the Radical Left party as a reform party of positivist and empirical scientists, Mazzini's Republican party of the right, the Nationalist party on the right extreme, and lastly, in 1919, the Catholic Popular Party. In the same year Benito Mussolini began to form his *fasci*, which were to become the nucleus of the Fascist party that was established formally in November 1921. At about this later date the major parties in power had split into factions. All of this political division resulted in very little constructive action. In October of 1922 Mussolini was appointed prime minister by the Crown. By 1925, with the completion of the establishment of a fascist bureaucracy in national and local government, Italy had become a totalitarian state. The monarchy and its apparatus, including the bicameral legislature, were retained. They received, however, only nominal powers, since Mussolini chose to govern at will and to legislate by decree.

Fascist rule endured until 1943, when Mussolini resigned and was arrested under the directives of the king, who named Marshall Pietro Badoglio to form another government. Fascist forces, however, continued resistance to the constitutional monarchy—particularly in the new form of the Italian Social Republic of Salò—until conquered by allied powers. In June 1944, King Victor Emmanuel III delegated the royal powers to Crown Prince Hubert II, who held the throne until a popular referendum in 1946 brought about, by a small margin, the establishment of a republican form of government.

The Current Political Structure

The current form of government is defined as a "parliamentary republic." It is the first truly democratic government which Italy has known. Although there is much similarity between the present political system and the apparatus of the constitutional monarchy, many important changes were instituted, and these can be seen particularly in the powers accorded to the executive and legislative bodies, and in the many new liberties accorded to the citizenry. Notable in this last respect is the extension of the right of franchise to all individuals of legal age—regardless of sex, economic, or educational status—and the provision that sovereignty resides in the people, all of whom share legal equality.

In the referendum of 1946 delegates were elected to the Constituent Assembly (1946–1947) to draft a constitution for the new republic. While taking its main inspiration from the ideals and needs of the Italian people, the committee which drew up the Constitution was guided to some extent by the provisions of the German (Weimar) Constitution of 1919, the postwar French constitutions, the Constitution of the Spanish Republic of 1931, and the French Declaration of the Rights of Man (1789). References are found also to the constitutions of the United States and of Soviet Russia and to the British constitutional systems. The new Italian Constitution was promulgated in December 1947 by the provincial president of the Republic, Enrico Di Nicola, and became effective on the first day of the following year.

One significant aspect of the current political system which deserves particular mention is that of the institutional holdovers from the Fascist regime. These institutional remnants are many and varied. We can mention in particular the numerous statutes, including the penal codes, which are not only essentially fascist but also as such remain inconsonant with the spirit of the new Constitution. Reform in these areas, of course, has been planned, but progress has been slow indeed.

The following description of selected aspects of the current political system of Italy is intended to provide a frame of reference for understanding the tenor of the political life of the nation, which is essential for a full appreciation of the material discussed in successive chapters.

President of the Republic

The President of the Republic is elected for a seven-year term by Parliament meeting in joint session along with three delegates from each region who are elected by the regional councils. Any citizen having reached fifty years of age and enjoying civil and political rights may be elected President. He is the head of the state and the symbol of national unity as well as commander in chief of the armed forces. The President promulgates the laws without veto power, ratifies international treaties approved by the Parliament, and retains the power to dissolve either or both houses of Parliament before the expiration of their terms and to call for new elections.

Government of the Republic

The Government of the Republic consists of the President of the Council (prime minister) and the ministers, jointly constituting the Council of Ministers. The President of the Republic appoints the President of the Council of Ministers, and, following the latter's proposals, the individual ministers. In spite of this procedure the Italian Government is a typical "parliamentary government," since it must enjoy the confidence of the two houses of Parliament. Moreover, the Government—except in extraordinary circumstances—cannot issue decrees with the value of law without express authority from Parliament. The actual exercise of executive power is to a considerable extent entrusted to the President of the Council, who is responsible to the President of the Republic and may be dismissed at any time.

Parliament

The bicameral parliament was retained in the Republic. Unlike the former monarchical arrangement, however, both houses now enjoy full and equal legislative authority, although their respective structure is different. The supreme power of legislation belongs to Parliament alone.

The Senate is elected on a regional basis. Each region is entitled to one senator for every two hundred thousand inhabitants or fraction over one hundred thousand. No region, however, may have less than six senators, with the exception of Valle d'Aosta, the smallest of the nineteen regions, which is entitled to only one senator. Voters over forty years of age are eligible for the Senate. The President of the Republic may nominate as senators for life terms five citizens "who have brought honor to the nation through their exceptional merits in the social, scientific, artistic and literary fields."[3] Former presidents of the Republic are by right senators for life unless they refuse the nomination. The Senate is elected for a term of six years in direct universal suffrage by voters over twenty-five years of age.

The Chamber of Deputies, the lower house of Parliament, is elected by direct universal suffrage of all those of the legal age of twenty-five years on the basis of proportional representation. There is one deputy for every eighty thousand inhabitants, or fraction thereof over forty thousand, in each of the electoral constituencies. The Chamber of Deputies is elected for a term of five years. Voters who are twenty-five years of age as of the day of election may be elected deputies.

Although the two houses of Parliament are constitutionally equal, the greater political power has tended to be located in the Chamber of Deputies. Mangone attributes this to the fact that its "membership contains a greater amount of talent and in part because its electorate is broader than that for the Senate."[4] Yet, whatever the circumstances, these facts may be offered. Since the establishment of the Republic, all the presidents of the Council of Ministers (the prime ministers) have with one exception come from the Chamber of Deputies. Moreover, the majority of the ministerial posts have gone to members of the Chamber, as have appointments to undersecretariats and to many other posts that are not legally part of the government and thus carry no executive authority. Any citizen, of course, meeting the legal requirements may be appointed to the government, but these appointments have traditionally been given to the members of Parliament. All the national leaders of the several political parties are members of the Chamber rather than of the Senate.

Political Structure of Parliament

For the purpose of political organization the party representatives in the Chamber, as those in the Senate, are organized into *gruppi parlamentari* (parliamentary groups). Any party with a representation of ten or more deputies is entitled to organize into a parliamentary group, which has its own president and secretary who function as the party leaders. The superior officer of these two leaders is usually the secretary, who in the Chamber groups is generally the national leader of the party. The presidency of the *gruppo* is somewhat of an honorary post that is often given in recognition of dedicated service to the party. Parliamentarians from any one party which does not number ten representatives are organized along with independent deputies into a *Gruppo Misto*. This group likewise has the respective officers who, in this case, serve merely as administrative functionaries. The officers and members of the *Gruppo Misto* are in no way politically bound to each other.

THE POLITICAL PARTY SYSTEM

Italy today has a multiparty political system, but it may be more appropriate to say, as did one deputy, that "Every Italian has his own party!" More than three hundred political parties came forth for the election of the First Republican Parliament in 1948. In the national election of 1958, which is the basis of this study, there were forty-four different political parties participating for parliamentary (Senate or Chamber) seats alone.[b] Many of these, of course, were only regional entities that did not appear throughout the country. Others are in the nature of "personal parties" which focus upon a single leader. Kogan claims that most Italians are too individualistic and too anti-ideological to become completely absorbed in a political organization.[5] This explanation becomes more significant if we consider the fact that several of these pluralistic political divisions are in many respects homogeneous.[c]

There are, nevertheless, eight major political parties that are established nationally. We shall confine ourselves in the discussion that follows to these major parties which are the basis of this study, and we shall consider to some extent their origins, ideology, platform, strengths, and social supports.

One of the principal characteristics which should be noted about the major political parties in Italy is that, unlike those of many other nations, they are distinguished in that each has its own ideology—a philosophy or doctrine—and its own political methodology. Less distinctive are the political platforms and the concrete interests, even though these, where diverse, reflect ideology and, where similar, may be founded upon different motivations. Thus, these Italian parties are more than merely political organizations that are distinguishable simply by individual platforms.

---

[b] Only seventeen of these parties did not receive any seats.

[c] Sixty percent of the deputies in our sample expressed a preference for a system that allows for a plurality of parties. Twenty-two percent ideally preferred a two-party system, but many of these stated that the day of realization for Italy "was very far off—given its history and tradition" or that it "did not correspond to the Italian mentality."

Christian Democracy (DC)

The leading party in Italy since the establishment of the Republic has been the Christian Democracy, which was established originally in 1919 as the Popular party—a Catholic lay organization with socialist orientations. The founder of this party was the late Luigi Sturzo, a Catholic priest and, at the time, a small-town mayor in Sicily. Although this party was to be based upon the tenets of Christian morality, Sturzo intended that it be separated completely from the control of the Roman Catholic Church. Said Sturzo, "Our party is a party of national integration. It cannot and will not take religion as its flag."[6] The formal position of this party, however, has been based upon the Catholic social doctrines that have emerged in the various papal encyclicals during the past seventy-five years.

The emergence of the Fascist regime forced Sturzo's party underground and many of its leaders into exile. When Fascism fell, the party reappeared under the name of Christian Democracy. Sturzo's original aims and positions, however, were modified. The Catholic Church did not remain neutral when the threat of Communism appeared formidable after World War II. Its lack of neutrality went beyond giving moral and theological support to anti-Communist forces; it openly "campaigned" for Christian Democracy, evidently as the political organization that best promised to protect the principles and interests of Catholicism.[7] Christian Democracy, for its part, seemed to narrow any gap that may have existed between it and the Church. In the drafting of the Constitution for the Republic the party originally inclined to include a series of declarations of allegiance to Catholic doctrine.[8] This radical change in attitude toward the Church may be seen in the following words of Alcide De Gasperi, then a major figure in the party and its postwar premier:

> We know that the state is completely independent in its relationship with the Church. We want, as the Church itself wants, to maintain this

independence. But we know that we have first of all the moral duty and, since the Concordat, the juridical duty as well, to surround the Holy See with the most absolute respect. And we must above all remember that in the last hundred years of Italy's history the activity of the clergy has been directed to the moral reconstruction of Italy and that of healthy and free democratic institutions.[9]

One might object that the Popular party and Christian Democracy are clearly not the same political organization. Nonetheless, Christian Democracy in its ideological and political position is the heir of Sturzo's party.

The issue of the role which the Catholic Church should have in the party still remains unsettled, and this matter has the party divided into factions. The organization is too clerical for some, not enough so for others. The clerical-minded factions favor an authoritative, but democratic, system of strong church control.[10] Many others feel that the alliance between the Church and the party is a difficult burden for each, particularly since this is a bitter point of criticism from the opposition, which often alleges that the Church is the sponsor of Christian Democracy.[11] The Church for its part shares the glories as well as the failures of the party's political combat, and this means those of the Italian government, which since the establishment of the Republic has been under the administration of Christian Democracy.

One problem with practically all of the Italian parties is that because of their factional composition it is often difficult to classify them in respect to any particular dimension. Each party has its own left and right, and sometimes center. This is perhaps particularly true for Christian Democracy, which is regarded as Italy's "rainbow party" by virtue of the fact that it contains within itself a broad range of practical orientation. It is often alleged that the Catholic Church maintains whatever unity may be found for the party's official centrist position.

This factionalism may be due in part to the fact that Christian Democracy receives its support from a widely contrasting electorate. The party is a heavily interclassist one that cuts across the socioeconomic stratification of the nation such as to be represented by and represent many camps. The primary support for Christian Democracy is seen by many to emanate from the Catholic Church and its host of auxiliary organizations that permeate Italian life—chief among which is the very strong Catholic Action movement, a lay organization in which over one-half of the Christian Democratic deputies have a long background. Italian women are reputedly much more responsive than men to Church guidance. Since the postwar inauguration of female suffrage, women have played a crucial role for Christian Democracy by yielding fifty percent of their total vote to the party. This accounts for more than two-thirds of the total support for Christian Democracy, which is the only party in which the female vote exceeds that of the males. Christian Democratic supporters undoubtedly include a substantial number of Catholic priests, brothers, nuns, and seminarians, who together amount to about 230,000.

The demographic profile of DC support is thought to reflect the differential presence of Catholic sentiment and practice in the respective areas. Generally speaking, the party has done best in the small towns and in the rural areas; its least impressive showings have been in the cities and in the industrial areas. Christian Democracy has captured an average of forty percent of the total popular vote during the past twenty years and thereby has remained the governing party since the establishment of the Italian Republic. Further consideration of the administration of the Christian Democrats will be given in a subsequent section.

Italian Social Movement (MSI)

One of the more significant inconsistencies in the Italian political system is the existence of a neo-Fascist party, the

Italian Social Movement. According to Article Twelve of the Transitory Provisions of the Constitution, the reorganization of the former Fascist party, in any form whatsoever, is prohibited. The Italian Social Movement is basically the modern version of the *Partito Nazionale Fascista* (National Fascist Party, PNF) of the Mussolini era, and is alleged to be just as fascist. "Even though the party was abolished, I have always been a Fascist," confidentially commented one MSI deputy during the course of our interviews. The same representative repeatedly referred to himself and his colleagues as "we Fascists." Twelve of the eighteen deputies in our MSI sample previously had belonged to the PNF. When asked the reason for "changing their political ideology," three of these said that they "changed parties" because the PNF went out of existence, but seven stated that there was "no change in political party" for them, thus implying that the MSI and the PNF are ideologically the same.[d]

That the MSI is basically a fascist organization is, of course, no secret to the Italian people. The thinking of the Government is based undoubtedly on the principle of "divide and rule" and that it is more desirable to tolerate an open and semilegal presence of the MSI than to force it into the secretive activity of underground existence. Nevertheless, the unconstitutional existence of the party is a source of much consternation to many Italians, politicians or not, and the focus of frequent public demonstration.

As the party of the extreme right, the Italian Social Movement attempts to continue the revolutionary fascist tradition, although there have been some apparent modifications of methodology, and admittedly of ideology, to fit the currently democratic political context. Primary among these is a paradoxically socialistic orientation, which has drawn its inspiration

[d] The other two deputies joined the MSI because of "ideological convictions."

from the Fascist Socialistic Republic that Mussolini established in Salò in 1943. Nonetheless the ideology of the party remains essentially fascistic.

One of the fundamentals of fascist philosophy is "the complete, conscious rejection of individualism and liberalism, and the complete, conscious assertion of the supremacy of the State. From this principle, all other elements of fascism follow."[12] The object of fascism is unlimited power in the hands of the dictator and the self-appointed and self-perpetuating senior hierarchs or elite. The MSI is thus a basically totalitarian, nationalistic, and class-conscious movement. It claims to be a Catholic party and offers in this respect the contention that the former Fascist party was the only party that ever reached an accord with the Catholic Church by means of the Lateran Pacts that were signed in 1929. Accordingly, it professes to be an even more devout defender of the faith than Christian Democracy.

The leadership of the MSI lacks the charismatic character provided by Mussolini, for whom within the party there still remains much nostalgia and reverence. Yet the current program of the neo-Fascists is confronted by the unhappy memories of the Mussolini era, and their relatively weak support may be partially due to this. The MSI has received about five percent of the popular vote in recent national elections. Of course, for a period of five years following the establishment of the Republic, the ex-Fascist leaders were not allowed any form of political activity. This too may have some bearing on the issue of popular strength. The supporters of the party are alleged to be predominantly ex-Fascists, children of former Fascists, university students, and war veterans. Poll data show the largest concentration of neo-Fascist voters in small communities, and ecological studies indicate that the party has been strongest in the less developed and less urbanized regions of the country, particularly those in the south.

The MSI generally supports the Christian Democratic governments, particularly from the "revolutionary" threats on the political right. It has taken part in several governing coalitions with the DC on the local level.

Italian Communist Party (PCI)

The Italian Communist party is the second largest party in Italy and the largest Communist party in the non-Soviet bloc. It has nearly two million "card-holding" members and receives about seven million votes, which account for approximately twenty-five percent of the national poll. The large mass of its members and voters come from the lower-income industrial workers, sharecroppers, landless peasants, and the unemployed. Its particular stronghold is in north and central Italy, especially in the regions of Umbria, Tuscany, and Emilia-Romagna, which coincides by and large with the area of the former papal states.[e] This is Italy's "red belt" in which the PCI receives two-fifths of the popular vote and an absolute majority in some cities. Rome is regarded as the "Red-est" capital of the Western world; nearly one-third of the Romans are reported to be Communists either by membership or political sympathy. The party, however, has been losing heavily in membership (about twenty percent in the last ten years), although its voting strength has not diminished—in fact, it has increased with each new national election.

There are relatively few convinced Marxists in Italy. Probably no more than twenty thousand members of the PCI are believing or knowledgeable Marxists. Much of this is due to the very minimal degree of formal education among the supporters of the party. The PCI is the most proletarian of the competing parties; ninety percent of the PCI voters have no formal education, or only elementary training. The party

[e] Contrary to many assumptions the strongest support of the PCI is not in the poverty-stricken and depressed areas of southern Italy. Moreover, its most recent increases in the popular vote have occurred in an era of unprecedented prosperity, especially for the cities of the north.

attracts only about two percent of Italy's university graduates. But since Communism means different things to different people, the strength of the Communist party has many explanations. It has been attributed, not to any special love for Russia nor to any desire to Sovietize the Italian economy, but perhaps more to the traditional influence of Marxist concepts of class struggle and popular discontent for rigid social stratification, the poverty of the peasantry, reaction to Fascism, chaotic and authoritarian bureaucratic administration, and a simple protest against the Catholic Church and the government of the Christian Democrats.

The Communist party came into existence as an offshoot of the Socialist party in 1921. It is clearly not a marginal movement, isolated and alienated, but rather deeply rooted in Italian life and society. Organization in the PCI extends everywhere. There are party locals in almost every village, and cells in every neighborhood in cities and towns. Only the network of Catholic parishes is as widespread as that of the Italian Communist party. While basically a revolutionary party, the PCI has acted consistently in a formally constitutional manner during the years of the Republic. Its allegiance is to Moscow, and it is clearly dedicated to Marxist principles. Nonetheless, the PCI has adopted as an official position in its recent congresses the achievement of socialistic reform through peaceful means and democratic processes. The party, nonetheless, remains split into internal factions over this question of political methodology. The Khrushchevian views of Palmiro Togliatti, the party's original and long-time leader, have been proclaimed as the official position of the Italian Communists, and they still remain the dominant orientation of the PCI today.

Italian Socialist Party (PSI)

One of the more controversial parties in Italy today is the Italian Socialist party, which dates back to the turn of the century. Historically, Italian socialism has been divided between the "revisionists" who emphasize reform and political democracy, and the "maximalists" who emphasize the overthrow of the bourgeois system and the establishment of rule by the working class. The former have comprised the dominant faction throughout the years, and in 1921 the extreme left split off to form the Communist party. The long-time leader of the Socialists, Pietro Nenni, claims that the secessionist movement on the part of the Communists was more for "motives of form than substance"[13] in that the Communists wanted a Bolshevik-type revolution in order to bring about a Socialist reform. To this, Nenni and his followers were opposed since they did not accept the principles of dictatorship and domination.[14]

The Communists and the Socialists, however, were united by pact in 1934 and 1946, and they offered joint electoral lists in 1953. Perhaps for this reason many can see little difference between Italian communism and Italian socialism. Nenni claims that these pacts were negotiated in order to take common action against Fascism, and now that the pacts have been broken, the two parties have returned to the positions which they would have taken forty years ago had they not assumed this common line of action.[15] In 1956, after the Soviet suppression in Hungary, Nenni returned the Stalin Peace Prize which Moscow had awarded him, and the PSI withdrew from its political alliance with the PCI. The two parties offered separate electoral lists in the national elections of 1958 and 1963.

Fundamentally the ideological doctrines of the two parties remain the same. The major differences between them seems to be the method of implementation. Nenni maintains that the Italian Socialist party is attached more strongly than most other European Socialist parties to the doctrine of scientific socialism, that is, Marxism.[16] The central platform of the party involves a dedication to democratic improvement in social justice for the working class and a commitment to neutralism in the international sphere. Nenni claims that the political alliance with the PCI was broken when "forced to the conclusion that our own route lay in the direction of what constitutes the basic problem of modern society, namely, democracy— democracy as a method, and as a goal for human action in the endeavor to create a new society."[17] Lenin's thesis of professional revolution, and its implicit concept of government stemming from the belief that the majority of the people are unable to think for themselves, is rejected totally by the Socialists, who seemingly believe—at least ideally—in democracy and majority rule within their own party and within the nation.[18]

According to Mangone, "The perennial problem of the Italian Socialist Party has been its lack of unity. Through its confusion on strategy, its dogmatic schisms, and its personal divisions it has lost the primacy it once held among workers and intellectuals in Italy to the Communists, the Democratic Socialists, and the left wing of Christian Democracy."[19] The party has been split into two major factions. The extreme left wing, headed by Tullio Vecchietti, favors alliance with the Communist party. His following represents about one-third of the party's membership, and in 1964 this faction split off and formed the PSIUP (Italian Socialist Party of Proletarian Unity). The controlling autonomists represent about fifty-eight percent of the party. It is the feeling of many that there remain within the PSI out-and-out dedicated Communists who threaten to secede and to join the Communist party. Quite recently, in fact, a group within the party caucused and declared themselves "national Communists" and established as guiding principles of their organization the development of the fullest democracy.[20]

Nenni considers the various dimensions within the PSI to be reflections of the diverse socioeconomic elements which the party represents: the poor peasants, the day laborers, factory workers, and the intellectuals.[21] Its strongest support is in the northern region of Italy, particularly Umbria and Tuscany, although it is gaining strength in the south. It captures about fourteen percent of the popular vote; most of its support is from the better educated and the more skilled segments of the working class. It is also more successful than the PCI in attracting followers among the middle class.

The PSI entered the coalition government of February 1962 (a government which made the unprecedented move toward a more socialistic orientation) and has remained in successive governments up to the present day.

Italian Social Democratic Party (PSDI)

The Social Democratic party, originally called the *Partito Socialista dei Lavoratori Italiani* (Socialist Party of Italian Workers), is an outgrowth of the Socialist party because of the withdrawal of Giuseppe Saragat (current President of Italy) and his followers in 1947 after the political alliance with the Communists had been renewed. More recent political developments have brought the two parties into much closer agreement and collaboration. Following national congresses of both parties in October 1966, the PSDI and the PSI formally agreed to a merger into a unified Socialist party. The organizational reunification, however, will not be complete until after the next national election in 1968.

The PSDI is a revisionist Marxist party that is dedicated to the democratic establishment of liberalism. Its allegiance is to the Western powers. Despite its Marxist origins the PSDI is not primarily a working-class party. It makes a greater appeal to the working elite—skilled workers, artisans, and clerical workers. Its main strength, however, is among the professional and higher income and educational categories. Strongest support is in the northern and central industrial regions of Piedmont, Liguria, and Lombardy. The strength of the PSDI, presently accounting for more than five percent of the popular vote, had been decreasing steadily and rapidly until the recent national election in 1963 in which it showed a considerable increase in the popular poll. It now numbers thirty-three deputies in the Chamber, which contrasts to the seventeen it won in the 1953 national election. The Social Democrats have been in coalition with the Christian Democratic governments for a number of years.

Italian Republican Party (PRI)

The Republican party claims an official center position on the political continuum. Yet, it, too, is marked by factions, and its dominant strength is oriented more toward a moderate leftist position. The party derives its name from its basic ideological position in favor of a republican form of government. It is the heir to the ideals of Mazzini and the tradition of the *Risorgimento.*

Since 1946, and the end of the monarchy, the PRI has had no substantial rationale for existence. The party does not receive strong support and has been in gradual decline for the past several years. In fact, it receives the least backing of all the major parties, which in the last two national elections amounted to 1.4 percent of the total vote. Its followers comprise the very staunch supporters of republicanism, along with voters with anticlerical sentiments; its strength is concentrated in the north. Despite its size (only six deputies in the Chamber) the PRI represents quite a range of political opinion and exercises a significant role on the national level. For a number of years the party has been in coalition with the Christian Democratic governments, in which it has retained ministerial posts.

Italian Liberal Party (PLI)

The Italian Liberal party is a basically conservative party that maintains a moderate rightist position. Some of its representatives, however, consider it to be a typically centrist party. Originally the PLI supported a conservative constitutional monarchy, and the separation of cross and crown. The party essentially seeks free enterprise in the economy and advocates the doctrine of liberty for the individual. Its primary support, as may be expected, comes from industrialists, large land-owners, and upper-income employees. In fact, the party is allegedly endorsed and financed chiefly by *Confindustria* (the Italian equivalent of the National Association of Manufacturers in the United States), for whose interest supposedly it is the parliamentary representative.[22]

It has also captured some of the ex-Fascist support on the right. The party's strongest support is localized in the urban centers of the northern and central regions of the country. The popular support of the PLI, up to the last national election of 1963 in which it doubled its strength, had been limited to about three percent of the total vote. The Liberals had participated in several coalitions with the Christian Democratic government until the formation of the Fourth Fanfani Government in 1962 shifted the DC toward a more leftist orientation.

Italian Democratic Party (PDI)

The Italian Democratic party is the result of a fusion in 1959 of two monarchist parties, the *Partito Monarchico Populare* (PMP) and the *Partito Nazionale Monarchico* (PNM). The former grew out of the PNM after the national elections of 1953 as a result of a power struggle and differences of opinion over political methodology rather than basic ideology. It accounted for about twenty-five percent of the PNM strength and found its chief support in south Italy. The monarchist parties—in whatever form—developed as a consequence of the 1946 referendum which rejected the monarchical form of government in favor of the Republic.

Originally the monarchists attracted considerable support, although their popularity has been located predominantly in the south, where every region voted in favor of the monarchy in 1946. And in the Campania (Naples district) region the vote was three to one against the Republic. Since 1958 the PDI has suffered a severe decline. During the course of the field work for this study in the summer of 1961, the parliamentary unit of the Democratic party began to disintegrate. Many of its deputies withdrew from the party and declared themselves "Independent Monarchists." One of these former PDI deputies, in fact, had announced at that time the formation of still another monarchical party. Evidently the same type of factional split that marked the PMP-PNM episode had come to life again. (This accounts, incidentally, for our relatively small sample of representatives for the PDI, although we interviewed several of the "Independent Monarchists.") The popular strength of the monarchists dropped from 4.8 percent in 1958 to 1.7 percent in the last national election in 1963.

The Democratic party represents the traditionalist elements which seek to defend throne and altar, and their separation. It is a basically nondemocratic movement that captures strong conservative support—from many major property owners as well as from some ex-Fascists—and a heavy vote from the peasantry. One of its obvious aims is the restoration of the House of Savoy to Italian rule. Some followers claim, however, that the monarchists have abandoned hopes of monarchical restoration and seek principally to defend the vested interests of their followers. Accordingly, the focus of party leadership allegedly has shifted from the exiled Umberto II of the House of Savoy to national figures that have been prominent in the history of the monarchical movement. Many local coalitions have been formed by the monarchist parties with the Christian Democrats and with the MSI.

General Party Organization

The major Italian parties have a similar organizational structure. The original model is that of the Soviet Communist party, which was adopted by the Italian Communist party and subsequently taken over by the other parties. The supreme organ is the national party congress composed of delegates selected from the general membership. These bodies meet annually or biannually and delegate power to a central committee which functions through an executive board that appoints the party secretary, who is the individual leader of the party.

In spite of the apparent democratic organization, power in the Italian parties is centered at the top. It is unusual for popular movements at the local level to have much success in removing the party hierarchs from their dominant positions. The party secretary controls most elections at all levels and in effect runs the party according to his wishes.

These descriptions of the major political parties, and the system of party organization in Italy, should serve as one indication of the political complexity which the nation offers. Particularly evident should be the fact that political ideologies are culturally relative, as is the affinity among the respective political movements within any one nation. We shall refer to these points in the chapters to follow. The popular support and strength of these major parties may be seen in Table 2, which indicates the results of voting and seat allocations for the Chamber of Deputies during the four national elections under the Republic and its preceding Constituent Assembly.

The Government of the Christian Democrats

Christian Democracy has been the governing power of Italy since the establishment of the Republic. As a result of the national elections in 1948 this party enjoyed an absolute parliamentary majority in both houses of Parliament. Since the national elections of 1953, however, the Christian Democrats have not enjoyed such success, and their strength has been declining steadily, although the party still continues to receive

TABLE 2*

RESULTS OF ITALIAN NATIONAL ELECTIONS, 1946–1963

	Constituent Assembly 1946			Chamber of Deputies 1948			Chamber of Deputies 1953			Chamber of Deputies 1958			Chamber of Deputies 1963**		
	Votes	%	Seats	Votes	%	Seats	Votes	%	Seats	Votes	%	Seats	Votes	%	Seats
DC	8,080,644	35.2	207	12,712,562	48.5	305	10,834,466	40.0	262	12,520,556	42.4	273	11,763,418	38.3	260
MSI				526,670	2.0	6	1,579,880	5.9	29	1,407,550	4.8	24	1,569,202	5.1	27
PCI	4,356,686	19.0	104	{8,137,047	31.0	}113	6,120,709	22.6	143	6,704,763	22.7	140	7,763,854	25.3	166
PSI	4,758,129	20.7	115	} People's Bloc			3,441,014	12.7	75	4,206,777	14.2	84	4,251,966	13.8	87
PSDI				1,858,364	7.1	33	1,222,957	4.5	19	1,345,334	4.5	22	1,874,379	6.1	33
PRI	1,003,007	4.4	23	652,477	2.5	9	438,149	1.0	5	405,767	1.4	6	420,746	1.4	6
PLI	1,560,638	6.8	41	1,004,889	3.8	19	815,929	3.0	14	1,047,073	3.5	17	2,142,053	7.0	39
PNM	637,328	2.8	16	729,174	2.8	14	1,854,850	6.8	40	659,956	2.2	11			
PMP										776,698	2.6	14			
PDI													536,653	1.7	8
Total[a]	22,968,286	92.1		26,220,150	97.6		27,087,601	95.4		29,413,823	96.6		35,428,595	98.7	

[a] Valid votes, excluding minor parties.

* Source: Annuario Statistico Italiano 1960 (Rome: Istituto Centrale di Statistica) pp. 144–148.

** Annuario Statistico Italiano 1965 (Rome: Istituto Centrale di Statistica), pp. 148–149.

the single high plurality of the popular votes. It controlled only forty-five percent of the seats in the Chamber in 1953 as compared to fifty-three percent in 1948. With this situation of declining power, Christian Democracy had to resort to coalitions, which in its many governments have been formed with other "centrist" parties: PSDI, PRI, and PLI.

Christian Democracy has been, as we indicated, a "rainbow party" that tolerates all shades of political complexion from left to right as long as they are within the Christian ethic. Other than this, its only initial unity seemed to be that it was anti-Communist. With time the threat of a socialist revolution which developed after World War II subsided, and no longer was an anti-Communistic platform sufficient for a political program. The Christian Democrats became saddled with factions and internal power struggles, which resulted in charges of *immobilismo* from the opposition. This, together with the loss of popular support, called for a new line of political thinking and orientation.

But, dependent upon their support, Christian Democracy was frozen solidly in the political center by the parties of the moderate left and the moderate right. Furthermore, these parties in coalition were losing popular strength. This situation placed Christian Democracy in an even more serious predicament, since the combined strength of these parties offered a majority that was too narrow for reliability. Greater coalition strength was needed; a turn to either the left or the right would mean the consequent loss of the respective parties already in coalition. Stronger and more pronounced polarization took place among the Christian Democrats, so that political neutrality was no longer possible. The balance of power shifted toward the left—the direction of the times as reflected in the trends of the popular vote. The major figures in Christian Democracy, particularly former Prime Minister Amintore Fanfani, advocated a more socialistic program.

The proposed move became known as *l'apertura à sinistra* (the opening to the left). The only choice for a coalition was obviously with the PSI, since any union with the PCI was unthinkable. Opposition to the plan on the national level was intense and fearsome, not only for practical political reasons but especially because of the previous pacts between the Socialists and the Communists, who remained allied in several municipal governments, particularly in southern Italy. The controversy held sway for a considerable length of time while pressure for action built up, particularly among the center-left parties of the coalition who threatened the withdrawal of their support.

In January 1961 the biennial congress of Christian Democracy met in Naples and there endorsed a plan presented by Fanfani and Aldo Moro, the party secretary, which provided for collaboration with the Socialist party. After sixteen years in a solidly centrist position the Christian Democrats had decided to open to the left. The party has continued this position through several governments until the present day. For the time being, at least, Christian Democracy has succeeded in securing the position originally established by Sturzo, and even by his very method.[f] Popular reaction to this new alliance, as judged in the poll returns from the 1963 national election, seems to be detrimental to the major parties concerned.

THE STATE AND THE CHURCH

No consideration of Italian politics would be complete, of course, without a realization of the major role of the Roman

[f] From 1919 to 1922 Sturzo attempted to obtain a common front among Social Democrats, Socialists, and Popularists for the formation of a government in which the Socialists would participate. See Mario Einaudi and Francois Goguel, *Christian Democracy in Italy and France* (Notre Dame: University of Notre Dame Press, 1952).

Catholic Church. Perhaps in no other nation have relations between Church and state been so controversial. The history of the one has been inseparable from that of the other.

The current situation is undoubtedly due in great part to the presence of the sovereign Vatican City within the Italian boundaries. To many people this unique situation necessitates special arrangements for the effective separation of Church and state. For others it has been the cause of fierce and extensive anticlericalism.

The Italian Constitution explicitly recognizes the Roman Catholic ethic as an integral part of Italian life and subsidizes it, despite the theoretical provisions for freedom of religion as given in the Constitution. The activities of the Vatican in many instances are recognized as major functions of the Italian state, as may be witnessed in such things as the publication of Church and papal functions in the political calendar of the Italian state, the listing of the hierarchy in the official parliamentary annual, and the state's official participation in the recent Ecumenical Council.

The relationships between the Church and the state are affirmed in Article Seven of the Constitution, which provides that "The State and the Catholic Church are within its own ambit, independent and sovereign. Their relations are regulated by the Lateran Pacts." These were incorporated by the Constituent Assembly into the Constitution of the Republic. Article One of the Pacts states: "Italy recognizes and reaffirms the principle embodied in article one of the statute of the kingdom dated the fourth of March 1848, according to which the Roman Catholic Apostolic religion is the sole religion of the state." Lest this be construed as an exclusive right accorded to the Catholic Church, however, Article Eight of the Constitution provides that "All religious denominations other than the Catholic are entitled to organize themselves according to their own creed provided that they are not in conflict with

Italian juridical organization. Their relations with the State are regulated by law on the basis of agreements with their respective representations."

This recognition of the Catholic religion as the sole religion of the state is interpreted customarily to mean only that whenever the state feels moved to participate in any religious act, it will do so through the agency of the Catholic Church.[23] Yet the recognition implies more than this. Article 36 of the Lateran Pacts provides for instruction in Christian doctrine in the elementary and secondary schools according to the Catholic tradition in a program agreed upon by the Holy See and the state. This instruction is to be given by teachers (laymen, clerics, or priests) approved and certified by the ecclesiastical authorities. Only textbooks approved by these authorities may be used for such religious teaching in the public schools. Furthermore, the Concordat—part of the Lateran Pacts—provides for the payment out of public funds for the maintenance of religious activity and exempts Church property from taxes. These pacts require mutual consent, and thus approval of the pope, for any modification. Experience shows, furthermore, that generally the Pacts have taken precedence over the Constitution whenever the two are not consistent with one another.[24] On the other hand, these arrangements are not all obligations of the state, since it retains the right to assert its powers in matters that relate to the appointment of bishops and the administration of ecclesiastical benefices.[25] For example, the Pacts require that all bishops in Italy be Italian, that they take an oath of loyalty to the state, and that these bishops be approved by the state.[26]

The Catholic Church is undoubtedly the most powerful non-party organization in Italy, and its influence is not exclusively spiritual. The clergy are to a great extent channels of access and influence in government, the public bureaucracy, and the parties; and they replace the parliamentarians in many instances. At election times the civic committee of the Catholic Action Movement conducts a major campaign. Nearly one-third of the Italian population will vote in a manner which is consistent with the directives of the Church, which have been traditionally supportive of Christian Democracy. But since the Christian Democrats for their part do not always follow the wishes of the Church, the power of the Church is more effectively negative than positive—it may more likely block rather than compel a particular course of action. Many of the other parties are quite respectful of the Church, but the Socialist parties, on the other hand, favor the principle *"libera chiesa, libera stato"* (free church, free state), which means in effect that the Church should disinterest itself completely from politics.

NOTES

[1] See Edward McNeil Burns, *Western Civilizations* (New York: W. W. Norton & Company, 1963), p. 736.

[2] Gordon A. Craig, *Europe Since 1815* (New York: Holt, Rinehart & Winston, 1961), pp. 339–340.

[3] Article 59 of the Constitution of the Italian Republic.

[4] Gerard J. Mangone, "Part IV: Italy" in Taylor Cole (ed.), *European Political Systems* (New York: Alfred A. Knopf, 1959), p. 509.

[5] Norman Kogan, *The Government of Italy* (New York: Thomas Y. Crowell, 1962), p. 41.

[6] Quoted in Mario Einaudi and Francois Goguel, *Christian Democracy in Italy and France* (Notre Dame: University of Notre Dame Press, 1952), p. 13.

[7] Einaudi, "The Italian Elections of 1948," *Review of Politics*, X (1948), 357.

[8] Einaudi and Goguel, *op. cit.*, p. 41.

[9] Quoted in Einaudi, "The Italian Election of 1948," *op. cit.*, p. 357.

[10] Einaudi and Goguel, *op. cit.*, pp. 84–88.

[11] E. A. Bayne, "Italy's Seeds of Peril," American Universities Field Staff, Reports Service, X (1962), No. 1, 4.

[12] Harold W. Metz and Charles A. H. Thomson, *Authoritarianism and the Individual* (Washington: The Brookings Institution, 1950), p. 210.

[13] Pietro Nenni, "Where the Italian Socialists Stand," *Foreign Affairs*, XL (1962), 213–215.

[14] *Ibid.*

[15] *Ibid.*, p. 217.

[16] *Ibid.*, p. 213.

[17] Pietro Nenni, "Progressive Forces in Italian Politics," *International Affairs,* XXXVII (1961), 213.

[18] William Ebenstein, *Today's Isms* (Englewood Cliffs: Prentice-Hall, 1961), pp. 209–210.

[19] Mangone, *op. cit.,* p. 495.

[20] Bayne, *op. cit.,* p. 12.

[21] Nenni, "Progressive Forces in Italian Politics," *International Affairs,* XXXVII (1961), 213.

[22] Bayne, *op. cit.,* pp. 3–14.

[23] Einaudi and Goguel, *op. cit.,* p. 40.

[24] See John C. Adams and Paolo Barile, *The Government of Republican Italy* (Boston: Houghton Mifflin, 1961), pp. 226–227.

[25] Einaudi and Goguel, *op. cit.,* p. 40.

[26] Herbert W. Schneider, *The Fascist Government of Italy* (Princeton: D. Van Nostrand, 1936), p. 20.

CHAPTER IV

Italian National Character

ONE ELEMENT ESSENTIAL to comprehending anything Italian is its national character, which perhaps is more intriguing and equally as mystifying as its political history. The problem is presented succinctly in the following statement from Sforza:

> The Italian—especially the common Italian—is at once so complex and so simple that one can only smile at the strangers who think that in a year or so on the peninsula they have discovered the key to the Italian character. Paradox or not, it is easier to discover the complexity of Italians than their simplicity.[1]

Much of this "complexity of Italians" seems to be due to the individualism of the Italian character—a rather proud independence of mind. Remarked one deputy: "It is difficult to understand Italy because we are very individualistic." Clearly this is manifested in the unusual plurality of political parties in Italy.

For what, we may ask, would bring about such a complexity of political organization? Much of this is due undoubtedly to the history and the tradition of the nation. Yet, without attempting to be reductive, we would attribute this plurality of political parties, and the diversity of political ideology which it represents, above all to the very dominant and pervasive characteristic of individuality which is fundamental in the Italian national character. The national modal character[a] of Italy may be described as one of "authoritarian individualism."

THE AUTHORITARIAN SOCIOCULTURAL SYSTEM

The political system of a nation usually is interrelated with and reflects the character of other institutional systems. It is somewhat of a truism that the institutional structure of Italian society is basically authoritarian. This situation is allegedly the chief agent of authoritarianism as a modal element in the Italian national character. That the Italian modal character is authoritarian is supported by our references in Chapter II to Italian studies which have used versions of the F-scale in an empirical investigation of this question.

No nation can escape the effects of its history. For Italy this includes the centuries of Spanish domination with its extravagant formalism, the bureaucratic centralization of the Piedmont Kingdom, and the years of enforced conformity to Fascism and its edification of the state.[2] Remnants from many of these historical elements are retained in the present political system. Particularly relevant are the holdovers of the Fascist civil and criminal codes, and the traditional bureaucratic apparatus which is literally medieval in many respects. Italian society is strongly bureaucratic and authoritarian, particularly in all aspects that comprise the state. One of the most conspicuous examples of the entire Italian social system is the intri-

---

[a] Modal character as used here refers to that type which is found so predominantly as to be designated the central characteristic or central tendency of personality within a given field.

cately complicated power structures and power relationships which result therefrom. Social activity in this context becomes primarily a power struggle.

Italian social life may be characterized as extremely formal, marked with a keen sense of status consciousness and social relations which are often caste-like in nature. One example, noticeable to even the least sophisticated observer, would be the distinctions of first- and second-class railroad travel, and the respectively separated waiting rooms found even in the infrequently used stations of very small towns. Often these facilities can be distinguished only by their physical separateness. Another reflection of this formality is found in the Italian language, which among other things provides *three* forms for addressing the second person.[b]

One would expect under such conditions that power and authority (whatever their origins) are apt to be central or dominant values in the Italian culture and that its people would be expected to manifest a keener search for personal power in virtue of a social system wherein the avenues for this have been limited extensively—not to mention the shallow and constricted distribution of political power. In turn this situation would lead most likely to the production of authoritarian personalities. There is little doubt that personality is partly the result of cultural and social influences, and fundamentally the product of socialization. Prothro and Melikian conclude from their research that "residence in an authoritarian culture (social, family, and political life of the Near East) leads to higher F-scores."[3] And, as Frenkel-Brunswik states: "It is true that the authoritarian character in a sense is a mirror of his society."[4] More particularly, personality in many respects may be seen as a microcosm of the societal macrocosm.

What are some of the historical and cultural factors which

[b] The Fascist regime tried to abolish the formal usages in an attempt to do away with any individual respect or personal deference, but apparently the conventional practice was resurrected after its demise.

would account for the Italian social structure manifesting an authoritarian nature and producing a national character of a similar kind? Italian society today retains those authoritarian structures which have been so much a part of its history. Aside from the medieval history of independent kingdoms, the subsequent constitutional monarchy—like all monarchies—was essentially authoritarian in structure. Monarchical forms of government are basically authoritarian—imposing clear and strong status distinctions upon their followings—and are marked with a unidimensional flow of authority from a supreme apex to an expansive, but weak, base. Some argue that the Italians desire and are prone toward the acceptance of charismatic leaders, perhaps even an individual leader such as a king. We can reiterate here that the monarchy was rejected by a very slim vote in the 1946 referendum; its supporters accounted for forty-five percent of the total vote. And many Italians feel that there was dishonesty in manipulating this vote in favor of the Republic.

Equally as important in this regard have been the centuries of widespread influence, and even temporal powers, of the very strong Roman Catholic Church, an organization which is structured in a highly authoritarian manner. Italy for all intents and purposes may be regarded as the most "Catholic" country in the world—perhaps not necessarily in terms of actual membership and practice but merely for the historical and institutional reasons which characterize the unique relationship between the Church and the Italian state. That the Catholic Church is basically authoritarian in doctrine and hierarchical in structure is reflected in the fact that Catholics score relatively high on the F-scale[5] as well as on the Dogmatism Scale.[6]

Under these historical and social circumstances one would expect the Italian family structure to be authoritarian, as it most certainly is. In this regard Linton has stated:

> Nations with authoritarian family structure invariably seem to develop authoritarian governments, no matter what the official government forms

may be. Latin American countries, with their excellent democratic
institutions and actual dictatorships, would be a case in point. In time
of crisis, a nation which has this authoritarian pattern will immediately
look for a dictator and individuals will find the emotional security in
complete devotion and obedience.[7]

Italy today remains a strongly centralized and authoritarian
political system, which is illustrated in the powers of the police
and provincial prefects as well as in the remaining aspects of
the Fascist bureaucracy and law, all of which combine to
impose serious limitations upon civil liberties in contrast to
those granted in many other free nations. This oligarchic pattern of decision-making is equally as true of Italian industry.
Banfield offers the view that "amoral familism" is the ethos
of the whole Italian society. This involves a type of individualism which is anticivic, and places a primacy upon personal
interests and emphasizes personal gain.[8]

There is one other explanation which may be considered for
the authoritarian nature of the Italian national character. May
this be due to the very broad lower-class base which characterizes Italian society? This hypothesis, of course, implies that
authoritarian personalities are found more prevalently in the
lower social strata. The argument is that both evidence and
theory suggest that these social levels are relatively more
authoritarian than others.[9] This, however, is based primarily,
if not exclusively, upon the "authoritarian syndrome" and findings derived from various versions of the F-scale which have
revealed correlations in this regard, particularly with the factor of education. Accordingly, authoritarianism is attributed
more so to the lower social classes partly because of their
lower educational attainments.

Thus, the Italian social system is basically and strongly authoritarian in the structure of its pivotal institutions—political,
religious, and familial, although it is obviously difficult to say
which of these is primary in influencing the others. The actual

situation is more likely one of mutual reinforcement which makes for greater intensification throughout the system.

Does the authoritarian nature of the Italian national character offer an explanation for the origin and widespread development and following of Fascism in Italy as contrasted to situations elsewhere? It is contended that Fascism, to appear and to take such a strong hold on the nation, needed certain disposing factors in the sociocultural milieu. We feel that these existed in the Italian social system. As Ebenstein points out, some people and some nations are more "dictatorship prone" than others and "the very existence of an authoritarian mass movement like Fascism depends on the *desire* of many persons to submit and obey."[10] But, what is it, we may ask, that on the more personal level leads to this "dictatorship proneness"? The phenomenon that is fertile soil for the rise of fascism anywhere, says Fromm, is "the insignificance and powerlessness of the individual."[11] Thus, with its sociocultural values and structures it would be "normal" for nations like Italy and Germany to provide for the rise of authoritarian and fascist governments, that is, from an authoritarian way of life to fascism may be only a step.[12] There is, therefore, an opening to argue that the authoritarian history and national character of Italy facilitated the development of Fascism. Nevertheless, little denial can be made that the effects of this ideology and its regime over the course of a generation strengthened the basic authoritarian tone of the social institutions. And the more important consideration is the penetrating influence which this kind of social system had on the Italian national character.

The Fascists did try to modify the national character. Part of the Fascist program under Mussolini, and especially under the secretary of the PNF, Achille Starace, was to change the Italian character into a new type by reforming certain Italian customs and thus the culture. States Germino, "The objective of the directives on Fascist 'style' was to make the Italians less

likeable and more ruthless. *L'uomo nuovo, il Fascista,* was to
be the inverse of the traditional Italian stereotype: he was
to be serious, efficient, hard, and militaristic."[13] He continues:
"The Fascist party was bent on nothing less than making the
Italian citizen over into a new man, a man who thought, acted,
and believed according to the dictates of the ruling ideology."[14]

Almost all students of national character agree that societies
which have experienced recurrent or prolonged authoritarian
government are inhabited by a large number of people that
have personality structures of an authoritarian or similar
nature. We might deduce from this evidence that the basic
personality structure of the Italian is authoritarian—or, as we
stated, may be described as one of "authoritarian individualism."[c] By speaking in this context of a "basic personality structure" is meant that personality configuration which is shared
by the bulk of the members of a particular society as a result of common experiences, particularly in the process of
socialization.[15]

DOGMATIC PERSONALITY STRUCTURES

The data for our nonpolitical control group (described in
Chapter II) may serve as a suitable indication of Italian
national character, particularly in the dimension of the authoritarian personality structure. The development of dogmatism,
as with that of authoritarianism, is a matter of the kind of
social *structures* to which one is exposed.

We found that of the total of 436 individuals, 74 percent

---

[c] Frenkel-Brunswik states: "He [the authoritarian personality] is not adapted
to change and thus lacks one of the most important requirements in all modern
societies." Else Frenkel-Brunswik, "Interaction of Psychological and Sociological
Factors in Political Behavior," *American Political Science Review,* XLVI (1952),
p. 64. One may wonder if this fact explains why Italy has remained so medieval
in function and so traditionalistic in spirit. At any rate, there is in evidence a
cultural lag which does not seem to be explained by economic factors alone.

scored positively (dogmatic) and 20 percent negatively (non-dogmatic) as determined along a possible score range of − 20 to + 20. The remaining six percent obtained neutral scores. The mean dogmatism score for the entire control group was 3.66 with a standard deviation[d] value of 5.36. The following table offers a categorical range of scores.

TABLE 3

DISTRIBUTION OF POSITIVE AND NEGATIVE DOGMATISM
SCORERS IN NONPOLITICAL CONTROL SAMPLE

Positive Scorers		Negative Scorers	
+ 1 to +10	282 (65%)	− 1 to −10	81 (19%)
+11 to +20	40 (9%)	−11 to −20	5 (1%)
Total	322 (74%)		86 (20%)

On the basis of these findings it would seem that closed-mindedness is apt to be a modal element of the Italian national character. Unfortunately, for lack of data we are not able to compare these findings with similar studies in other cultures. A legitimate objection may be raised that this sample is composed predominantly of Romans, which are more likely to be southern in mentality.[e] One nevertheless would expect the

[d] The *standard deviation* is a statistical measure of the distribution or amount of variability of scores around a mean. One standard deviation value on each side of the mean represents 68.26 percent of the scores; two standard deviation values on each side of the mean represent 95.44 percent of the scores.

[e] No statistically significant difference in mean dogmatism score was found for those residing in the province of Rome more than five years and those not in this category. Residents: $M = 3.69$, $S. D. = 5.43$, $N = 355$; nonresidents: $M = 3.75$, $S. D. = 4.77$, $N = 69$. t-value is .078.

southern mentality to be more closed-minded than its northern counterpart since the kind of structures which are productive of dogmatism are found both more intensively and extensively in the south. Moreover, voluntary respondents particularly would constitute a biased sample of low scorers. Volunteers in psychological studies have a greater tendency to be less fascist-minded, less conventional, less anti-intraceptive, less dogmatic, and less authoritarian.[16] It was found that in one study using an F-scale the individuals willing to be interviewed differed significantly from those not willing (the more authoritarian).[17]

The strong individualism which is characteristic of the Italian mentality would appear to be an indication of open-mindedness. On the other hand, it can be—and apparently is more likely in the Italian case—a correlate of an ethnocentrism which not only is central to the Italian national character but also is elemental in the authoritarian syndrome. This attitude has been expressed traditionally in the history of a regionalism which persists today, albeit in a rather modified and tempered fashion, as an integral part of Italian life. The nineteen regions that constitute administrative entities of the Italian Republic are fundamentally the historical and geographic subdivisions of Italy. These regions have a most curious and interesting importance in whatever attempt is made to understand anything Italian. Each has its own native customs, dress, food, dialect, history, and even form of government in some instances. As Schneider remarks, "Among strangers Italians are so obviously Italian that the foreign observer cannot appreciate the extent to which among themselves they are Venetians, Tuscans, Neapolitans, Sicilians, etc."[18] Essentially, these subdivisions are the same as those that were in existence during the Middle Ages. The people of these regions were fierce enemies and rivals for centuries, and not all of this feeling has disappeared. Even though the development of communication and transportation has broken down many of their separating barriers, these distinct subcultures continue to endure. Nevertheless one must realize that in the history and life of these regions there is not only an individuality but also a unity of Italian mentality. Strangely paralleling the persistent hatreds and rancors that these regions have borne each other is a keen sense of nationalism which, in an extreme form, is another indication of an authoritarian ethnocentrism.

Perhaps today such regional ethnocentrism is more pronounced in the relations between northern and southern Italy, which are separated so widely by realistic socioeconomic differences that one frequently hears references to "the two Italies." Aside from cultural, lingual, sociological, psychological, and even biological differences, the most disturbing discrepancy between these two areas is economic. The south is a backward agricultural area, much of which is depressed miserably; the north is a rapidly developing and prosperous industrial area.[f]

This socioeconomic cleavage has had serious consequences for the social rapport between northern and southern Italians. The former tend to display an attitude of superiority toward their latter compatriots. The typical Italian of the south, says Carlo Sforza, is to the Italian-in-general what the latter is to northern Europeans, with the same accentuation of qualities and defects.[19] One might say that northern Italians are as anti-Italian as the United States Congress which passed the immigration statutes of 1921 and 1924 if by "Italian" is meant the southern Italian to whom these laws were directed primarily.[g] Despite these situations all Italians are thoroughly and profoundly Italian, and share within this regional diversity

[f] One reason among others advanced for this situation is the geographical separation brought about by the existence of the former papal states in central Italy. See Carlo Sforza, *The Real Italians* (New York: Columbia University Press, 1942), p. 69.

[g] It may be noted that the American stereotype of the Italian is typically that of the southern Italian. Likewise, the Italo-American subculture is based overwhelmingly on that of southern Italy. This may be explained by the differential Italian migration to the United States between 1890 and 1910.

and ethnocentric spirit a common heritage and a unity of Italian culture and mentality. Yet this pronounced regional temperament and national spirit undoubtedly is related in some way to the relatively strong degree of closed-mindedness which apparently is distinctive of the Italian national character.

Any meaningful concept of a distinctive political personality must be related to its sociocultural milieu and viewed analytically in such a context. This consideration of Italian national character—as with that of the nation's political history and structure—will be an important frame of reference for our considerations in the chapters that follow.

NOTES

[1] Carlo Sforza, *The Real Italians* (New York: Columbia University Press, 1942), p. 77.

[2] Gerard J. Mangone, "Part IV: Italy" in Taylor Cole (ed.), *European Political Systems* (New York: Alfred A. Knopf, 1959), p. 507.

[3] E. Terry Prothro and Levon Melikian, "The California Public Opinion Scale in an Authoritarian Culture," *Public Opinion Quarterly*, XVII (1953), 353–362.

[4] Else Frenkel-Brunswik, "Interaction of Psychological and Sociological Factors in Political Behavior," *American Political Science Review*, XLVI (1952), p. 64.

[5] Milton Rokeach, *The Open and Closed Mind* (New York: Basic Books, 1960), p. 111.

[6] *Ibid.*, p. 351.

[7] Ralph Linton, "The Concept of National Character" in Alfred A. Stanton and Stewart E. Perry, *Personality and Political Crisis* (Glencoe: The Free Press, 1951), p. 146.

[8] Edward C. Banfield, *The Moral Basis of a Backward Society* (Glencoe: The Free Press, 1955), p. 7.

[9] See Seymour M. Lipset, *Political Man* (London: William Heineman, 1960), p. 101.

[10] William Ebenstein, *Today's Isms* (Englewood Cliffs: Prentice Hall, 1961), p. 101.

[11] Erich Fromm, *Escape From Freedom* (New York: Holt, Rinehart & Winston, 1941), p. 240.

[12] Ebenstein, *op. cit.*, pp. 100–101.

[13] Dante L. Germino, *The Italian Fascist Party* (Minneapolis: University of Minnesota Press, 1959), p. 26.

[14] *Ibid.*, p. 27.

[15] Abram Kardiner, *The Psychological Frontiers of Society* (New York: Columbia University Press, 1945), pp. 23–46.

[16] See Ephraim Rosen, "Differences Between Volunteers and Non-Volunteers for Psychological Studies," *Journal of Abnormal Psychology,* XXXV (1951), 185–193.

[17] Lorraine P. Kruglov and Helen H. Davidson, "The Willingness to be Interviewed: A Selective Factor in Sampling," *Journal of Social Psychology,* XXXVIII (1953), 39–47.

[18] Herbert W. Schneider, *The Fascist Government of Italy* (Princeton: D. Van Nostrand, 1936), p. 4.

[19] *Ibid.*, p. 71.

CHAPTER V

The Political Personality

HAVING DESCRIBED the research process, as well as the relevant sociopolitical aspects of Italy and its national character, we shall turn to our findings with a treatment of the first general question—the political personality. As we have seen in the introductory chapter, several statements previously published have suggested that the professional politician may be distinguished by the possession of a distinctive personality, particularly one which is characterized by strong orientations toward power as a personal value.

Our specific concerns in this chapter will be a consideration of the nature of the personality structure of the professional politician in terms of the dogmatism syndrome, the relationship of this political personality to that similarly measured for the nonpolitical individual, and the question of power-orientation as the distinctive mark of the professional politician.

The Empirical Evidence

Politicians and Dogmatism

The first hypothesis to be considered is stated as follows:

> The political personality is characterized by a structural syndrome of authoritarianism or dogmatism to a relatively strong degree.

Our data show that professional politicians appear to be generally dogmatic in personality structure. Seventy-six percent of our sample scored positively on the D-10 instrument, and twenty-four percent negatively, within the possible range of -20 to $+20$. The categorical range of scores is given in Table 4. The mean dogmatism score for this sample is 5.51, with a standard deviation of 6.75.

TABLE 4

DISTRIBUTION OF POSITIVE AND NEGATIVE DOGMATISM SCORERS IN POLITICAL SAMPLE

Positive Scorers		Negative Scorers	
$+$ 1 to $+10$ = 61 (47%)		$-$ 1 to -10 = 26 (20%)	
$+11$ to $+20$ = 37 (29%)		-11 to -20 = 1 (1%)	
Total	98 (76%)		27 (21%)

Politicians and Nonpoliticians

These data become significant only when seen in some kind

of a comparative perspective. For this purpose we introduce Hypothesis II, which is stated as follows:

> There is a significant difference in the dogmatic personality structure between politicians and nonpoliticians such that the former are more closed-minded than the latter.

The test of this hypothesis will be made by comparing the dogmatism data for the political sample with that for the nonpolitical control group. Table 5 gives the distribution of dogmatism scores obtained for the two samples.

TABLE 5

COMPARISON OF DOGMATISM SCORERS IN POLITICAL
AND NONPOLITICAL SAMPLES

Sample	Positive	Negative	Totals	Mean	S.D.
Political	98 (76%)	27 (21%)	125 (97%)[a]	5.51	6.75
Nonpolitical	322 (74%)	86 (20%)	408 (94%)[b]	3.66	5.36

$X^2 = .03,\ df = 1,\ p > .05$ $\qquad\qquad$ $t = 3.245,\ p < .01$

[a] 4 neutral scores.
[b] 28 neutral scores.

The application of a chi-square test to this distribution indicates that there is not a statistically significant difference between the two samples. Relatively speaking, there are neither more nor less dogmatic individuals among politicians than among nonpoliticians. Nonetheless, since dogmatism is a continuous rather than a discrete variable, the hypothesis requires a more precise testing in terms of degree. This can be secured by comparing the difference between the mean dogmatism scores of the political and nonpolitical sample. These data are given in Table 5.

The statistical application of Student's t technique to the means of these two samples yielded a t-value of 3.245, which is statistically significant at the .01 level of probability. This evidence substantiates the general research hypothesis that there is a difference in personality type between politicians and nonpoliticians as well as the more specific hypothesis that the political personality is characterized by a syndrome of dogmatism (closed-mindedness).

The discrepancy in statistical significance between the chi-square technique and the test of difference between means indicates that the dogmatic personality is found among politicians to a greater extent only as a matter of degree. This serves further to substantiate our general methodological position that any meaningful concept of a distinctive political personality must be related to its cultural, and perhaps even social, milieu in order to determine whether or not such a personality type indicates an accentuation relative to the normal expectancy, such as the national modal character, of a particular society.

When we utilize our control group as an indication of national character, the findings for the political sample take on significance. We find dogmatic closed-mindedness to be distinctive even more particularly of politicians within a basically authoritarian sociocultural system wherein power apparently is ranked high in relation to other values, and in a national character setting that appears to be dogmatic. This fact would tend to underscore Lasswell's assertion that "anyone who accentuates power in such a setting closely approximates the most drastic, popular and scientific idea of what constitutes the *homo politicus*" in his conception.[1]

A legitimate objection may be raised that the control group is composed predominantly of Romans, and as such is likely to be substantially southern in mentality.[a] This may be true; however, one would expect the southern mentality to be more closed-minded than its northern counterpart. Seen in this light, the difference between the political and the nonpolitical samples is all the more significant. Moreover, the skewness of the control sample is in the direction of those religious and political factors—specifically, Catholicism and Christian Democracy—with which higher dogmatic elements have been found to be associated.[b] This, too, lends further credence to the significance of our findings.

This consideration of the closed-minded political personality may be pursued with an analysis of the comparative political and nonpolitical findings for each of the major political parties. By using Student's t a test of difference was applied to the mean D-10 scores for each party. As we may see in an inspection of Table 6, the political sample mean is higher than that of the nonpolitical sample in all except three parties: PCI, PSI, and PLI. No statistically significant differences were found, however, between the respective means in these three parties.

Statistically significant differences were derived for all other parties with the exception of the PRI: for DC and the MSI at the .001 level, for the PSDI at the .01 level, and for the PDI at the .05 level. There is one other interesting finding in these data. For both the political and the nonpolitical sample the distribution of party means was subjected to an analysis of variance. The F-ratio derived for the political sample indicates statistical significance at the .01 level, while that for the nonpolitical sample shows no such significance at the .05 level. This suggests that political leaders and political followers may tend to differ among themselves in personality structure along

[a] See note e on page 87 in Chapter IV.
[b] We shall elaborate on this in Chapter VIII.

TABLE 6

MEAN DOGMATISM SCORE COMPARISONS OF POLITICAL
AND NONPOLITICAL SAMPLES FOR INDIVIDUAL PARTIES

Party	Political Sample			Nonpolitical Sample				Level of
	N	Mean	S.D.	N	Mean	S.D.	t-value	Significance
DC	31	7.96	6.48	139	3.91	4.58	4.069	.001
MSI	18	9.55	3.90	60	3.91	5.58	3.949	.001
PCI	25	.92	5.49	35	2.88	5.01	1.425	NS
PDI	3	9.33	4.64	28	3.07	4.86	2.059	.05
PLI	11	4.00	5.29	44	4.52	5.36	.285	NS
PRI	5	8.00	3.52	28	4.10	5.09	1.590	NS
PSDI	8	9.00	3.39	37	1.41	7.30	2.804	.01
PSI	21	2.23	7.70	40	5.20	5.57	1.692	.1
Totals[a]	129	5.51	6.75	436	3.66	5.36	3.245	.01

$F = 4.368, \ p < .01$ $\qquad F = 1.729, \ p > .05$

$dfb, \ 7; \ dfw, \ 114$ $\qquad dfb, \ 7; \ dfw, \ 403$

[a] Includes minor party affiliates.

the lines of political party affiliation. This is a question which will be considered at length in the chapter to follow. It is important, however, to bear in mind that "political party affiliation" in regard to the nonpolitical sample is merely a matter of expressed preference.

These data for the two samples reveal a pattern which shows that politicians and nonpoliticians, both of the political center and the political right, tend to differ in personality structure, whereas similarities in personality structure tend to be found for parties on the political left. The exceptions are the PLI and the PRI.

An explanation for this may be the greater disparities in the social backgrounds of leaders and followers of parties of

the political right and center than of those of the political
left. Research shows that political decision-makers tend to be
drawn disproportionately from higher social class categories,
and the higher the authority level of the decision-makers, the
more marked is the difference between the decision-makers
and the ordinary citizens.[2] From this principle it would follow
that those parties showing statistically significant differences
between leaders and followers are marked by a greater disparity in their respective social bases than for the exceptions
of the PRI and the PLI (although the latter shows only a
slight difference in mean dogmatism score between the two
samples). These are smaller parties which have appealed not
to the "man in the street," but more to the professional and
managerial classes, as is revealed by their limited popular
support. This interpretation, of course, implies a relationship
between personality structure in terms of dogmatism and social
backgrounds, which, however, is not consistent with our findings (Chapter VIII) that show no such relationships except
on the basis of religion, which in this study is not an indicator
of socioeconomic status. Further consideration of this question
will be given in the subsequent section on data interpretations.

Politicians and Power-Orientations

Our third consideration is the question of power-orientation
in the political personality. As we have mentioned, the major
statements about the political personality contend that it is
distinguished by a dominant orientation toward power, that
is, the incorporation of power as a personal value. People seek
power, not for its own sake, but rather for its instrumental
value in gaining a variety of ends. The same goal may be
cathected by different motives, just as the same role, such as
a political one, may be instrumental for the attainment of different goals. We suggest that different motivations for power
attract different types of personality.

As we indicated in Chapter II, the power variable in the

authoritarian syndrome involves the two seemingly contradictory elements of authoritarian aggression and authoritarian submission. Accordingly, the orientation of the authoritarian
personality to power is one of personal aggression and submission as contrasted to the more "impersonal" and "democratic"
orientations. For the authoritarian personality the drive for
power is defined characteristically as personal power over
people, a power which is used to assuage one's own psychological needs. Thus it is not power which is sought so much for
its manifest functions, but rather it is the latent functions of
power which constitute the principal goal. For the democratic
personality, on the other hand, the drive for power is defined
characteristically as that of "strength" over problems which
are external to the power holder.[3] The position which we are
stating, therefore, is that the hypothetical power-orientation
of the political personality is essentially one of an authoritarian
nature. Hypothesis III may be stated as follows:

> The political personality is characterized by an author-
> itarian orientation toward power.

The question now is whether or not there is an association
between the dogmatism syndrome and such a power-orientation. That is to say, is it possible to infer from closed-mindedness an authoritarian conception of personal power? This
question was answered affirmatively in the methodological
considerations of Chapter II, wherein it was shown that the
basic defining characteristic of dogmatism is the extent to
which there is reliance upon absolute authority. The rationale,
however, may be restated logically as follows. The focal element of the authoritarian syndrome is power; dogmatism is an
alternative to authoritarianism. Accordingly, dogmatism should
serve suitably as an indication of power-orientation in the
authoritarian conception.

The data on the dogmatic findings for the political sample
which were elaborated above substantiate the hypothesis as

qualified. We have, nonetheless, other data which may be
used to test this hypothesis more precisely.

The political personality which is personally oriented toward
power, in the authoritarian conception presented here, would
be expected most likely to manifest somewhat of an unprinci-
pled method in the pursuit of power as a personal value. In
short, he should be Machiavellian in this regard. This, in fact,
is essentially the basis of the positions that allege power-orientation as the distinctive mark of the professional politician.
Spranger's conception exemplifies this when in describing his
"political type" he states: "Human beings are like pawns or dollars and cents. . . . For politics man is a means to an end, in a
favorable case a means to his own good."[4] Thus, political man
is presented as a basically ruthless, amoral, and unscrupulous
opportunist.[5]

This issue may be approached by means of one of the neutral items that was included in the D-10 scale. The item reads
as follows:

> The ends and the objectives of political ideology are much more im-
> portant than the manner and the methods used to realize them.

If anything, this question is a Machiavellian statement that
actually is content-biased toward authoritarianism of the political right. Machiavellian philosophy is part and parcel of fascist ideology: "Mussolini . . . had no firm principles of his
own, and, at the beginning of his career in power, was given
to boasting that Fascism needed none either, that the Fascists
were the 'gypsies of politics,' and that action was more important than philosophy."[c] Agreement with such a Machiavellian

---

[c] Gordon A. Craig, *Europe Since 1815* (New York: Holt, Rinehart & Winston,
1961), p. 595. This seems to be substantiated by the findings which show that
the neo-Fascist MSI party had the highest mean response (1.22 out of a possible +2) for this question. These data for the individual parties may be compared in Table 38 given in Appendix F. Commented one MSI deputy in
answering: "Yes—the logical answer for a Fascist!" And another: "Certainly, I
agree . . . it's Machiavellian!"

and fascist principle would tend to indicate the existence of an authoritarian personality. The question was answered in the same format as that indicated for the personality inventory. Table 7 gives the distribution of responses and other related data.

TABLE 7

RESPONSE AND DOGMATISM SCORES FOR
MACHIAVELLIAN QUESTION

Response	Dogmatic Scorers	Nondogmatic Scorers	N^*	%	Mean	S.D.
1) Partly agree	70 {33	9} 15	44	34.1	6.06	6.39
2) Completely agree	{37	6}	44	34.1	7.29	6.22
3) Partly disagree	27 {14	7} 12	22	17.0	1.77	6.70
4) Completely disagree	{13	5}	18	13.9	4.66	7.02
Totals	97	27	128			

* Includes neutral scorers.

The overwhelming number of deputies, sixty-eight percent, gave "Machiavellian" responses, that is, either agreeing completely or partially with the statement. No statistical significance is obtained in chi-square testing the response for the four categorical answers in terms of dogmatic and nondogmatic scorers ($X^2 = 2.37$, $df = 3$).[d]

[d] No analysis of variance was performed on the dogmatism means of these four response categories. Student's t tests, however, were applied to the various combinations of answers. Only two of the six possible combinations were found to be statistically significant. These are 1 and 3, a t-value of 2.491 at the .02 level; 2 and 3, a t-value of 3.258 at the .01 level.

These data become significant in a more realistic application of the following procedure. A very sharp difference is found in combining the dogmatism means for the two categories of positive response and the two categories of negative response. Positive responders have a mean of 6.67 ($S. D. = 6.35$), and the negative responders have a mean of 3.07 ($S. D. = 6.95$).[6] A Student's t test applied to these two combined means yields a t-value of 2.805 which is statistically significant at the .01 level. A chi-square test on these combined categories, while in the hypothetical direction, is not statistically significant ($X^2 = 3.04$, $df = 1$).

The findings indicate that particular kinds of personality structure tend to be involved differentially in the forms that the orientation to power and the pursuit of it may take. The Machiavellian individual is more likely to be a dogmatic individual. Perhaps these data may be interpreted logically as follows. Machiavellian respondents are more closed-minded than the non-Machiavellian respondents. Or, in other words, the more closed-minded are Machiavellian. Therefore, the dogmatic, or the more closed-minded, tend to be authoritarian personalities. As a consequence of this it would follow that the more dogmatic are oriented toward power in an authoritarian manner. The overwhelming number of respondents in the political sample are both dogmatic (seventy-six percent) and Machiavellian (sixty-eight percent). Thus, there is in these data a substantiation for our hypothesis that the professional politician is personally power-oriented in personality structure. In short, the professional politician tends to be a basically authoritarian personality as described in Chapter II. This would tend to suggest that personal power may be a potent incentive to political activity.

The empirical data, in summary, support the three research hypotheses proposed and considered in this chapter. The personality structure of the professional politician may be characterized as dogmatic. Politicians are distinguishable from non-politicians on the basis of such a personality structure. Moreover, the evidence shows that the professional politician is oriented toward power in an authoritarian manner. The findings, therefore, affirm Dahl's distinction of the *homo politicus* and the *homo civicus*, as well as more particularly the theses of Spranger,[7] Michels,[8] Lasswell,[9] Schumpeter,[10] Downs,[11] and others that the political personality is distinguished by the search for the pursuit of power as a personal value.

INTERPRETATION OF THE FINDINGS

While our hypotheses are supported, the data show nevertheless that not all individuals, or all parties, manifest the political personality in the conception presented here. By no means, of course, are we maintaining that professional politicians are all of the same type or kind—on whatever criteria of classification. As stated previously, we have hypothesized the existence of only a modal type, and this has been found in terms of our theoretical and methodological procedures. The question remains to account for the patterns of variation which are observable in the data. Some explanation is in order for the fact that not all of the political sample achieved high dogmatism scores, and likewise not all of the nonpolitical sample yielded low dogmatism scores. What is it, then, that distinguishes the low scorers and the high scorers among themselves as well as within respectively high and low dogmatic categories?[e]

Perhaps our findings may be assessed more meaningfully by delineating different types of political man and, more specifically, different types of professional politicians. The Italian

[e] In the individual cases, as Rokeach suggests, there may be a host of other personality factors at work to account for higher or lower scores. Milton Rokeach, *The Open and Closed Mind* (New York: Basic Books, 1960), p. 120.

Chamber of Deputies in many ways appears as a heterogeneous body of political men, particularly in terms of fundamental
occupation. One finds nearly every walk of life represented in
Parliament. Sartori, in his study of the Italian parliamentarian,
distinguishes three categories of "professionalization to political life." These are the nonprofessional politician (the gentle-
man politician), the semiprofessional politician (one who has
another occupation and is not involved in politics primarily
for party interests), and the professional politician.[f] We suggest that a more precise delineation of the professional politician in terms of a classification such as this is apt to reveal
significant differences in the political personality structure.

   References may be found to other classifications which have
been suggested for political man. Lasswell distinguishes the
"institutional type" and the "functional type."[12] He speaks further of a second classification consisting of political "agitators,"
"administrators," and "theorists," and various combinations of
these which may be distinguished according to the character of
the functions which they perform or are desirous of perform-
ing.[13] Each of these types, it is suggested, has significant dif-

   [f] The political status of these three types, says Sartori, may change at any
time, particularly at election time when they all seem to become "professional"
politicians. He found these types to represent respectively five, thirty-eight,
and fifty-seven percent of his subjects. The nonprofessional politician, exemplified by cultural leaders and major industrialists, are found mainly in the smaller
parties. Giovanni Sartori, "Parliamentarians in Italy," *International Social Science Journal*, XIII (1961), 583–599.
   We may mention that in our own study none of the thirteen monarchists
(PDI or Independents) or Republicans claims to have a professional vocation
to politics. Moreover, the parliamentarian role for many other subjects is a
part-time activity. These men give the impression of "squeezing in" the duties
of parliament with those of their respective professions. Sartori found that fifty-
eight percent of Italian parliamentarians conducted either complete or partial
professional activity during their parliamentary tenure. Giovanni Sartori, *Il
Parlamento Italiano* (Naples: Edizioni Scientifiche Italiane, 1963), p. 30. Several
of our interviews were conducted in professional environments, such as the
offices of physicians, lawyers, journalists, publicists, industrialists, and business
executives; newspaper plants; and even in one hospital.

ferences in its developmental history. Barber offers a similar classification for state legislators in terms of the nature and the degree of their legislative activity.[14] And a classification based more in terms of sociological origins may be found in Matthews' operational definitions of United States Senators.[15] We mention these classifications simply as illustrations.

Then, too, we may recall here the question raised in Chapter II concerning the nature of political recruitment. Would significant differences be found by discerning between the elective (self-recruited) and the appointive (recruited) politician? This is an issue that, given the Italian electoral system, seems particularly significant. Our hypotheses have been directed exclusively toward the former type, but it is possible that both types are present in our sample. Even in more democratic political systems there is always some "selection" of candidates. This pattern is true more especially in the upper echelons of the political structure. The selection process (the type and methods of recruitment into political office) may be a crucial device through which the internal structure of political systems and parties could be analyzed to shed light on the attraction of personality types. We shall return to this explanation.

One particularly significant issue in this regard is the element of factions within the individual parties. Other factors that may be involved in a more precise analysis of such data would include 1) the status-level of political office within the system, 2) the function of the particular political office (including the overlapping executive branch or other political functions) within the sytem,[g] 3) successful politicians and unsuccessful political candidates, 4) the type of social routes that

---

[g] We are suggesting that party representatives be distinguished in terms of "leaders" and "representatives." Lasswell speaks on this question when he offers this hypothesis: "Intensely power-centered persons tend to be relegated to comparatively minor roles." That is, he claims this to be true more likely of dogmatic and authoritarian personalities. Harold D. Lasswell, "The Selective

are used to reach political office, 5) political opportunism, and 6) self-images and conceptions of the political (parliamentary) role.[h] This brief list is not intended to be exhaustive. Nevertheless, the question is the same in all cases: Are certain types of politicians apt to be more dogmatic and power-oriented than others? Unfortunately, our data are such that we are not permitted to analyze the findings in terms of all of these more specific considerations. Some of them, however, will be taken up more thoroughly in the chapter to follow. We suggest the others as possible explanations for appropriate variations in our findings and offer them as considerations for future research.

On the whole the data show that politicians are more dogmatic and closed-minded than nonpoliticians. Nevertheless we must explain the outcome of the three parties which show higher dogmatism means for the nonpolitical samples, although the difference in means in each case is not statistically significantly different. One of these, the PLI, shows an extremely slight difference. It is curious that the other two parties are both on the political left—the PCI and the PSI, both of which incidentally indicated the lowest dogmatism scores.

Two explanations seem valid to account for this deviation from the general pattern. One includes a question of fundamental ideology, and the other is that of political recruitment.

Effect of Personality on Political Participation" in Richard Christie and Marie Jahoda (eds.), *Studies in the Scope and Method of "The Authoritarian Personality"* (Glencoe: The Free Press, 1954), p. 222.

[h] One of the focal aspects of the relationship of personality to occupational structures should concern the conceptions of the social roles which are involved and the specific role behavior which takes place. Our data suggest that among the parliamentarian subjects there is by no means a homogeneous conception of their political role, in terms of either what it is or what it ought to be. Relevant in this regard would be a delineation in terms of such role-taking conceptions as 1) parliamentarian, 2) representative, and 3) clientelistic, which have been developed by John C. Wahlke, H. Eulau, W. Buchanan, and L. C. Ferguson, *The Legislative System* (New York: John Wiley & Sons, 1962), Part IV.

Both elements are not necessarily unrelated to one another.

There are correlations between membership in the two parties of the political left and adherence to Catholicism and its practice. In the political sample ninety-two percent of the PCI representatives professed no religion, whereas in the nonpolitical sample for the PCI sixty-one percent claimed to profess Catholicism. For the PSI political sample sixty-two percent as opposed to eight percent of the nonpolitical sample claimed to be nonbelievers.

Our findings show, as do others,[16] that the factor of religion is related significantly to the dogmatism syndrome. In cross-tabulating for religion and its practice in the political sample it was found that the lowest dogmatism mean (1.73) was derived from nonbelievers, whereas those professing Catholicism yielded means in the various categories of practice that average about 8.00, which clearly reveals a marked discrepancy.[i] An analysis of variance applied to the mean scores for the religious categories of the nonpolitical sample is not statistically significant at the .05 level. A similar application for the political sample is statistically significant at the .01 level.[j]

The point that we are advancing is that politicians of the PCI and the PSI should be expected to be more committed to party ideology (dialectical materialism) than the nonpolitical followers of such parties.[k] Therefore, in the cases of the PCI and the PSI we would expect to find more atheists among the political samples, and more Catholics among the nonpolitical samples, given the religious orientation of the nation.[l]

[i] See Table 14 in Chapter VIII for the categories of religious practice.

[j] This question of religion and dogmatism is relevant to other parties, particularly the DC, and will be treated at greater length in Chapter VIII.

[k] It should be borne in mind that "political party affiliation" for the nonpolitical sample refers simply to a matter of preference.

[l] Given the popular following of these parties, we would question the intellectual receptivity for Marxism on the grounds of educational and literacy levels. This ideology has many different personal meanings for the Italian people.

This may account for the lower degree of dogmatism in the political samples of these two parties. Such an interpretation, however, does not exclude the second of our explanations.

As we have suggested, recruitment procedures are likely to be significant in accounting for patterns that may be discerned along the lines of political parties in terms of personality structure. Under the election system used in Italy[m] the political parties are able to exercise considerable control over the candidates which are offered to the voters, and to a great extent actually determine the results of the popular elections and thus those who will be recruited into the system. That the *cursus honorum* in this system may be more in the nature of an ascribed rather than an achieved social status is an important consideration to keep in mind for the analysis of our data.

Methods of recruitment are not consistent in the individual parties. There is some evidence that the parties of the political left—the PCI and the PSI—are the least democratic in the selection of candidates, or the recruitment of representatives. About one-fourth of our political sample—and these came almost exclusively from the two parties in question—stated that the decision to offer their candidacies for the Chamber was not their own, but that of their party. As one deputy remarked, "The parties are run by the secretaries who keep out competition and independent thinkers."

The differences in dogmatism scores for the individual political parties may be influenced strongly by the various methods of recruitment. There may be a selective bias operating in that party leaders apparently choose—knowingly or unknowingly—individuals with particular kinds of personalities. We suggest that they do so because these particular kinds of personalities are functionally necessary for the party and its political system. This, then, raises the question of whether such political representatives should be considered as recruited

[m] See Appendix G for a brief description of the Italian electoral system.

(appointive) or self-recruited (elective) professional politicians.

In fact, a more pertinent question for these political samples is whether or not the political individuals in these parties, or how many of them, are the actual power holders?[17] That is, does political power really reside at the address of these deputies? What we are dealing with is referred to often as the *visible* political elite. It would seem that many of these individuals have no or only limited powers; all power resides with the party leaders. One would expect that under this kind of (recruitment) system power-oriented individuals are less apt to gravitate to political office in order to fulfill aspirations of personal power, since the possibility and the opportunity to hold and to exercise political power are either nonexistent or only minimal.[n] This explanation relates to the suggestion made above concerning the differential attraction of personality structures according to the level and the function of the political office.

These individuals of the visible political elite, nonetheless, occupy a social position that confers a considerable amount of status and the manifestation, as well as the exercise, of another "kind" of power.[o] Thus, they may not hold the actual political power, or have independent power and authority, but to a more or less degree they hold a *position* in the power structure and share limitedly in the decision-making process. Political man has been characterized also by intense and ungratified cravings for deference and respect, and as one who seeks political office primarily as an attempt to acquire these goals. One such reward for the Italian deputy is found in the title of "honorable." Honorific pressures to become and to remain a

[n] In fact, the PCI (least dogmatic) had the lowest percentage of its representatives selecting "political power" as the "most important personal benefit derived from the office of deputy."

[o] The sense of importance, as well as that of "being in on things," which politics offers are closely related as psychic lures to that of power-orientation. Donald R. Matthews, *U. S. Senators and Their World* (Chapel Hill: University of North Carolina Press, 1960), p. 49.

parliamentarian are apparently quite strong. Kogan feels that "the hunt for titles [in this authoritarian milieu] is more persistent in these days of the republic than it was in the monarchy."[18] Such motivations, of course, are consistent with the authoritarian personality structure. We asked our subjects to indicate which personal advantage they considered to be most important among those which they were able to derive as parliamentarians. Thirteen percent of our sample, all scoring dogmatically, selected "social respect" and achieved the highest categorical mean for dogmatism (9.61, S. D. = 4.19) in this response.

On the basis of our general findings, we would be inclined to agree with Lasswell and state: "It is tempting to suggest that politicians tend to be recruited—self recruited—from power-centered personalities in all forms of government and in all periods of crises (or non-crises). But this is exceedingly doubtful."[19] This may not be true in nondemocratic political systems. The evidence seems stronger that where self-recruitment is allowed to operate, politicians come from dogmatic and power-oriented personalities. Where the recruitment process is controlled, the evidence suggests that a differential selection of personalities may be operating according to the needs of the system. Thus, in this latter case our theoretical conception of the political personality may or may not obtain. This element of differential recruitment, in terms of our findings, should serve to substantiate further our research hypotheses that the self-recruited professional politician is both dogmatically closed-minded and power-oriented in an authoritarian manner. We shall return to this consideration of political recruitment in the following chapter.

Politics and the Cursus Potestatis

An apropos question to be considered is why political activity should be selected as the route to the attainment of personal power. Politics, of course, is not the only way one may achieve power, since power-oriented individuals are found in all walks of life. Nonetheless, they should be expected most particularly in those occupations which have strong power-gratification potential.

This question is even more interesting when we consider that the public opinion toward politics consists in great measure of an unwholesome attitude. Politics to many is nearly equivalent to dishonesty and corruption, an attitude manifested in the well-known expressions "to play politics," "the politics of it," and "he's a real politician!" While such unwholesome attitudes may. be culturally limited, there is sufficient reason to expect such an orientation in political systems which are basically similar in structure and function.[p] And this situation becomes all the more paradoxical, as Matthews remarks, if political activity is entered into for motives of prestige, even though many successful politicians do enjoy considerable prestige.

While political office may reward the individual with power, prestige, and perhaps even fame, we would agree with Matthews that "the price of power is high."[20] For example, the cost to become a member of the United States Senate is astounding. The minimum expense is $100,000 and the average is $500,000.[21] Moreover, the maintenance of this office nearly always exceeds the salary by a few thousand dollars.[22] We suspect that a similar situation—even if somewhat on a lesser scale—is true for the Italian parliamentarian. Of course, in Italy much of this, if not all, is a party expense rather than a personal one. Nevertheless, the individual deputy experiences a personal financial "loss." Furthermore, the office of the

[p] Meynaud suggests that by and large parliamentarians are not held in high esteem. Jean Meynaud, "General Study of Parliamentarians," *International Social Science Journal*, XIII (1961), 527–528; and Kogan states that since World War II Italians have exhibited a revulsion from political activity and hold a certain cynicism toward the motives and behavior of politicians. *Op. cit.*, p. 35.

Italian parliamentarian is established as a more or less part-time activity. And notwithstanding the unemployment and underemployment situation of the nation, we doubt that many of these men engage in politics for supplementary financial returns.[q] This fact becomes even more decided when we consider that in many countries no actual salary is paid to the parliamentarian, as was the case during Italy's constitutional monarchy. In other nations the stipend is deliberately kept to a minimum, as seems to be the case in Italy.[r] Both of these situations would tend to aggravate the difficulties incumbent upon the individual politician.[23]

We are attempting in this section to discern the personal motives from the public reasons that individuals have for seeking and taking political roles. One would expect that the drive for power is expressed usually in a disguised or sublimated form.[s] The person who seeks power, especially that of an authoritarian type, cannot openly admit to such a personal motivation, but rather he must rationalize his search in other terms which are more consistent with the value-orientations of his sociocultural environment. Most politicians contend that

[q] Despite the fact that Italian parliamentarians are probably among the highest paid in Europe, not a single subject indicated that "greater financial returns" were his most important personal benefit from parliamentary office.

[r] The members of Parliament receive a monetary compensation as established by law. This currently amounts to 65,000 lire per month. In addition, the parliamentarian is granted an expense allowance amounting to 385,000 lire per month during the period that parliament is in session. Members, however, are docked 5,000 lire for each absence from a session of parliament and 2,000 for each absence from a commission meeting. Moreover, party dues for these people are especially high, nearly fifty percent of their salaries in most cases. (One thousand lire exchange for about $1.60.)

[s] We offer the following comments from deputies who seemed sufficiently dauntless to select "political power" as their most important personal benefit from parliamentary office: "Political power, of course! . . . We are respected only because we are strong, and it's a sad thing. . . . It would be nice to be respected even if not a deputy" and "Political power is without a doubt the most important personal advantage for a politician. . . . It's useless to be in the politics of no power."

they are in politics to be of service to the public.[t] Thus, while it could be argued cogently that public reasons, such as civic duty, defense of the nation, political ideology, social reform, and so forth, are rationalizations to a great extent in many cases, there remains nevertheless the question that such situations may have been the external attraction which provided the circumstantial answer for the individual's "choice" of politics rather than other activity as a route to power. We cannot disregard, for example, the role of the family in shaping political careers. There is evidence that political attitudes are formed early in life as part of the general process of socialization.[24] Children who are reared in strongly politically oriented families are more likely to be imbued with motives and attitudes favorable toward politics as a professional enterprise.[u] Often, too, as Matthews states, family name and experience may be a decided advantage in achieving political goals.[25] Sufficient instances of this in the United States document the point well, and there are evidences of a similar kind in the Italian situation.

The thesis in the general proposition of this study is that certain occupations have a particular attraction for the power-oriented individual such that he constitutes the modal character of these occupations. If this kind of individual may be found in other occupations, then which ones are these? An

[t] Harned in her study of ward chairmen found that those ranking high in authoritarianism limited the rationales for their jobs to such things as party support, political issues, and images of the public welfare. Louise Harned, "Authoritarian Attitudes and Party Activity," *The Public Opinion Quarterly,* XXV (1961), 393–399.

In this study, thirty-seven percent of the deputies gave as their purpose for entering politics such things as "civic duty," "honor of nation," "justice and democracy"; and another sixteen percent, "to oppose ideologies" not considered in the interests of the nation. And seventy-five percent of these respondents were dogmatic scorers.

[u] Seven percent of our political sample offered "family tradition and family interest" as their reason for entering political life.

answer here perhaps would shed more light on why politics is a *cursus potestatis.*[v] A definitive answer would obviously require a thorough analysis of the social structure of all the occupational systems involved. Lasswell offers a partial answer when he refers to situations that are functionally, if not conventionally, comparable.[26] This would imply, among other things, that such occupational roles would have a strong potential for power gratification.

One explanation for politics as a popular route to power is found in the structure of the sociocultural system as the context of these political roles. First of all, these roles have sanctioned legitimacy. Not only are power holding and power wielding considered necessary, but these functions appear manifestly in the interest of the public and not that of the individual. The element of social recognition in these roles is a most important one as is seen in the considerable amount of social status which is attached to them. Furthermore, these offices carry the broadest and most extensive application of power, much more than is possible in any other limited position in the social system. In the uppermost echelons of the political system these roles experience somewhat of a geometric expansion in their powers. This situation would seem to be enhanced in Italy, whose sociocultural system is, as we have shown, basically authoritarian in structure and, as such, not only offers a limited number of legitimate avenues to power but sanctions all the more the political offices with considerable social status and prestige due to their functional significance. Our point is that the political roles have the greatest status recognition of all the social roles within a mutual context of their sphere of activity. On this basis, then, we suggest that

[v] It may be significant to point out that following the traditional pattern, nearly one-third of our political subjects were pursuing careers in the field of law. See Table 23 in Appendix A for the occupational backgrounds of our political subjects.

the more strongly power-oriented individuals will be attracted to political office because of this very structure which it has as the *cursus potestatis*.ʷ Whether or not they actually are found there remains an objective for further research involving comparative studies of social roles.

Development of the Political Man

The question that faces us now is to answer, in Dahl's terms, how the *homo politicus*—as we have delineated him—develops out of the *homo civicus*. Political opportunities are provided by the social structure, but it is the personality structure which provides political motivation. Only in this light is it possible to explain why the political opportunities affect some people and not others. The degree of political success which one experiences, of course, is a consequence of many other elements—not the least of which is the development and the possession of appropriate political skills.

Political motivation in our view involves the generation of a drive or motive for and the pursuit of power. The most specific contribution that we have for the development of the personally power-oriented political man is the explanation suggested by Lasswell: Private motives (the intense and ungratified cravings for power and deference that characterizes the political man) are displaced unto public objects (persons and practices connected with the power process) and rationalized in terms of public interests.[27] The distinctive mark of the *homo politicus* is this rationalization, since he shares the private

---

ʷ Lasswell does not, of course, restrict his concept of the power-oriented *homo politicus* to the political sphere, but in fact suggests that "It is probable that the most aggressive, power-lusting individuals in modern society find their way into business, and stay out of the legislature, the courts, the civil service, and the diplomatic service." Harold D. Lasswell, *Psychopathology and Politics* (New York: The Viking Press, 1960), p. 45.

motives in common with every man, and the displacement mechanism with some.[28]

Yet the more basic consideration which remains is why the power motive, why the power-orientation in certain persons. This more specific question implicitly seeks the origin of the authoritarian and the dogmatic personality. Such a consideration is an independent theoretical question which is actually beyond our scope and purpose here, but we may offer a brief mention for the curiosity of the reader.

Any one of several psychological theories could be applied to this context. The explanations that we have, however, are generally psychoanalytic in tone. These imply an element of deprivation and compensation. Says Lasswell, "Our hypothesis about the power seeker is that he pursues power as a means of compensation against deprivation. Power is expected to overcome low estimates of the self, by changing either the traits of the self or the environment in which it functions."[29] Spranger had offered the same explanation for his political type.[30] This notion of powerlessness is, of course, the essential thesis of Fromm,[31] the originator of the concept of the "authoritarian personality," who states that the search for power is a defense against low self-estimates which are so escaped. This kind of character, according to Fromm, is essentially a reflection of the "social character."

Others, however, have spoken of the "naturalness" of the "power instinct," either as a universal human phenomenon[32] or more limitedly as a normal quality of the politician.[33] Be that as it may, people are not born wanting power—just as they are born neither open-minded nor closed-minded, neither authoritarian nor democratic, neither liberal nor conservative. These orientations are rooted basically in attitude development.

It is the predominant opinion among students of national character that the authoritarian and dogmatic personality arises mainly out of the socialization process, and particularly influential is the family.[34] Others challenge the influence of the socialization process in this respect and favor instead the later influences of adulthood experiences.[35] In either case, we have tried to suggest (Chapter IV) that specific organizational structures are apt to produce certain kinds of personality structures. The dogmatic personality, and thus the political personality, is essentially the product of dogmatic and authoritarian social structures to which the individual has been exposed or subjected.

Notes

[1] Harold D. Lasswell, *Power and Personality* (New York: W. W. Norton, 1948), p. 33.

[2] Richard C. Snyder, "A Decision-Making Approach to the Study of Political Phenomena" in Roland Young (ed.), *The Study of Politics* (Evanston: Northwestern University Press, 1958), p. 367.

[3] A. H. Maslow, "The Authoritarian Character Structure," *Journal of Social Psychology*, XVIII (1943), 401–411.

[4] Eduard Spranger, *Types of Men* (Halle: Max Niemeyer Verlag, 1928), pp. 191–192.

[5] Robert E. Lane, *Political Life* (Glencoe: The Free Press, 1959), pp. 124–125.

[6] Methods for this computation are according to Henry E. Garrett and R. S. Woodworth, *Statistics in Psychology and Education* (New York: Longmans, Green and Company, 1958), p. 56.

[7] Spranger, *op. cit.*

[8] Robert Michels, *Political Parties* (New York: Collier Books, 1962).

[9] Harold D. Lasswell, *Psychopathology and Politics* (New York: The Viking Press, 1960) and *Power and Personality* (New York: W. W. Norton, 1948).

[10] Joseph A. Schumpeter, *Capitalism, Socialism, and Democracy* (New York: Harper & Row, 1950).

[11] Anthony A. Downs, *An Economic Theory of Democracy* (New York: Harper & Row, 1957).

[12] Lasswell, *Psychopathology and Politics*, pp. 38–64.

[13] *Ibid.*, p. 262.

[14] James D. Barber, *The Lawmakers: Recruitment and Adaptation to Legislative Life* (New Haven: Yale University Press, 1965), pp. 212–217.

[15] Donald R. Matthews, *U. S. Senators and Their World* (Chapel Hill: University of North Carolina Press, 1960), p. 61.

[16] See Milton Rokeach, *The Open and Closed Mind* (New York: Basic Books, 1960), p. 351.

[17] See C. W. Cassinelli, "The Totalitarian Party," *Journal of Politics*, XXIV (1962), 111–141.

[18] Norman Kogan, *The Government of Italy* (New York: Thomas Y. Crowell, 1964), p. 63.

[19] Harold D. Lasswell, "The Selective Effect of Personality on Political Participation" in Richard Christie and Marie Jahoda (eds.), *Studies in the Scope and Method of "The Authoritarian Personality"* (Glencoe: The Free Press, 1954), p. 221.

[20] Matthews, *op. cit.*, p. 90.

[21] *Ibid.*, p. 72.

[22] *Ibid.*, pp. 88–89.

[23] Jean Meynaud, "General Study of Parliamentarians," *International Social Science Journal*, XIII (1961), 527.

[24] Herbert H. Hyman, *Political Socialization* (Glencoe: The Free Press, 1959).

[25] Matthews, *op cit.*, p. 49.

[26] Lasswell, *Power and Personality*, p. 14.

[27] Lasswell, *Psychopathology and Politics*, pp. 75–76; and Lasswell, *Power and Personality*, p. 38. This theory is restated in less "clinical" terms in his more recent work, "The Selective Effect of Personality on Political Participation," *op. cit.*, pp. 215–216.

[28] Lasswell, *Psychopathology and Politics*, p. 262.

[29] Lasswell, *Power and Personality*, p. 40.

[30] See Lasswell, *Psychopathology and Politics*, p. 52.

[31] Erich Fromm, *Escape From Freedom* (New York: Holt, Rinehart & Winston, 1941), p. 172.

[32] Alfred Adler in his system of Individual Psychology conceives of the "will to power" as an innate fundamental need that constitutes the basic human motivation (*Practice and Theory of Individual Psychology* [New York: Harcourt, Brace & World, 1924]); Hans Morgenthau states, "The lust for power is common to all men" (*Politics Among Nations* [New York: Alfred A. Knopf, 1956], p. 33); similarly, Robert Michels contends that it is an elementary psychological fact that the "love of power" and the "desire to dominate"—for good or for evil intentions—are universally inherent in human passions (*Political Parties*, p. 206).

[33] Max Weber, *From Max Weber: Essays in Sociology*, trans. H. H. Gerth and C. W. Mills (New York: Oxford University Press, 1958), p. 116.

[34] Alex Inkeles, "National Character and Modern Political Systems" in Francis L. K. Hsu (ed.), *Psychological Anthropology* (Homewood: The Dorsey Press, 1961), pp. 200–201.

[35] Hyman, *op. cit.*, p. 201.

CHAPTER VI

The Political Personality and Political Ideologies

OUR CONCERN in this chapter shall be the proposition that distinctive personality structures are found in association with various political parties and political ideologies. We intend to show that political parties may be distinguished by distinctive personality structures in terms of the dogmatism syndrome and that significant differences and similarities of personality structure exist with regard to extreme and moderate ideological positions and with regard to the positions of the political left and those of the political right.

It is highly unlikely that a particular personality type will be associated with varying forms of political systems, and such an improbability should remain valid even with subsystems, such as political parties. The considerations in the preceding chapter already have shown this to be true. Our general proposition, to repeat, is that a particular type of personality (or personality structure) is more responsive and attracted to a particular political party or ideology to such an extent that it constitutes the "modal character" for that party or ideology. The demonstration of this basic position with the plurality of parties that we have is not as difficult as may appear at first consideration. Since we are dealing fundamentally with just one type of personality structure, we have to consider only the degree to which the dogmatism syndrome is found sufficiently to indicate real distinctions between parties. Positive results here would indicate the extent to which open-minded or closed-minded personalities are attracted to particular political ideologies. To this end we should be able to demonstrate that personality may be a determinant of political ideology and party preference.

The Italian political system, unlike many others, offers an opportunity for a more precise measurement of the role of personality in relation to political behavior. Again the plurality of political parties should make for a maximization of the influences of personality upon political activity. Our proposition here is that the precision of the relationship between personality and political ideology is related to, and dependent upon, the effective range of ideological alternatives which are available. As Levinson states, "The greater the number of options for participation, the more can the person choose on the basis of personal congeniality. Or, in more general terms, the greater the richness and complexity of the stimulus field, the more will internal organizing forces determine individual adaptation."[1] Further significance is found in the fact, already pointed out, that one major distinction between political parties in Italy and those of many other nations is that each of the former is not merely political in nature but also has its own ideology, a doctrine or philosophy.[a] This should introduce more theoretical precision in our analysis.

[a] One would suspect that in the United States, for example, personality would be less related to the Democratic and Republican parties, but would perhaps reveal greater differences based on liberal and conservative factions within each of these.

We shall test in this chapter Hypotheses IV, V, and VI in the same general procedures as were used in the preceding chapter. Our data, however, will be limited to the political sample, so we shall be speaking only of political "leaders" rather than political "followers."

THE EMPIRICAL EVIDENCE

No political party has a monopoly on dogmatism. Yet there are discernible patterns in regard to the degree of variation among the individual respondents in the several parties. Table 8 gives the categorical range of scores for each party. This will offer a perspective for a consideration of our findings.

TABLE 8

DISTRIBUTION OF POSITIVE AND NEGATIVE DOGMATISM SCORERS BY PARTY IN POLITICAL SAMPLE

Score Range	DC	MSI	PCI	PDI	PLI	PRI	PSDI	PSI	Totals
+ 1 to +10	12	10	11	1	7	4	5	10	60
+11 to +20	15	8	1	2	1	1	3	3	34
Total Dogmatic	27	18	12	3	8	5	8	13	94
— 1 to —10	4	–	9	–	3	–	–	8[a]	24
Total	31	18	21[b]	3	11	5	8	21	118[c]

[a] Includes one score of —12.

[b] Four representatives had neutral scores.

[c] Omits neutral scores and minor parties.

Political Parties and Dogmatism

The more general consideration to be treated in this chapter, Hypothesis IV, is stated as follows:

> The dogmatic political personality varies along the political continuum such that significant differences in personality structure may be discerned among political parties.

There is a considerable variation among the major political parties in terms of the dogmatism syndrome as may be seen readily in Table 9. In an application of an analysis of variance we obtained an F-ratio of 4.368, which is statistically significant at the .01 level. Every pair combination of parties was given a Student's t test for statistically significant difference between their mean dogmatism scores. Three of these are significant at the .001 level. Every pair combination of parties was given a Student's t test for statistically significant difference between their mean dogmatism scores. Three of these are significant at the .001 level. These involve the PCI and the PSDI, MSI, and DC. Ten other combinations of the total of twenty-nine are statistically significant at the .05 level or beyond. These data may be inspected in Table 30, which is given in Appendix E. Thus, every party manifests statistically significant difference with at least one other party.[b]

[b] This same kind of analysis was done with the nonpolitical sample. The analysis of variance gave an F-ratio of 1.729 which is not statistically significant at the .05 level. (See Table 6 in Chapter V.) Out of twenty-eight paired combinations only two are statistically significant, and these not at the necessary .001 level. In fact, the over-all pattern of response is not consistent with that of the political sample. Political affiliation as determined for the nonpolitical sample, of course, is merely a matter of expressed preference. Italians in general are not ideologically committed, except in terms of religious tenets, in their political behavior. Seen in such a perspective, this finding offers further substantiation for Hypothesis IV. Moreover, it supports our previous consideration (Hypothesis II) that there are significant differences in personality structure between politicians and nonpoliticians.

TABLE 9

MEAN DOGMATISM SCORES OF PARTIES
IN POLITICAL SAMPLE

Party	N	Mean	S.D.
DC	31	7.96	6.48
MSI	18	9.55	3.90
PCI	25	.92	5.49
PDI	3	9.33	4.64
PLI	11	4.00	5.29
PRI	5	8.00	3.52
PSDI	8	9.00	3.39
PSI	21	2.23	7.70

$F = 4.368$ dfb, 7; dfw, 114. $p < .01$

The distribution of party scores may be more meaningful when arranged along a political continuum. As may be seen in Chart 1, there is somewhat of a progression of scores from the political left to the political right, with the highest and the lowest mean scores found respectively on the right and the left extremes. In fact, the lowest two means are found on the left extreme, and the highest two means are on the right. This in itself is significant. The generally accepted view is that the PCI and the MSI (or Communists and fascists of whatever variety) are identical in terms of authoritarianism and, both being totalitarian, should exhibit the highest degrees of dogmatism.

Although the centrist parties show general similarity in means, no statistically significant differences exist among them. Nonetheless, Christian Democracy, the center party, is not statistically significantly different from the parties of the political right, but it is so different from the two parties of the political left. The MSI on the right extreme scored as expected. Since this party represents neo-Fascism, it would be expected —given the tenets of its ideology—to be totally authoritarian.[c]

CHART 1

CONTINUUM DISTRIBUTION OF MEAN DOGMATISM
SCORES OF PARTIES IN POLITICAL SAMPLE

PCI	PSI	PSDI	PRI	DC	PLI	PDI	MSI
.92	2.23	9.00	8.00	7.96	4.00	9.33	9.55

There was not a single negative or open-minded score in the MSI sample. The fact that this party scored so heavily lends credence to the validity of the D-10 instrument. Some may object, however, that in contrast to the lower scores on the left extreme, the scale is weighted with content toward the political right. Notwithstanding the evidence given in Chapter II for the validity of the scale, further proof is suggested here. High dogmatism means are found on the political left, as in the cases of the PSDI and PRI; and a low dogmatism mean is found on the political right for the PLI. These means upset the pattern of progressive dogmatism scores from the political left to the political right. One explanation for this condition might be that the PSDI as an offshoot of the PSI is but its conservative wing, while the PLI is but the liberal segment

[c] As we have mentioned, one of the elements of the authoritarian syndrome is ethnocentrism or, as it is often expressed, nationalism. The high mean score of the MSI, as well as that of the PDI, undoubtedly reflects this factor which is central to their ideology.

of the conservative right ideologies. The PRI score is more difficult to explain in these terms, except to say that it is basically a socialist party of conservative orientation. Subsequent discussion will consider this implication of differential personality structure in association with varying orientations to a given, general ideology.

Our data clearly substantiate Hypothesis IV. Every party showed a statistically significant difference with at least one other party in terms of the dogmatism syndrome. Some indicated as much with two and even three other parties. The political personality does vary along the political continuum such that political parties may be distinguished in terms of the personality structure of their representatives. These findings shall be amplified with the treatment of the more specific hypotheses concerning political ideologies.

Moderate and Extreme Ideologies

The first of these, Hypothesis V, concerns moderate and extreme political orientations, and is stated as follows:

> Politicians maintaining extremist ideologies tend to be more dogmatic than those maintaining moderate ideologies.

Some evidence already supports this hypothesis from the data presented above for the more general Hypothesis IV. We have, however, two more particular procedures for testing this particular hypothesis. Our data are derived from two specific questions of the interview schedule which made use of a traditional left-to-right continuum in order to determine political complexion.[d] The subject was asked to indicate the locus where

---

[d] These questions replace the Opinionation Scale technique used by Milton Rokeach, *The Open and Closed Mind* (New York: Basic Books, 1960), pp. 80–87. It was not expedient to use these scales with our subjects due to their length, detail, and other problems which, as mentioned in Chapter II, we tried

he would place himself and the locus where he would place his party.[e]

The respondent was asked in Continuum I to place himself at one of the indicated loci of the political continuum. The following operational definitions are established in terms of political locus: one and six, extremes; two and five, moderates; three and four, centrists. The mean dogmatism score for these loci are given in the following figure.

With one exception there is a steady progression of mean scores from the left extreme locus to that of the right extreme. The low mean of 1.66 for locus five (moderate right) upsets the progressive pattern.[f] An analysis of variance applied to this distribution of means yielded an F-ratio of 5.069, which is significant at the .01 level. Of the fifteen pair combinations in tests of significance with Student's t, seven indicated statistically significant difference at the .05 level or beyond. Each locus is statistically significantly different from at least one other. These data may be inspected in Appendix E (Table 31).

The research hypothesis asserts that there are significant differences in the dogmatism syndrome between extreme ideological positions and moderate ideological positions. There are two ways to apply a test of this hypothesis: 1) by compar-

to avoid. This procedure may not offer as precise an indication of ideological tendencies as those of Rokeach. Nevertheless, the mechanism indicates how the individual perceives both himself and his party in reference to other parties (and political ideologies). Furthermore, in this way it is possible to discern discrepancies between personal and party ideology.

[e] The analysis of political systems in terms of "left, center, and right" stems from the time of the First French Republic when delegates were seated in a continuous semicircle according to their political ideology, from the most radical and egalitarian on the left to the most reactionary and aristocratic on the right. The Italian Chamber of Deputies is organized in this fashion, and our mechanism of the political continuum attempts to reflect this conception of political alignment.

[f] We look upon this as a spurious result not only because it is not in the line of theoretical expectation but more so because of the limited number of three cases upon which it is based. These three cases are PDI $+3$, I. M. $+4$, and I. M. -2.

CHART 2

DISTRIBUTION OF MEAN DOGMATISM SCORES IN LOCI OF POLITICAL CONTINUUM I — PERSONAL IDEOLOGY

N	27	27	37	14	3	16
MEAN	1.25	3.70	6.78	9.50	1.66	9.62
	├── 1 ──┼── 2 ──┼── 3 ──	── 4 ──┼── 5 ──┼── 6 ──┤			
S.D.	6.13	7.12	6.43	4.95	2.62	3.99

$F = 5.069$ dfb, 5; dfw, 118 $p < .01$

ing the extreme and the moderate means on each side of the continuum and 2) by comparing a combination of the two extreme means with a combination of the two moderate means. First let us test each extreme mean against the moderate position on its own side of the continuum.

On the basis of Student's t no statistical significance is found between locus one and locus two; but between one and three we have statistical significance at the .01 level. Between four and six, nothing; between five and six there is a statistically significant difference, but we decided not to consider this due to the limited number of cases. We conclude, therefore, that there is no statistically significant difference on the political right between extremes and moderates. On the political left there is a statistically significant difference only between the extreme locus and that of the left center—left and right center showing no such difference. Now, then, let us see if the two extremes show difference with the total centrist positions (loci three and four).

When locus one is compared to three and four combined, we get a t-value of 2.443, statistically significant at the .02 level. Locus two compared to the centrist combination is not statistically significant ($t = 1.412$), as are locus five ($t = .807$)

and also locus six (t = .563). This again shows that statistically significant differences between extremes and other ideological positions (moderate and centrist) are found only on the political left. What is all the more interesting is that the above difference is in the opposite direction of the research hypothesis—the extreme is less rather than more dogmatic.

The only other tests we could have done would be to test loci one and six against a combination of loci two, three, four, and five. But these would not have been very meaningful, since we prefer to show differences between liberal and conservative orientations on the same side of the political continuum. Moreover, the combined mean of the two extremes would have balanced out to that of the moderate means.

Taking the second method (combination of two extreme means versus combination of two moderate means), we have the following data. For the extremes, M = 4.36, $S.D.$ = 6.77, N = 43; for the moderates, M = 3.49, $S.D.$ = 6.83, N = 30. The t-value for this equals .530, which is not statistically significant at the .05 level.

We can repeat the test of this hypothesis by utilizing this time the data from Continuum II, in which the subject is asked to indicate the locus on the traditional political continuum where he would place his party. This continuum is essentially the same as the preceding one with the exception that it has just five loci, only one being offered for the political center.[g] The following operational definitions are established

[g] Generally the pattern of ranking party and self were similar. Nine respondents, however, showed differences in these two perceptions. Two MSI's who placed their party on the right extreme placed themselves on loci two and three—both loci of the political left. Two PSDI's placed their party on locus three but placed themselves more to the left on locus two, as did one PRI. One PDI deputy placed his party on locus four (center) and himself also on locus four (moderate right). One DC deputy placed his party on locus two, himself on locus three. One PLI deputy placed his party on locus two, himself on locus four. One PSI deputy placed his party on locus one, himself on locus two.

in terms of political locus: one and five, extremes; two and four, moderates; three, center. The mean dogmatism scores for these loci are indicated in the following figure.

CHART 3

DISTRIBUTION OF MEAN DOGMATISM SCORES IN LOCI OF POLITICAL CONTINUUM II – PARTY IDEOLOGY

N	26	29	50	4	15
MEAN	.69	4.51	7.04	7.50	9.66
	1	2	3	4	5
S.D.	5.51	7.27	6.24	4.03	3.82

$F = 5.724$ dfb, 4; dfw, 119 $p < .01$

The party continuum is nearly identical in dogmatism description to that of the personal ideology continuum. There is substantial difference between all the loci, and here there is a consistent progression of increasing dogmatism means from the political left extreme to the political right extreme.[h] An analysis of variance applied to this distribution of means yielded an F-ratio of 5.724, which is significant statistically at the .01 level. Of the ten pair combinations in tests of significance with Student's t, five were statistically significant at the .05 level. Each locus is statistically significantly different from at least one other, and all loci are in such manner different from locus one. These data are given in Appendix E (Table 32).

[h] The moderate right position (locus four), while still containing very few cases, yielded a mean that is in the line of theoretical expectation. These four cases included three Monarchists and one Liberal, all scoring positively. This makes for a complete progression of scores from the left extreme to the right extreme.

We repeat the test of our hypothesis. First, on the political left, between loci one and two, the mean difference is statistically significant at the .05 level. Between four and five on the political right there is no statistically significant difference. The left extreme is statistically significantly different from the center at the .001 level; no statistically significant difference exists between the center and locus five. Between two and three, and between three and four, there is no statistically significant difference, that is, the center and the moderate loci are not dissimilar. Again, significant differences between the extremes and the moderate loci or the center are found only on the political left.

Utilizing the second testing technique, we take the combined mean of the two extreme means ($M = 3.97$, $S. D. = 6.58$, $N = 41$) and test versus a combination of the two moderate means ($M = 4.87$, $S. D. = 7.03$, $N = 33$). The t-value for this comparison is .559, which is not statistically significant. Here the extremely high and low means of the extremes are balanced out by less dissimilar moderate means. The difference between the two combined means is .90, which by inspection would not indicate a statistically significant difference.

The evidence we have presented here substantiates the research hypothesis, but with qualification. The data show that individuals maintaining extreme and moderate ideologies on the political left do differ significantly on the basis of dogmatism to the extent that the extremes are more open-minded than the moderates. Individuals maintaining extreme and moderate ideologies on the political right do not differ significantly from each other on the basis of dogmatism; both of these tend to be relatively closed-minded.

Evidence that extremists (left and right) differ from moderates (left and right) is inconsistent, and this is partly the result of the progression of dogmatism scores from one pole of the political continuum to the other. These data indicate, however, that the more left one leans politically, the more open-minded he tends to be. Conversely, the more right one leans politically, the more closed-minded he tends to be. This supports the often-claimed thesis that the political right is traditionally more authoritarian than the political left. Or, conservatives tend to be more authoritarian than liberals.

This position can be supported further. For Continuum II the combined mean of the two left loci ($M = 2.70$, $S. D. = 5.26$, $N = 55$) was tested against the combined mean of the two right loci ($M = 9.20$, $S.D. = 4.00$, $N = 19$). The t-value for this equals 4.850, which is statistically significant at the .001 level. This verification can be duplicated by following the same procedure for Continuum I. The combined mean for the two left loci ($M = 2.47$, $S. D. = 6.75$, $N = 54$) was tested against the combined mean for the two right loci ($M = 8.36$, $S. D. = 4.79$, $N = 19$). The t-value for this equals 3.464, which also is statistically significant at the .001 level.

We offer for more descriptive evidence Chart 4, which gives the distribution of open-minded and closed-minded individuals in the various loci. These show rather convincingly the predominance of open-mindedness on the political left and that of closed-mindedness on the political right. Chi-square tests are statistically significant in all instances. This liberal-conservative correlation is in the line of theoretical expectancy with the concept of the dogmatism syndrome.

Rokeach's findings show that closed-mindedness has a somewhat greater affinity with right-of-center ideologies. He states:

Nevertheless, the data stubbornly suggest that people to the right of center are somewhat more prone to authoritarianism and intolerance than people to the left of center. The dogmatism scores show slight but consistent positive correlations with conservatism. So do the opinionation scores. Also, the dogmatism scores correlate more highly with right than with left opinionation.[2]

CHART 4

DISTRIBUTION OF POSITIVE AND NEGATIVE DOGMATISM
SCORERS IN LOCI OF POLITICAL CONTINUA

Continuum I:

	63			30		
Dogmatic	13	19	31	12	2	16
Nondogmatic	10	8	7	1	1	0
		25			2	

$X^2 = 6.59$
df, 1; $p < .05$

Continuum II:

	34			19	
Dogmatic	12	22	42	4	15
Nondogmatic	10	7	8	0	0
		17		0	

$X^2 = 8.47$ $X^2 = 10.45$
df, 1; $p < .01$ *df,* 2 (center used); $p < .01$

Perhaps the first explanation that would come to mind is, as Rokeach mentions, that despite efforts to construct ideologically contentless scales, the Dogmatism Scale—particularly the D-10 version—still contains some content that may be weighted more to the right than to the left. Rokeach admits that this cannot be ruled out without further research.[3] Neither can it be accepted as highly likely in the light of the construction and validation procedures as explained in Chapter II. The more plausible answer, suggested by Rokeach, is that there is a theoretically necessary reason for authoritarianism to have a somewhat greater affinity with right than with left ideologies. This explanation involves the distinction between the content and the structure of an ideology, and whether or not these two elements are compatible with each other.[4] We shall consider this further in the section below on the interpretation of the findings.

Liberal and Conservative Ideologies

There remains one more consideration in this context of political ideologies. As we mentioned above, it is a rather common thesis that political extremism is marked by a general syndrome of authoritarianism or dogmatism.[5] Our findings thus far would tend not to support this position—at least not without qualification. The question, however, may be considered more thoroughly with Hypothesis VI:

> Politicians of the extreme political left and those of the extreme political right differ significantly from each other in terms of dogmatism.

We can test this hypothesis by utilizing the data from the two questions utilizing the political continuum. First, the test for Continuum I. Student's t applied to loci one and six yielded a t-value of 4.763, which is statistically significant at the .001 level. For Continuum II we tested similarly between locus one and locus five. This yielded a t-value of 5.442, which is statistically significant at the .001 level. Furthermore, if we want to take the mean of the PCI and that of the MSI to test for a significant difference, we get the same result: t equals 5.573, which is likewise statistically significant at the .001 level.

These data substantiate the research hypothesis that the political left extreme and the political right extreme do reveal significant differences based on the dogmatism syndrome. This evidence challenges the position often advanced that the two political extremes are identical such that the political continuum may be seen as a "closed circle" with the opposite poles joining together. With regard to personality structure, at least, political ideologies still follow the traditional bidimensional continuum. Dogmatism, or closed-mindedness, is distributed along a unilinear scale. Thus, these findings further challenge the position that both of the political extremes are similarly strongly authoritarian.[6] The political left is substantially open-minded, and the political right is substantially closed-minded.

We can substantiate this position further by considering the data for the moderate loci. For Continuum I a Student's t test between locus two and locus five gives a value of .475, and for Continuum II the same test between locus two and locus four gives a value of .779. Neither of these values is statistically significant—not even at the .1 level. And still further, for Continuum I the center loci (three and four) yield a t-value of 1.398, which also does not achieve statistical significance at the .1 level.

In summary, our data have supported the three research hypotheses presented in this chapter. We have demonstrated that the dogmatism syndrome does reveal significant differences among the various political parties and ideologies. Specifically, the political right tends to be more closed-minded, while the political left tends to be more open-minded. Moderate exponents of liberal ideology tend to be more dogmatic than extreme exponents of the same ideology, while moderates and extremists of conservative ideologies do not differ in this respect. This has shown that distinctive personality structures are found in association with various political ideologies.[i] By so doing, the concept of the political personality has been cast into more precise significance.

[i] We must repeat once again that our hypotheses are limited to politicians as defined in this study. The same kind of analysis with data from the nonpolitical sample is contradictory. The continuum questions were not used for this sample. Nonetheless, we arranged the mean dogmatism scores for the various parties along a continuum, as was done in Chart 1, and tested the leftist parties against

INTERPRETATION OF THE FINDINGS

We shall present in this section some interpretations—theoretical and practical—for the findings that have been derived. The general problem, of course, is to account for the variation in the dogmatism syndrome among the several political parties and ideological orientations. Specifically, we shall offer explanations for the antithetical dogmatism pattern between the political extremes, and consider more particularly the predominance of open-mindedness on the political left. The practical explanation of differential recruitment which was suggested in the preceding chapter will be extended in this context. And, finally, a consideration will be given to party factions to explain the range of open-minded and closed-minded scorers within the individual parties.

the rightist parties while we held the center constant. These data are given in Table 6, Chapter V. The combined mean of means for the leftist parties (3.40) was compared to that for the parties of the right (3.93). Standard deviations are respectively 6.03 and 5.38; N's are respectively 140 and 132. Clearly, from inspection no statistically significant difference should be expected. The t-value for this equals .609, which is not statistically significant at the .05 level. By way of contrast, we can follow the same procedure for the political sample (see Chart 1). The combined mean for the left is 3.08, the S. D. is 6.75; the mean for the right is 7.62, and the S. D. is 5.20. The t-value equals 3.289, which is statistically significant at the .01 level.

Thus, our evidence shows different patterns for political leaders and political followers if we assume that our latter sample is truly representative, even though it is skewed somewhat toward the upper social levels. Political affiliation as determined for the nonpolitical sample is merely a matter of expressed preference. There may be a bias too in the fact that many nonpolitical people who were approached either refused or were apprehensive about indicating a political party preference. Perhaps this was true particularly of the more closed-minded. (See reference for note 17 in Chapter IV.) And we would suspect this to be more true in regard to supporters of the "unpopular" or "banned" parties, specifically the PCI and the MSI. To repeat once again, however, Italians in general are not committed ideologically, except in terms of religious tenets, in their political behavior. Seen in such a perspective, this contrast in findings offers further substantiation for Hypothesis II regarding significant differences in personality structure between politicians and nonpoliticians.

The first question to be considered is that of the significantly different personality structures representing the extreme political left and the extreme political right. Since our data indicate that the representatives of these two ideological positions were nearly exclusively Communists and Fascists respectively, we shall speak in these terms.[j]

As we have indicated, the PCI has the lowest dogmatism mean, and the MSI presented the highest. Such a result, undoubtedly, will be most surprising to many. Since the PCI represents an extreme ideology and since Communism throughout the world has been a dictatorial and totalitarian movement, the generally accepted conception is that Communists are highly authoritarian individuals—just as much as the similarly operating Fascists of the right extreme—and therefore would be expected to be as highly dogmatic. This position was suggested by many of our parliamentary subjects, excluding, of course, those representing the two parties in question: the PCI and the MSI are "two birds of the same feather" that could easily unite into a coalition. Actually, these two parties are vehement enemies—the most bitterly inimical pair of parties in Italy.

The standard view maintains in effect that political alignment forms a "closed circle" rather than a "finite line" of the traditional continuum; the two extremes have a contiguous relationship to each other and, as such, are basically identical in all political respects. Yet at least on the basis of personality our data do not confirm this position. The explanation for one

[j] The data from the continuum questions show that twenty-five and twenty-six out of the twenty-seven left extremists were from the PCI, and all of the right extremists were from the MSI.

The MSI is the modern version of the *Partito Nazionale Fascista* of the Mussolini era. Twelve of the eighteen deputies in the MSI sample previously had belonged to the PNF. The MSI attempts to continue the revolutionary fascist tradition, although there have been some apparent modifications in methodology. The ideology of the party, however, is essentially fascist.

totalitarian extreme being open-minded and the other totalitarian extreme being closed-minded is found in the very
nature of the dogmatism syndrome.

Ideological Content and Ideological Structure

Rokeach maintains that there is a theoretically necessary
reason for authoritarianism to have a somewhat greater affinity
with the political right than with the leftist ideologies. The
explanation involves the distinction between the content and
structure of an ideology and the compatibility of these.[7] A
"unitotalitarian" approach to the study of modern dictatorships
has been a major theme in recent political analysis.[8] The differences of the divergent "isms" have been thought to be
less important than their similarities. These "unitotalitarian"
approaches have focused attention upon the common means
employed by dictatorships. This perspective emphasizes what
totalitarian movements do rather than what they ideologically
or propagandistically profess. Communism and fascism are
the most extreme forms of political liberalism and conservatism respectively. Both ideologies may be said to be authoritarian from the point of view of ideological *structure*. This
may be asserted on the similarity of the two movements in
the matter of methodology or political tactics, such as rigid
discipline, powerful pressure among their members, rejection
of opposition, and oligarchy or dictatorship. Thus, from the
point of view of the structure of the movements and their
operations, both Communism and fascism are quite similar,
if not identical. Seen, on the other hand, from the aspect of
ideological *content*, Communism and fascism have little in
common. As Rokeach explains:

> Communism, considered purely as an ideology, is humanitarian and
> anti-authoritarian. Its ideological aim is to establish a classless society,
> to wither away the state, and to take care of the individual according to
> the doctrine: "From each according to his abilities, to each according to

his needs." However, in the case of fascism, particularly Nazism, its ideological content is frankly anti-humanitarian. It advances as its ideological aim the establishment of the Aryan race as master-race, to rule and subjugate forever the rest of mankind.[9]

Fascism, according to the doctrine espoused by Mussolini himself, is anti-individualistic, disciplinarian, authoritarian, insists upon the superglorification of the state, rejects the possibility or utility of perpetual peace; therefore it is warlike, militaristic, antipacifist, and totalitarian.[10] The fundament of fascist theory is the complete, conscious rejection of individualism and liberalism and the complete, conscious assertion of the supremacy of the state.[11] In rejecting the welfare state, fascism considers individuals as but means to the state.

The "democratic fallacy" that people are capable of governing themselves is rejected by fascism. Only a small minority qualified by right of birth, social standing, and education is capable of understanding what is best for everyone.[12] Communism, in theory at least, does not advocate the supreme rule of a dictator, or apparently that of the *classe dirigente*. Thus, one maintains the principle that the majority of the people are unable to think for themselves, and the other does not.[k]

Whereas fascism advocates the inequality of men, Communism stresses the equality of mankind. Communism espouses "world brotherhood and sharing"; fascism glorifies nationalist supremacy and aggressive power. Communism theoretically is essentially humane and humanitarian; fascism is basically prejudicial, ethnocentric, and nationalistic. Communism condemns racism and imperialism as well as other ideological tenets that are exclusively or fundamentally fascist.[1] Our results are in the line of these theoretical expectations.

[k] Looking at the data for Item #5 in the D-10 Scale ("Most people don't know what's good for them"), sixty-eight percent of the PCI representatives answered negatively, but ninety-four of the MSI representatives answered affirmatively.

[1] Rokeach found that Communists scored very low on the Ethnocentrism Scale and, as expected, very high on the scale of Left Opinionation. Rokeach, *op. cit.*,

On numerous occasions during the field-work phase of this study the writer visited the PCI *gruppo* secretariat in the Parliament office buildings. One particular thing that captured his attention, because of its inconsistency and contrast with the typical Italian scene, was the informality that marked the social relations among the Communist deputies, but more especially those between the party officials and the "office girls." We may mention as an example of this the general use of the most informal *tu* form of the second person and words such as *compagno* (comrade). All of this undoubtedly is in keeping with the Communist doctrine of classless and equal brotherhood. Nonetheless, that this should exist in an extremely formal and status-conscious society, particularly involving the status-relationships mentioned, is all the more significant. Expediently or theoretically, this operation is democratic.

Considering the development of interests in politics, we find that the majority of the open-minded respondents claim to have entered political activity 1) for reasons of "social justice, democracy, and liberty" and 2) for the purpose of fighting Fascism. Thirty-two percent of the PCI sample responded in each of these two categories. In contrast, none of the MSI representatives (all closed-minded scorers) entered politics in the interests of "social justice, democracy, and liberty." Forty-four percent of the MSI deputies offered "defense of party and personal ideology" and another twenty-eight percent of these gave "nationalistic" (civic duty, honor of country) answers consistent with fascist ideology. None of the PCI representatives gave such answers. This pattern of response appears to be in keeping with the profile of the open-minded and closed-minded personality.

p. 115. Richard Christie has presented evidence indicating that adherents to Communism score low on the F-Scale. This is consistent, of course, with the ideological bias of the F-Scale toward authoritarianism of the political right. "Authoritarianism Re-examined" in Richard Christie and Marie Jahoda (eds.), *Studies in the Scope and Method of "The Authoritarian Personality"* (Glencoe: The Free Press, 1954), pp. 130–133.

Now, on the operational level fascism and Communism have much in common. The two are basically nondemocratic in organization, structure, and procedures. Communism actually does function through the *elite concept* of government. Both are totalitarian and authoritarian in this sense. This must be seen, however, as a de facto form of Communism and not as the ideally advocated de jure Communism, whereas in fascism there is no discrepancy between the de jure and the de facto aspects of the ideology.[m]

What does all this mean? Simply that this is a situation of two antithetical objectives, ends, or political ideologies being sought and pursued by identical means, procedures, or political methodology. In the case of fascism there is an authoritarian ideology and authoritarian methodology, both of which support each other in a very compatible manner. In the case of Communism there is a situation of a democratic ideology and an authoritarian and nondemocratic methodology, each of which is incongruous with the other. Rokeach explains this situation in the following manner:

> We thus see in the case of fascism that ideological content and structure support each other. There is no incompatibility between them and thus psychological conflict is not engendered nor guilt feelings aroused. For this reason, authoritarian ideological structures may be psychologically more reconcilable—more easily "attachable"—to ideologies that are anti-democratic than to those that are democratic in content. If a person's underlying motivations are served by forming a closed belief system, then it is more than likely that his motivations can also be served by embracing an ideology that is blatantly anti-equalitarian. If this is so, it would account for the somewhat greater affinity we have observed between authoritarian belief structure and conservatism than between the same belief structure and liberalism.
>
> But in the case of a person who embraces Communism there is a

[m] For example, in the Machiavellian question on "means and ends" (see previous chapter) the MSI had the highest mean response (1.22), while the PCI had the lowest (.28). The difference between these values, however, is not statistically significant. These data may be compared in Table 38 given in Appendix E.

sharp discrepancy between content and structure. Such a person may have seen a lot of social injustice around him and may want to do something about it. He may read the literature of Marxism and discover that it proposes humanitarian, equalitarian solutions. He may join the Communist party in the hope of alleviating or eliminating such injustices. But somewhere along the line he may become aware, at one level or another, that the methods advocated, the discipline, and the hierarchical structure of the party are somewhat at odds with the humanitarian aims advocated. He may sense, perhaps without being quite able to make it explicit, that there is an inherent conflict between the content of communist ideology and its structure.[13]

We concur with Rokeach's conclusion: "The analysis of conflict or harmony between ideological content and structure seems to suggest that there is a compelling theoretical reason for our finding a somewhat greater affinity of authoritarian belief structure with political conservatism."[14]

The following evidence may be offered for this interpretation. Rokeach suggests the disillusionment of the many Communist followers when sooner or later they find themselves experiencing this conflict. It is this situation that supposedly accounts for the tremendously high turnover rate among members of the American Communist party as well as the wholesale defections from Communist parties as a result of the Nazi-Soviet Friendship Pact in 1939 and the suppression of the 1956 Hungarian revolt by the Soviet army.[15] Moreover, we could mention the enormous number of defections from Communist East Germany during the past several years.[n] Mangone makes a similar point in stating that the de-Stalinization in Russia and the harsh suppression in Hungary on the part of the Soviet Union had the same detrimental effect on the PCI by bringing about innumerable defections during 1956 and 1957, especially among its intellectual leadership.[16]

[n] The Communist subjects in our nonpolitical sample had a relatively low mean score for dogmatism. This did not indicate any statistically significant difference, however, from that of any of the other political classifications.

We may mention another verification of this disillusionment, namely, the severance on the part of the PSI of its political alliance with the PCI when the latter pressed for a Bolshevik-type revolution to bring about a socialistic reform.[17] Pietro Nenni, the long-time leader of the Italian Socialists, claims that the PCI originated as a secessionist movement from the PSI "for motives of *form* more than substance."[18] He asserts that the PSI has a "method" all its own and that the antihumanitarian and Machiavellian methodology of the PCI is not acceptable to the Socialists' preference for democracy as a political methodology.°

These events seem to become more understandable if one thinks of (political) disillusionment as a psychological state in which the person experiencing it becomes aware of a discrepancy between ideological content and ideological structure, between what he believes and how he believes, between what he says and what he does. This discrepancy is so painful, claims Rokeach, that only the inner core of party members, by virtue of heavy investments, can withstand it long.[19] The rest seem to defect sooner or later. He claims that this state of disillusionment is experienced far more often by adherents to causes of the left than those of the right.[20] As Ebenstein states:

> The *main weakness of Communism,* however, is the *discrepancy between ideal and reality.* Its leaders proclaim lofty ideals for the renewal of mankind and yet use inhuman means, age-old instruments of oppressive despotism. One of the deepest insights of the liberal way of life is that *means and ends cannot be too sharply separated* from each other, and that the nature of the means employed in realizing an end will determine the character of the end itself. Communism acts in total disregard of this axiom, and purports to build a new fellowship of love and fraternity with the knout and the slave labor camp.[21]

° It may be well to point out at this point that no statistically significant difference exists between the mean dogmatism score of the PCI and that of the PSI in either the political or the nonpolitical sample.

This interpretation clarifies the position that totalitarian regimes and systems cannot be classified into a single category. As Rokeach explains, political ideologies at opposite extremes both may be authoritarian in basic ideological structure by sharing the same general conception of authority, power, and leadership. Yet they may disagree sharply in ideological content. Thus both may take the same route to essentially diverse goals or may seek the same goals with different means. It seems clear, however, that political ends and political means cannot be inconsistent with each other. This challenges the notion that authoritarianism is the psychological root of political extremism—at least of all extremism. Ideologically Communism and fascism attract different types of personality. We shall return to this question subsequently with the consideration of political recruitment.

The data for the extreme political right fulfill theoretical expectations. But, the more striking finding, particularly in the light of the discussion above, is that of relative open-mindedness on the extreme of the political left. Thus, the question still remains of reconciling in this context the apparent discrepancy between ideological content and ideological structure. We shall elaborate upon this consideration in the section to follow.

Communism and Dogmatism

Our findings of dogmatism in Communists are inconsistent with those obtained by Rokeach. He found that Communists scored higher than other political groups on the entire sixty-six–item version (Form D) of the Dogmatism Scale.[p] Rokeach's data, however, are quite limited. His Communist sample of British university students, who usually may be expected to be rather conservative, consisted of only thirteen individuals.[22]

Also there are theoretical inconsistencies in Rokeach's data.

[p] None of the mean differences, however, achieved statistical significance at the .05 level. Rokeach, *op. cit.*, p. 115.

The British Communists have the lowest score on the Anxiety Scale,[23] but Rokeach has shown that dogmatism and anxiety correlate with each other as two elements of the same syndrome.[24] He explains, moreover, that these British Communists did not score higher than others on the entire sixty-six–item instrument, but rather generally on only those statements that tap primarily the structural and formal aspects of belief systems. They scored lower on items tapping the dynamic or functional aspects of belief systems.[25] No such pattern is evident in our use of the D-10 version of the dogmatism instrument.[q]

We do not doubt the validity of Rokeach's findings on British Communists despite their theoretical inconsistency. Neither, however, can we reject the validity of our own. A basic explanation for the discrepancy in these findings may be that of an apparent difference between political leaders and political followers in terms of personality structure, which of course is the principle thesis of this study. And another is that concerning different kinds of Communism.

More specifically, our claim is that committed Communists and Communist sympathizers or followers may be distinguishable in terms of dogmatism. Rokeach's samples of theistic nonbelievers[r] scored low in dogmatism,[26] and all our low-scoring Communists with two exceptions claimed to be nonbelievers. Many in fact openly declared themselves to be atheists, a sign of their being committed Marxists. We have contended that the majority of our nonpolitical sample of Communists are not committed to Marxian ideology.[s] This we suspect to be the case likewise for Rokeach's British Communists. We suspect that if the Dogmatism Scale were to be administered to Russian people, there would be differential results for Communist

[q] See Appendix D for mean responses to each item.

[r] Again, quite limited. Six students in one and fifteen in another.

[s] Only thirty percent of the nonpolitical PCI sample were nonbelievers.

party members and the not-so-committed Russian populace.[t] Furthermore, the same situation we suspect would obtain in other Communist environments.

In a similar type of analysis based on different instruments, Eysenck claims to have found British Communists to be "tough-minded radicals" and fascists to be "tough-minded conservatives."[27] This again presents the position of similar personality structure in both types of extremists. The "tough-minded" concept[u] is claimed to be similar to that of the "authoritarian" and the "dogmatic" personality. Yet independent studies relating the various instruments for the authoritarian syndrome found that there was no relationship between tough-mindedness and authoritarianism as it is usually defined.[28] Moreover, Rokeach and Hanley, in a methodological criticism of Eysenck's research, claim that his data actually indicate that Communists are the most "tender-minded" of all political groups and thus reject his contentions about Communists.[29] If there is a negative association between "tender-mindedness" and dogmatism, then Eysenck's results—in terms of Rokeach and Hanley's criticism—substantiate our findings.

Another most important explanation remains to be considered. It is well known that an ideology, including a political one, is affected and modified by its cultural environment. The Italian Republic is certainly a rather unique example of democracy. Moreover, the European, and more specifically the Italian, connotation of the words "liberal," "republican," and "conservative" shows that these concepts are relative to a particular political context. Much too often people think of all Communists—no matter from which country—as being com-

---

[t] For a consideration of the differential recruitment of certain personality types among the Russian people into the Soviet political system, see Alex Inkeles, Eugenia Hanfmann, and Helen Beier, "Modal Personality and Adjustment to the Soviet Socio-Political System," *Human Relations*, XI (1958), 3–22.

[u] Derived from William James.

pletely identical in political ideology and methodology. Yet even in the parent Soviet party we have witnessed different kinds of Communism advanced during recent years. This suggests that every ideology should be seen in the perspective of its cultural and social (political) context. Such an explanation may be a potent one for our findings. As Gross has stated:

> Within every nation, every culture, we may find a variety of political ideologies, but every one of them is in some way or another influenced by the national ethos. For his political affiliation an Englishman may choose among conservatism, liberalism, and socialism, yet each of these will have a common tinge of British culture. In the same way, although British, French, or Spanish socialists share many values, ideas, and views, nevertheless, certain elements of their ideology will differ as a result of differences in national culture and in social, economic, and political conditions.[30]

It is generally known that Italian Fascism during the Mussolini era was but one expression of this ideology. To what extent were Nazism and Peronism *cultural* and *social* variations of a theoretical fascism?[v] We suggest that these fascist movements were significantly different from one another in terms of cultural elements. Furthermore, the fascist parties existing today in various countries throughout the world differ from one another, including the MSI, on the same basis. The implicit principle, of course, is that such cultural variations may be reflected in differences of personality structure for the followers of these movements.

Specifically, then, are there different types of Communism or Communist movements? Are the Communist parties of Russia, China, and those in other Communist nations identical to each other or distinguishable from one another? Does the political machinery function identically in all Communist nations? Do Communist parties in democratic political systems

[v] Lipset has attempted to distinguish these three fascist movements as factional variations discernible in terms of social bases. Seymour M. Lipset, *Political Man* (London: William Heineman, 1960), pp. 173–174.

function differently than those in totalitarian nations?[31] We ask
these questions notwithstanding the fact that there are certain
fixed principles and themes to which all Communists subscribe.
The proper question is, then, Are the various Communist
parties *structurally* different?

Recently the world has witnessed the lack of harmony between Chinese Communism, which prefers a Leninist-Stalinist
conception of Marxism, and the current brand of Russian Communism as formulated and advanced by Nikita Khrushchev.
The Lenin-Stalin position is one of revolution, war, violence,
and whatever means are necessary to effect the establishment
of world Communism. Stalin was an orthodox Leninist in the
fundamentals of Communist doctrine. Everywhere he adapted
and implemented the ideas of his master.[32] Lenin's most important single contribution to the theory of Marxism is alleged
to be his concept of the *professional revolutionary*.[33] The Stalinist position, as adopted by the Chinese Communists (and
its colleagues in Albania) is one of strict ideological rigidity
(dogmatism) which allows no deviations from the established Leninist patterns, and the denunciation of all revisionist
attempts or tendencies. In contrast, the Khrushchevian position, which is continued officially by Russia at the present
time, is one of "democratic coexistence" that stresses nonvio-
lent means toward the expanding establishment of Communism. The difference in these positions is fundamentally that
between the classic Bolshevistic and Menshevistic orientations.
Nonetheless, Soviet (and by and large international) Communism has been somewhat more ambivalent on doctrine, and
even more particularly on political means.[w] Freedom is ex-
panded and contracted, the cold war is frozen or thawed, and
the Communists have been dominant or submissive according

---

[w] "It would be extremely harmful to try to fit revolutionary processes in this
extremely varied world into ready molds, as the dogmatists are trying to do."
Attributed to Nikita Khrushchev. *Time*, January 18, 1963, p. 25.

to the particular situation much more than was the case under the rule of the unyielding, immobile, steadfast, and authoritarian position of Stalin. As Meyer states:

Obviously, communism is protean; its meaning depends on time and place, circumstance, and on the point of view of the observer. Even its articulate ethos, Marxist theory, clothes itself in garbs of many hues. The theory itself distinguishes different levels of understanding and tries, accordingly, to speak to different publics. It also views reality on different levels of concreteness or abstraction, so that it takes long-, short-, and intermediate-range views of the setting, the goals, and the strategies of the communist movement. Outsiders, meanwhile, note the tendency toward the development of an esoteric communist language which, some maintain, serves as a complicated code only the initiates know how to decipher.[34]

More specifically on the Italian scene, the long-time secretary of the PCI, Palmiro Togliatti, upon his return from exile in Moscow in 1944, stressed the need for a "new type of party" (*Partito di Tipo Nuovo*) which is to be a progressive, democratic, and constitutional party.[35] Togliatti, once a Stalinist, accepted the possibility of a peaceful road to Socialism and later became a loyal Khrushchevite. He thus retained his allegiance to Moscow. In his "Memorandum on Problems of World Communist Tactics," written just before his death at Yalta in August 1964, Togliatti endorsed the Khrushchevian position and urged Communists everywhere "to overcome every form of dogmatism."[36] Luigi Longo, Togliatti's successor as leader of the Italian Communists, states in an introduction to this "Memorandum" that it was published posthumously as a precise statement of the current position of the PCI on the problems of the international Communist movement.

The growing disunity and diversity within the international Communist movement is in sharp contrast to the popular image of Communism in the Western world, where it has been seen as an entirely undifferentiated bloc, a monolith that is well defined and uniform.[37] But the question is, What is the methodological position of the PCI? Is this party Leninist-Stalinist or Khrushchevian in its structural operations? Evidently the PCI was faced eventually with this problem of choosing between the two camps, and the latter faction emerged victoriously.[38] The majority of the PCI favor continuing the policy of Togliatti, who led the party to its present strength as the largest Communist party in the Western world by stressing its purely Italian character and by eschewing violently doctrinaire militancy.[x] The PCI prefers ideally, of course, a one-party system, but in recent national congresses has adopted the official position that its ideological program can be achieved by working in a democratic fashion through the multiparty system so long as this democratic advance toward a socialistic revolution is neither interfered with nor prohibited.[y] On this basis one would suspect that the PCI, having accepted the Khrushchevian orientation, would not find itself in the incongruous content-structure dilemma. Our dogmatism findings support the dominant orientation of the party.

Furthermore, as another point of difference from international Communism, Italian Communists in the past have spoken for a polycentric world movement, that is, one providing for more "central offices" than the singularity of Moscow.[39] Togliatti described himself as a decisive champion of the autonomy of Communist parties. In his "Memorandum" he urged, for the development of the international Communist movement, the essential establishment of a democratic organization that respected with tolerance and open-mindedness the position of all Communist parties throughout the world. Togliatti contended that the unity of world Communism has to be achieved in the diversity of concrete political positions and

[x] One PCI deputy curiously referred to Togliatti as an "open-minded" individual: *"una mentalità più aperta."*

[y] This program of coexistence, and its implicit de-Stalinization, resulted in a number of defections from the PCI. *New Haven Register,* March 3, 1963.

by using working methods that conform to the political ambient and to the degree of Communist development in each country. Recently this issue of autonomy has become a crucial one within the Communist world, and in some respects it may be regarded as a third major variety of Communism.[z] One well-known form of "national Communism" is that of Titoism, which insists on remaining free of foreign domination and rejects the imperialism within the Soviet world.[40] A similar situation exists in Poland. Since Wladyslav Gomulka's triumph in October 1956, Communism there has moved steadily away from Stalinist totalitarianism to a Communist variation of authoritarianism in government and relative liberty in thought, religion, and literature.[41] Does this decentralization and factionalization of the authoritarian Communist rule indicate anything in the direction of a more open-minded approach on the part of Italian Communists?

There seems to be ample evidence to maintain that all Communist parties do not fit into a monolithic mold. More particularly, while Communist theory may be everywhere the same, its political methodology does show social and cultural diversity. Meyer claims that unity for Communism has become a mere historical fact. He states that three distinct doctrines, currents, and practices have emerged in the Communist bloc since the 1956 Hungarian revolt: 1) the democratic "left" wing which is loyal to patterns established by Stalin, 2) the autonomists, and 3) the mediators of the Soviet Union, who sometimes support one and sometimes the other.[42]

Another indication of the sociocultural relativity of politics may be seen in the following. We asked our political subjects

[z] Within a recent period of time a group within the PSI caucused, declared themselves "national Communists," and established as guiding principles of their organization the development of the fullest democracy. E. A. Bayne, "Italy's Seeds of Peril," American Universities Field Staff *Reports Service*, X (1962), No. 1, p. 12.

to select a world leader who was typical of the kind of personality considered best suited for Italy. Several parliamentarians stated that Italy needed an Italian: "Outsiders cannot understand Italy!" Apparently these respondents could not imagine political leaders of other nations expressing the same political platform effectively or successfully in Italy. Some comments of these individuals are the following: "I cannot imagine a successful foreign politician in Italy"; "Would Stalin be a good leader for Italy?"; "Adenauer in Italy would not be the same man"; and "I cannot envision Churchill or Khrushchev in Italy. . . . The man must be matched to the situation." Evidently this is just as true in regard to ideologies.

One other aspect of this contextual relativity of political ideology is that of the political context. For example, do Communist parties operating in totalitarian systems and those in democratic systems differ from each other? It would seem that a Communist party in a free political structure would have to function more "democratically," not so much to gather support, but more so because this is the functional structure of the system within which it must operate. Meyer speaks of the competition of Communist parties with other socialist parties, particularly for the allegiance of workers and other voters: "They fight within the present social and economic system, not against it."[aa] Then, too, there is a question of the legality and constitutionality of the Communist party in many nontotalitarian countries. This fact undoubtedly influences the political methodology that is employed.

Rokeach has shown that ideologies or movements are apt to become more closed-minded when their activity or existence is threatened.[43] As situational threats increase, there is a cor-

[aa] Meyer claims that where there are other socialist parties, the Communists are distinguished, not by greater revolutionary force, but only by their unquestioned loyalty to the USSR. Alfred G. Meyer, *Communism* (New York: Random House, 1960), p. 172.

responding increase in institutional dogmatism. He says, "The more concerted or widespread the attacks on authority or the authority's belief systems (which amounts to the same thing), the more closed or dogmatic the reaction to be expected."[44]

Threats to the activity or existence of ideological movements, such as severely challenging oppositions, should lead to the manifestation of closed systems on the part of these movements, at least as long as the threat endures. This situation should hold true for those political parties which in whatever nation are banned, controlled, considered unconstitutional, or in any sense not given full recognition. The Communist party in Britain, although not banned, is certainly fighting for a fully accepted and legitimate existence equal to that of other national parties. While the legal aspects are not identical, a similar problem confronts the American Communist party. The PCI, however, enjoys complete constitutional sanction and freedom, and its strength and popularity are by no means even approached by any other Communist movement outside of the Soviet bloc. Would this situation account for the relatively low dogmatism of the PCI, and the high dogmatism found for the British Communists, as well as the authoritarian stereotype usually attributed to Communists in other free countries?

To be sure, there is much agitation for the annihilation of the PCI. It appears, nonetheless, that this party does not feel threatened. The PCI is the second largest party in Italy and the largest Communist party in the entire free world. Furthermore, the strength of this party has increased steadily in each of the four national elections which have been held since the establishment of the Italian Republic. Recall, too, the party's platform of rejecting the usual revolutionary means in favor of the democratic process to bring about its socialistic reform.

It is interesting to note in this regard that the more open-minded parties in our political sample are those that have gained progressively in strength; the more closed-minded parties are those that have lost strength, even to the point of passing out of existence. Table 10 illustrates this situation.

TABLE 10

POLITICAL PARTY STRENGTH* AND DOGMATISM SCORES

Progressively Gaining Strength

PCI	.92
PSI	2.23
PLI[a]	4.00

Losing Strength

DC	7.96
PRI	8.00
PSDI	9.00
PDI	9.33

Constitutionally Banned

MSI[b]	9.55

* Based on parliamentary strength from 1946 to 1958 (see Table 2). Results for the national elections of 1963, subsequent to the time of this study, substantially reveal the same patterns with the notable exception that the PSDI increased its parliamentary strength by 75 percent.

[a] This party has fluctuated in strength, but showed a major increase in the last two elections as compared to its poll in the 1952 national election.

[b] The MSI, however, has gained appreciably in strength.

These data support the explanation of dogmatism correlating with threatened existence. The greater and the more imminent the threat, the more closed or dogmatic the reaction.

Furthermore, this explanation may account for the higher dogmatism means of the PRI and the PSDI as compared to the other parties of the political left, and the lower dogmatism mean of the PLI in contrast to the other parties of the political right. We submit this interpretation as a plausible explanation for our findings.

We have offered here more specific explanations for the findings of low dogmatism on the political left. Once again the question of a significant difference in personality structure between political leaders and political followers has been suggested. Introduced is the consideration of the social (political), and more particularly the cultural, context of an ideology which is apt to reveal important modifications in theory and practice. The element of institutional threat offers some significance in this regard. These explanations, while they offer plausible interpretations for our findings, are meant by no means to be confined to Communist ideology. We shall continue our interpretation of the findings with further considerations that are applicable to all ideologies.

Political Recruitment and Dogmatism

We referred in the previous chapter to the influence of recruitment procedures upon the types of personalities which are apt to be attracted to the political system and to the individual political parties. Here we shall elaborate further on this matter; however our consideration is directed more particularly to an explanation for dogmatism as a party pattern rather than as a variation among individuals.

Political office in all Italian parties is a bilateral affair that requires considerable compromise. Italian parties in principle operate democratically, but in fact are generally disciplined ones that operate by oligarchic control. Party leaders expect their party colleagues to vote and to act as the party leadership dictates. Voting in the Italian Parliament is frequently by roll call—only rarely is the secret ballot used—a practice which affords the party an open control on its representatives. Parliamentary power thus is usurped by the party executive boards, which become the locus of all top decision-making. Under such arrangements even the governments and the individual ministers are responsible to these executive boards. So prevalent and common is such highly centralized and concentrated decision-making in Italian politics that the term *partitocrazia* has been coined to describe the tendency of party organizations to encroach upon the whole sphere of political life and thereby make subservient to themselves the authorities who legally are responsible to the citizens.[45] As one deputy commented, "The deputy does not represent the people"; and in the words of another, "The deputy is in the hands of his party and represents its interests." LaPalombara contends that the functions of interest groups and those of political parties in Italy are not sufficiently differentiated.[46] The political parties in his view are "essentially transmission belts" for introducing into the legislature and other sectors of government the particularistic demands of a host of interest groups. Hence the Parliament consists principally of the representatives of these respective groups.

Little doubt exists that in Italy an individual is not at complete liberty to offer his candidacy for Parliament; the Italian parties have considerable control over the selection of their parliamentary representatives. This may be summed up in quoting one PSI deputy: "The party places our candidacy and in large measure, under the Italian electoral system, even determines the elections. . . . The party actually elects the candidate." Although this prerogative is exercised throughout the system, presumably the amount of personal decision which is left to the individual is a matter of degree depending upon the policy of his respective party. It appears that the political left leaves no choice to the individual, while greater freedom of candidacy is allowed on the political right and in the center. Twenty-two of the forty-six deputies from the PCI and the PSI freely remarked that their candidacy was placed by their party and not themselves. Only one deputy from the DC and another from the MSI made the same comment. Apparently for the nonleftist parties the individual has a more personal role in the decision. Another MSI deputy stated that candidacy in his party was "a combination of individual determination and party choice. The party rejects those it does not want for moral reasons, but generally places all those who so desire." Presumably, to greater or lesser degree, the other parties follow this mode of operation. Thus under the Italian electoral system[bb] the electors determine how many parliamentary seats each party shall receive, but it is the party organization that determines who shall occupy them. The executive bureau of each party retains the final power to approve or to disapprove the lists of candidates which are submitted from the electoral districts. Such a procedure would provide a fine mechanism for eliminating independent and rebellious thinkers and thereby would prevent the emergence of factions within the party ranks.

Personality is an important element in the dynamics of social control. We suspect, as mentioned already in the preceding chapter, that recruitment within the Italian parties is being made, among other things, on the basis of personality structure. As far as the political right is concerned, the data are in support of the theoretical structure of the respective ideologies. Furthermore, with evidently greater freedom of personal determination on the political right, and even the center, the data also substantiate our major proposition that the dogmatic individual is self-recruited to politics.

The more puzzling situation concerns the parties of the political left. If, as we have shown, the true ideology of the

[bb] See Appendix G for a note on the Italian electoral system.

PCI and the PSI is one of humanitarian, liberal, equalitarian, and democratic ideals, then the low dogmatism means for these parties are not inconsistent with this ideology. That is to say, even though these parties are selecting their representatives, the recruitment is of relatively open-minded personalities. Moreover, in order to avoid the theoretical dilemma of incongruous ideological content and ideological structure, these parties would have to recruit or to select nondogmatic individuals.

Yet there is much to suggest that this discrepancy between ideology and methodology does exist. That is, despite the content of their ideologies, the PCI and the PSI are authoritarian in their structures. First of all, of course, there is this very question of candidate selection. Then, too, there is no such thing as split parliamentary voting for these parties. They vote *en bloc* in contrast to the other parties. In the PSI the bloc vote is determined by a democratic majority of the *gruppo*, but in the PCI the vote on any legislative issue allegedly is decided by the party leader (or leaders). The remainder of the party's representatives unanimously follow this directive— and apparently under the sanction of expulsion from the party. Instances of such punishment for the violation of party discipline are not uncommon.[cc] Within such a party structure the role of the deputy consists principally of providing strength in numbers by following the dictates of the party leaders and perhaps keeping the party in contact with the political masses.[47] This would seem to be a manifestation of the submissive dimension of the authoritarian personality, but it is unlikely

[cc] For example, two Socialist deputies (and twelve senators) were suspended from the PSI for breaching party discipline by refusing to support the center-left coalition government that was installed in December 1963. A similar incident occurred in the PRI when a former party leader, serving his fifth term in Parliament, was expelled from the party for a breach of discipline on the same issue.

that the power-oriented (in this case, dogmatic) individual would be attracted to such systems.[dd]

There are clearly old-guard Stalinists in the PCI and self-declared Communists in the PSI who consider themselves to be farther to the left than the Communists themselves.[ee] It is interesting to note in this context that shortly after this study Togliatti reportedly undertook a quiet but intensive purge to surround himself with younger men in order to give the PCI a new appeal to voters. The purge affected several old-guard members in municipal and provincial posts, and reportedly this de-Stalinization was planned to include nearly one-third of the party's parliamentary candidates in the general elections of 1963.[ff] Togliatti admits in his "Memorandum" that even some party leaders had to be expelled from the PCI ranks because they were responsible for violating party discipline and for engaging in the formation of factions within the party. Nevertheless, while factions do exist within these parties, they are more in the nature of covert and internal ones confining their dissensions to themselves rather than to public expressions. This type of activity is characteristic of the dogmatic individual.[gg]

Now if the PCI and the PSI are authoritarian in structure,

[dd] Barker has shown that the dogmatics of the political left, center, and right are similar in all authoritarian criteria except submission to authority. Edwin N. Barker, "Authoritarianism of the Political Right, Center, and Left," *Journal of Social Issues*, XIX (1953), p. 66.

[ee] One major leader of the PCI, when asked his occupation, remarked: "My profession is a Communist. . . . Professional revolutionists—that's what we are!"

[ff] *South Bend Tribune,* November 18, 1962. A parliamentarian may be purged by such indirect methods as shifting his future candidacy from a "safe" area to a constituency in which he is certain not to gain re-election. Kogan contends that there are not enough safe constituencies to go around; those that get them are likely to be docile to their party's dictates in order to reassure nomination. Norman Kogan, *The Government of Italy* (New York: Thomas Y. Crowell, 1964), pp. 95–96.

[gg] See Item #1 of the D-10 Scale ("The worst crime a person can commit is to attack publicly the people who believe in the same thing he does"), for which the PCI had a relatively high mean response, as did the PSI.

what is the explanation for their attraction of more open-minded personalities? Of course, the attraction and the recruitment of open-minded people would be in theoretical harmony with the PCI's orientation along the lines of Khrushchevian or Togliattian Communism[hh] as well as with the expressed principles of the PSI. Nonetheless, there may be a significant difference in personality structure between party leaders and the other representatives (followers) of the parties. The leaders, in the light of the consideration above on closed party structures, in fact may be highly dogmatic and authoritarian personalities.[ii] We cannot offer much evidence on this since our sampling included only a few leaders.[jj] As for the "followers" in these parties, the system may be recruiting a fair number of political opportunists. Only open-minded people would be expected to be opportunists, since closed-mindedness (rigid commitment) and opportunism are contradictory. Accordingly, inasmuch as this pattern would not be expected in the more dogmatic parties, the explanation seems all the more plausible. Of course, this is not to deny—as we suggested in the preceding chapter—that particular individuals in the other parties may be political opportunists.

An opportunist is an individual with neither principles nor

[hh] To reiterate our preceding consideration, different political methodologies require different personalities. As Gross explains, "A change in the ideology of power of a political movement, even a change in tactics, may have its impact on the process by which its members are drawn into the movement." Felixs Gross, *The Seizure of Political Power* (New York: Philosophical Library, 1958), pp. 14–15.

[ii] We would, therefore, challenge Lasswell's position that "It is improbable that the top leaders of an established totalitarian regime in an industrial society are recruited from authoritarian personalities." Harold D. Lasswell, "The Selective Effect of Personality on Political Participation" in Richard Christie and Marie Jahoda (eds.), *Studies in the Scope and Method of "The Authoritarian Personality"* (Glencoe: The Free Press, 1954), p. 223.

[jj] One known leader of the PCI scored + 9. Moreover, the three or four direct refusals for interviews which we received in these parties came from party officials and "faction" leaders, who seemed to be most apprehensive about this research.

convictions. As such, he has no system of beliefs about which
and for which to be dogmatic or closed-minded. He is, therefore, open-minded to whatever ideology or methodology may
satisfy his expedient desires. The opportunist in this regard
is a multivalent personality which—as defined by Gross—is
inconsistent and functions not on one, but on many, often contrary, value systems.[48] Such an individual would experience
little difficulty in switching his political allegiance to another
political party, given that he has no political convictions and
thus exhibits no ego-involvement with the ideology of any
particular party. Thus, motivated by personal expediency,
opportunistic individuals are expected to be open-minded personalities that would manifest very low measures of dogmatism.

Opportunists are usually thought to be dogmatic and authoritarian people. Indeed, this was the basis of our consideration
of Hypothesis III in the preceding chapter. In that respect we
offered evidence to support the contention that dogmatic people have an authoritarian orientation toward power and, as
such, are Machiavellian. Our explanation here is intended to
suggest that there are different kinds of opportunists.[kk] While
not dogmatic (and perhaps not power oriented in the authoritarian sense), these individuals do apparently "live off" politics in contrast to the more ideologically committed and closed-
minded individuals who may actually "live for" politics. Barzini, himself a deputy, points out in his study of the Italian

[kk] This whole question of opportunism, especially in relation to dogmatism and
authoritarianism, is a very complex one. It deserves much more analytical attention than it has been given so far. In the light of this situation our explanation
for these political findings is offered, of course, as a merely tentative one. Some
evidence, however, supports this course of action. Richard Christie reports (in
personal correspondence) that the F-Scale and Machiavellianism—as measured
by scales based upon the writings of Machiavelli—correlations have hovered
around −.10 in nine varied samples. It is interesting to note that while none
of these correlations is statistically significant, the relationship is moving in the
opposite direction from that which is usually hypothesized.

character: "Many Italians are not technically opportunists; they do not find it difficult to weave in and out of political parties, conceal their thoughts, accept whatever official ideas are being imposed from above merely because they want to avoid risks; they do all this also because they are skeptical."[49] Such skepticism, of course, is a mark of the open-minded individual.

Kogan claims that Italians in general have a widespread utilitarian attitude toward government. Political institutions and principles, he says, evoke no loyalties in their own right.[50] Many Italians are concerned simply with achieving purely private goals. The quality of representation is least impressive in the PCI and the PSI as we may see in an inspection of the educational and occupational backgrounds of our sample. An offer of one of the highest public positions to such individuals, particularly in an extremely status-conscious society, is most gratifying, even if it means surrendering one's independence and declaring allegiance to a particular ideology for which the individual does not necessarily have any personal commitment. It has been suggested that patronage is a characteristic tactic of these parties in that they are interested in the immediate consequences of political office for their functionaries.[51] A good salary and a life pension after six years of parliamentary service may be sufficient inducement and reward for obedience and submission to party dictates.[11] The latter benefit requires at least one re-election, for which the parliamentarian is dependent upon his party. Kogan contends that parliamentarians want desperately to be re-elected and that this pressing desire makes them prisoners of the party organi-

[11] It should be noted that the salaries of the Communist and Socialist deputies are paid directly to the respective parliamentary groups. A portion of the salary, based on personal needs, is given to the deputy and the rest is retained by the party. See John C. Adams and Paolo Barile, *The Government of Republican Italy* (Boston: Houghton, Mifflin, 1961), p. 159.

zation.[52] Dedicated obedience thus is rewarded with a high degree of security. At the same time, of course, the allocation of parliamentary positions is to an extent a recognition and reward for loyal service to the party.

We maintain that it is more advantageous for a party to work with the open-minded individual. As an opportunist he is a willing follower and would offer very little, if any, opposition. Furthermore, such an arrangement would minimize the development of factions or power struggles of another kind within the system. As Spitz maintains, "It is precisely among authoritarians that the greatest ideological divisions are likely to occur; for here the driving force is said to be not ideology but ambition, the craving for power."[53] It is the more dogmatic individual (the authoritarian power seeker) who objects to party discipline.[mm]

Political systems with various methods of recruitment "attract" different personality types. We submit that this partly accounts for differences in the dogmatism scores of the various political parties. The parties with relatively low dogmatism scores (open-mindedness) actually select their representatives; the high dogmatism scores (closed-mindedness) of the other parties is a function of the comparatively uninfluenced self-recruitment of the individual politicians. This explanation supports the interpretation given in the preceding chapter.

Personality and Party Factions

One thing that remains to be discussed is the variance of individual dogmatism scores within the political parties.

[mm] There seems to be a positive parallel between the degree of dogmatism that characterizes a party and the degree to which its representatives consider party discipline to be excessive. Sartori's study reveals that party discipline thought to be "excessive" shows a pattern of least response (eight percent) for the PCI to an eighty-three–percent response for the MSI. Giovanni Sartori, *Il Parlamento Italiano* (Naples: Edizioni Scientifiche Italiane, 1963), p. 115.

Closed-mindedness or open-mindedness, as we have indicated, is not an all-or-none characteristic of political parties. Several parties, on the basis of our measurements, are represented by "both" types of people. This syndrome, we must recall, is continuous rather than discrete or absolute. As such, its presence in everyone is a matter of degree. The figure that follows shows the range of scores for each party.[nn]

CHART 5

RANGE OF DOGMATISM SCORES FOR POLITICAL PARTIES

— 20 18 16 14 12 10 8 6 4 2   0   2 4 6 8 10 12 14 16 18 20 +

DC	—7_____+17
MSI	+2_____+16
PCI	—7_____+15
PDI	+3_____+14
PLI	—4_____+12
PRI	+4_____+14
PSDI	+5_____+15
PSI	—12_____+16

If we judge from the variation of the dogmatism scores within the individual parties, it would seem that personality structure may not be the sole determinant of party membership, even though in some parties there is a pronounced consistency. In the preceding chapter, speaking in terms of

[nn] Standard deviations given in Table 9 may be consulted for a similar indication. Consult also Table 8 for the number of positive and negative scorers.

the professional politician as a general category, we offered several possible explanations for this variation. Undoubtedly, some of those, such as the status-level and the function of the individual's role within the political system, would also explain the variance within particular parties. One specific consideration in this respect is that political parties in Italy are not completely homogeneous: each has its own left and its own right, and sometimes even center. We should like to advance the thesis that the range or variation of dogmatism within parties is a reflection of their factional structure.

The data show that the more closed-minded parties have a relatively narrow range of dogmatism and that the more open-minded ones have a much wider variation of individual dogmatism scores. These latter parties are represented by both negative and positive scorers, that is, open-mindedness and closed-mindedness in terms of our measures, in contrast to the more dogmatic parties, which are represented exclusively by positive scorers. Both types, however, are found in the relatively high-scoring DC.

We suggest that those parties with the wider range of scores are more apt to be marked with factions—or, at least, by more acute dissensions. Interestingly enough, the least dogmatic parties, as we have indicated, are characterized by more "methodological" factions than some of the more dogmatic parties. Yet it would also be in keeping with theoretical expectancies to find that the more dogmatic parties are more homogeneous in their range of scores, for the idea of factions within authoritarian political systems is somewhat contradictory. In a highly dogmatic and authoritarian system one would expect to find a rather complete unity of mind and absolute obedience to singular authority. Thus, the greatest number of "ideological" factions would be expected in those parties that are the least dogmatic—the most open-minded.

This may seem to be a contradiction of the position stated

previously that the greatest number of factions would be expected in authoritarian systems, wherein the goal is said to be simply power. Again we assert this to be quite correct. Nonetheless, it is important to distinguish between factions based upon varying views of methodology within the same political ideology, and those rooted in simply personal goals of power which may or may not involve differences in political methodology. Moreover, wherever possible, power struggles among authoritarian individuals would manifest themselves more likely as independent parties. Recall our mention that the plurality of parties in the Italian political system is in great measure due to the individualism and the authoritarian structure of the Italian national character.

On this basis we advance the position that factions of whatever variety would be relatively less prevalent within parties that comprise a multiparty system than in those that form one-, two-, or three-party systems. The greater the differences among the parties, the less likely is the probability of differences within the individual parties. Factions are more apt to exist as independent parties within a multiparty system. This is certainly the situation for some of the Italian parties, as we have seen. The PSDI in its establishment was an offshoot of the PSI, out of which also originated the PCI. These parties may be seen respectively as conservative and liberal wings of Socialism. The PSI more recently has been divided between the "revisionists" who emphasize democratic reform and the "maximalists" who emphasize militant revolt. A group of the latter, under the leadership of Tullio Vecchietti, bolted from the PSI in 1964 and re-formed the Italian Socialist Party of Proletarian Unity (PSIUP). Former monarchical parties, specifically the *Partito Monarchico Populare*, came into being as the result of factional splits, particularly as an alleged power struggle based upon differences of opinion over political methodology rather than basic ideology. And the PLI is but the liberal segment of conservative ideologies of the political right.

The achievement and the maintenance of party unity depends in part upon the correspondence between its methodology and the personality structure of those involved. We propose, therefore, that factions which exist within political parties can be distinguished on the basis of the personality structure of their supporters. Given our findings, and their theoretical consistency, we would hypothesize that open-minded and closed-minded individuals characterize liberal and conservative factions respectively. Such a distinction, of course, would be a relative one, not necessarily yielding any highly significant differences from a statistical perspective. This would be contingent upon the nature of the factions and the degree of dissension between them. To repeat, the greater the range of scores, the more likely the factions and the more apt is their difference to be significant.

What evidence is there for this? We would like to categorize our subjects into the respective factions of their party and then to test for significant differences between the means of the factional subsamples. Unfortunately our data does not permit us, particularly with such small samples, to make meaningful distinctions in terms of party factions. One indication of this thesis, however, is found in Continuum I (personal ideology). This continuum contains two centrist loci intentionally so designed to distinguish the left-of-center individuals from those right-of-center in their political ideology. Our data show that these loci are represented by six of the eight major parties. The exceptions are the PCI and the PSI.

There is an appreciable difference in the mean dogmatism score for the two loci (left center: $M = 6.78$, $S.D. = 6.43$; right center: $M = 9.50$, $S.D. = 4.95$). The t-value obtained (1.398) is statistically significant only at the .1 level in a one-tailed test. The data are not completely factional since they cut across party lines; however, a difference, statistically significant at the .01 level, was obtained for the mean dogmatism score of the Christian Democrats in these two loci (left center: $N = 23$, $M = 6.51$; right center: $N = 6$; $M = 12.50$; $t = 3.307$). The evidence points in the hypothesized direction and serves to illustrate our thesis that liberal-conservative partisans of an ideology may be distinguished by their personality structure.

Another indication for this thesis is the following. The three "factions" which may be discerned both on the political left and on the political right—all in the form of individual parties —reveal more open-mindedness on the left wing and more closed-mindedness on the right wing in each instance. Specifically, on the political left the PCI, PSI, and PSDI show a progression of mean dogmatism scores, as do the PLI, PDI, and MSI. Moreover, in both cases the respective left and right wings are statistically significantly different from each other.

Some would argue that these "factions" are distinguished from each other by their social bases. Lipset, for example, has presented the thesis that all political ideologies are characterized by left, center, and right expressions which are distinguishable in terms of social bases and suggests that "each major social stratum has both democratic and extremist (authoritarian) political expressions."[54] But can this explanation be applied to factions within parties—particularly where there is such a multiplicity of them? Lipset speaks primarily of ideologies; however, he refers also to political groups. We interpret this to include political parties. Moreover, since Italian parties are ideological in nature, it would seem that Lipset's thesis should be applicable to the Italian system.[oo] That intraparty factions within a multiparty system are based primarily upon social class is questionable. Such factions are distinguished essentially in terms of political methodology,

oo That factions within political parties may be due to social bases does not negate the thesis that they are due likewise to personality structure. This simply indicates that personality structure and social class may be correlated. This question will be considered in Chapter VIII.

while ideology remains substantially constant. Political methodology rather than ideology shows greater significant relationships with dogmatism. To repeat once again, it is not so much *what* one believes, but *how* one believes, that characterizes the dogmatic individual.

This is not meant to be reductive in a psychological dimension. Rather, we are subscribing to Levinson's proposition, stated above, that the more specific the alternatives, the more likely that political party selection will be made on the basis of personality and its congruity with the political system. Our thesis, therefore, is an extension of this proposition, namely, that insofar as factions exist within political parties, they too can be discerned in terms of the personality structure of their supporters (which, at least in terms of dogmatism, cuts across social class categories). We offer this only as another, yet most plausible and potent, explanation for the variation of dogmatism within political parties.

The various explanations considered here for the variation of dogmatism both among and within the political parties are meant to be neither exhaustive nor mutually exclusive. All of these explanations, however, seem to be valid for the Italian political system, and in the case of a particular party one specific interpretation may be a more applicable explanation than another. It should be emphasized, nevertheless, that these several interpretations by no means are unrelated to one another.

NOTES

[1] Daniel J. Levinson, "The Relevance of Personality for Political Participation," *Public Opinion Quarterly*, XXIII (1958), 9.

[2] Milton Rokeach, *The Open and Closed Mind* (New York: Basic Books, 1960), pp. 125–126. Other research with American subjects has substantiated these findings. See Edwin N. Barker, "Authoritarianism of the Political Right, Center, and Left," *Journal of Social Issues*, XIX (1953), p. 70.

[3] Rokeach, *op. cit.*, p. 126.

[4] *Ibid.*, pp. 129–130.

[5] For references see Alex Inkeles, "National Character and Modern Political Systems" in Francis L. K. Hsu (ed.), *Psychological Anthropology* (Homewood: The Dorsey Press, 1961), p. 193. This position has been particularly common among psychoanalysts. See, for example, Franz Alexander, *Our Age of Reason* (Philadelphia: J. P. Lippincott, 1951); Augusta Bonnard, "On Political Creed and Character," *Psychoanalysis* (1954), 2:55–59; and David Drake, "A Psychoanalytic Interpretation of Social Ideology," *American Imago* (1955), 12:193–198.

[6] Discussions on this question may be found in Edward A. Shils, "Authoritarianism: 'Right' and 'Left'" in Richard Christie and Marie Jahoda (eds.), *Studies in the Scope and Method of "The Authoritarian Personality"* (Glencoe: The Free Press, 1954), p. 38; and Alex Inkeles, *op. cit.*, p. 193. See also Irving A. Taylor, "Similarities in the Structure of Extreme Social Attitudes," *Psychological Monographs* (1960), 74, Whole issue, No. 489.

[7] Material here based on Rokeach, *op. cit.*, pp. 126–130.

[8] For a treatment of this question see Alexander J. Groth, "Isms in Totalitarianism," *American Political Science Review*, LVIII (1964), 888–901.

[9] Rokeach, *op. cit.*, pp. 126–127.

[10] Benito Mussolini, "The Doctrine of Fascism" in Lyman J. Gould and E. William Steele (eds.), *People, Power, and Politics* (New York: Random House, 1961), pp. 171–178.

[11] Harold W. Metz and Charles A. H. Thomson, *Authoritarianism and the Individual* (Washington: The Brookings Institution, 1950), p. 210.

[12] William Ebenstein, *Today's Isms* (Englewood Cliffs: Prentice-Hall, 1961), p. 17.

[13] Rokeach, *op. cit.*, p. 127.

[14] *Ibid.*, p. 128.

[15] *Ibid.*

[16] Gerard J. Mangone, "Part IV: Italy" in Taylor Cole (ed.), *European Political Systems* (New York: Alfred A. Knopf, 1959), p. 503.

[17] Pietro Nenni, "Where the Italian Socialists Stand," *Foreign Affairs*, XL (1962), 213–223.

[18] *Ibid.*, pp. 215–217. Italics mine.

[19] Rokeach, *op. cit.*, p. 128.

[20] *Ibid.*

[21] Ebenstein, *op. cit.*, p. 77.

[22] Rokeach, *op. cit.*, p. 350.

[23] *Ibid.*, p. 352.

[24] *Ibid.*, p. 364.

[25] *Ibid.*, p. 352.

[26] *Ibid.*, p. 35.

[27] H. J. Eysenck, *Sense and Nonsense in Psychology* (Baltimore: Penguin Books, 1957), p. 298. A more complete treatment of this may be found in H. J. Eysenck, *Psychology of Politics* (London: Routledge & Kegan Paul, 1954).

[28] Barker, *op. cit.*, p. 65.

[29] Milton Rokeach and Charles Hanley, "Eysenck's Tender-mindedness Dimension: A Critique," *Psychological Bulletin,* LIII (1956), 169–176.

[30] Felixs Gross, *The Seizure of Political Power* (New York: Philosophical Library, 1958), pp. 1–2.

[31] See C. W. Cassinelli, "The Totalitarian Party," *Journal of Politics,* XXIV (1962), 111–141.

[32] Moshe Decter, *The Profile of Communism* (New York: Collier Books, 1961), p. 131.

[33] Ebenstein, *op. cit.,* p. 24.

[34] Alfred G. Meyer, *Communism* (New York: Random House, 1960), p. 2.

[35] Interview with Leo Wollemborg, correspondent in Rome for the *Washington Post,* January 28, 1961.

[36] *New York Times,* September 5, 1964.

[37] Meyer, *op. cit.,* p. 169.

[38] E. A. Bayne, "Italy's Seed of Peril," American Universities Field Staff *Reports Service,* X (1962), No. 1, 12.

[39] Meyer, *op. cit.,* p. 173.

[40] Decter, *op. cit.,* p. 112.

[41] Ebenstein, *op. cit.,* p. 82.

[42] Meyer, *op. cit.,* p. 182.

[43] See his examination of councils of the Roman Catholic Church. Rokeach, *op. cit.,* Chapter 21.

[44] *Ibid.,* pp. 387–388.

[45] Jean Meynaud, "General Study of Parliamentarians," *International Social Science Journal,* XIII (1961), 536.

[46] Joseph LaPalombara, *Interest Groups in Italian Politics* (Princeton: Princeton University Press, 1964), pp. 84–85.

[47] See Cassinelli, *op. cit.*

[48] Gross, *op. cit.,* p. 19. For a more elaborate treatment of multivalent man see Alfred McClung Lee, *Multivalent Man* (New York: George Braziller Publisher, 1966).

[49] Luigi Barzini, *The Italians* (New York: The Atheneum Press, 1964), p. 226.

[50] Norman Kogan, *The Government of Italy* (New York: Thomas Y. Crowell, 1964), pp. 35–40.

[51] Meyer, *op. cit.,* p. 172.

[52] Kogan, *op. cit.,* pp. 95–96.

[53] David Spitz, *Democracy and the Challenge of Power* (New York: Columbia University Press, 1958), p. 142.

[54] Seymour M. Lipset, *Political Man* (London: William Heineman, 1960), p. 131.

CHAPTER VII

Personality Structures
and Political Consensus-Cleavage

PERHAPS THE MOST pertinent question concerning the relationship between personality structure and political ideology is the value which this may have for behavior within the political system. Specifically, does such a relationship have any significance for the decision-making process?

One of the principal concerns in political sociology is the general question of political consensus and political cleavage, factors directly bearing on decision-making. Recent sociological work has attempted to treat this question through a consideration of social bases. Notwithstanding the merits of this approach, we should like to pursue in this context the general theoretical approach of this study. Our question, then, is whether or not political consensus and/or cleavage are in any way a function of personality structure.

Two political issues which involve the element of consensus-cleavage are those of political alliances and changes in political party affiliation. We shall attempt to relate our dogmatism data to specific Italian political issues of these kinds.

Political Alliances

Christian Democracy has been the ruling party in Italy since the establishment of the Republic. Since the national elections of 1953, however, it has not had an absolute majority in Parliament. As a consequence of this, the Christian Democrats have had to form coalitions with other "centrist" parties in order to exercise the powers of the government. Until recent years these parties have been the PSDI, PRI, and PLI. The question, then, is whether or not there is a similarity of personality structure between Christian Democracy and these parties as well as among themselves.

Returning to the dogmatism data given in Table 9 (Chapter VI), we applied Student's t in a test of difference between the mean of the DC and that of all the other parties.[a] None of the differences between the DC and the three parties with which the Third Fanfani Government (that which was in force during the time of this study) was in coalition achieved statistical significance at the .05 level. The following results were obtained for the four parties not in coalition: PCI, significant at the .001 level; PSI, significant at the .01 level; PDI and MSI were not statistically significant.

This evidence shows that those parties (both left and right) in coalition with the DC do not differ significantly from it or generally from one another[b] in terms of personality structure. Two other parties with similar personality structures, however, were not in the coalition. These are both on the political right. Statistically significant differences were found between the

[a] These data are given in Appendix E (Table 30).

[b] There was one statistically significant difference between two of the coalition parties, the PSDI and the PLI.

DC and the two parties on the political left. Apparently the DC has a greater affinity and coalition potential with the conservative dimension of the political continuum. The data suggest, nevertheless, that coalitions may not be formed solely in terms of ideological and personality structure. Other factors also, and presumably that of ideological content especially, may be particularly important in this regard.

Our attempt in this chapter is to show that, while each of the Italian parties has an ideology and a program which are different from those of the others, some of these parties do apparently "think" alike. Rokeach hints at this kind of explanation as instrumental in the formation of political coalition when he speaks of the perceived similarity of belief systems, that is, believing or thinking *in the same manner* as each other.[1] The findings presented tend to substantiate this position.

During the past few years the Christian Democratic government—as established in coalition with the above-mentioned parties—still remained confronted with the problem of achieving majority support in Parliament. It and the coalition parties have been experiencing somewhat of a progressive loss in strength, and the majority of the Government has been a most precarious one. Accordingly, attempts were made to seek another party or parties with which an alliance could be formed in order to strengthen the governing coalition.

In terms of our data on personality structure, it seems unlikely at first sight that the DC would form any political alignments with either the PCI or the PSI, but such moves seem more probable with either the PDI or the MSI, or even both.[c] The Tambroni Government of 1960, in fact, was put into power with the support of the MSI.

[c] The PDI and the MSI have been in alliance with the DC in several municipal governments. Moreover, the MSI was the only ally of the DC during a factional split involving the formation of the regional government of Sicily in 1959.

Parenthetically, an interesting aspect that needs to be pointed out is the similarity between the DC and the MSI. The Student's t test applied to their mean dogmatism scores yields a value of .925, which of course is not statistically significant. Likewise, in analyzing the data derived from Continua I and II no significant differences were found in similar tests between the center loci and that of the right extreme. Christian Democracy is comparatively strongly dogmatic and authoritarian, and some allege that it is basically fascistic in character.[d] As we previously mentioned, the administration of the government—especially its bureaucracy and legal structure—retains much from the Fascist era. Then, too, the DC—more so than parties on the political left—is supported by former members of the *Partito Nazionale Fascista*. Several of the current Christian Democratic leaders reportedly were associated with the Fascist regime of former years. We may mention, too, that the clerico-fascist wing of the Popular party split off in 1924 to support, and subsequently to merge with, the Fascists. Undoubtedly these elements have had some influence in accounting for the striking similarity in dogmatism between the DC and the MSI. Nonetheless, although not significantly different in structure, other factors must be operating to preclude the establishment of a formal political alignment between these two parties.

We would like to predict, on the basis of dogmatic personality structures, the potentials which exist for the formation of

[d] The MSI alliance with the Tambroni Government (often called the neo-Fascist government) led to considerable public protest and rioting. Many alleged that order was restored by the use of "Fascist methods" that breached the limits of democratic conduct. This government was forced to resign immediately thereafter by the executive bureau of the Christian Democracy. Such reaction shows that what happens on the party level may not be acceptable to the nonpolitical masses, who—as we have shown in the preceding chapters—do not have the same personality structures as their parliamentary representatives in many cases.

future coalitions. This may be done in terms of the statistical significance of t-values derived from testing the difference between dogmatism means for the DC and the other parties. Table 11 gives these data arranged according to the parties accepted in the coalition of the Third Fanfani Government, and those similarly rejected.

TABLE 11

COALITION POTENTIALS FOR CHRISTIAN DEMOCRATS

Parties Accepted			Parties Rejected		
PRI	.010	NS	PCI	4.246	S
PSDI	.424	NS	PSI	2.839	S
PLI	1.782	NS	MSI	.925	NS
			PDI	.345	NS

These data show that the party more likely to be accepted (from the significantly different rejectees) would be the PSI; the party most likely to be rejected from the accepted and significantly similar parties would be the PLI. This is exactly what happened in the formation of the Fourth Fanfani Government in February 1962—about six months after the completion of the field work for this study. The controversial *l'apertura à sinistra* (opening to the left) was brought into realization.[e] There was no intention of turning to the conserva-

[e] This was not an entirely new action. The DC and the PSI were allied already in the municipal governments of Milan, Genoa, Florence, and a number of other cities in northern and central Italy as a result of the administrative elections of November 1960.

tive—yet structurally similar—parties of the PDI and the MSI. The dominant ideological orientation in the DC was toward the political left. Moreover, it was in this direction that popular sentiment was shifting.

Such a course of political action is a bilateral affair. Obviously, an opening to the left is also an opening to the right. Our data, however, show that a coalition with the PSI would not appear likely, since this party is significantly different from the DC in personality structure. Yet such an alliance had been debated for years. Christian Democrats split widely on this issue. The conservative right wing was opposed categorically, while the liberal interests of the left were more willing to take such a political venture. It was this latter faction that held the balance of power within the party. The reaction of the PSI to such a proposal was similarly divided on the bases of party factions.

In view of the factional composition of the DC this political maneuver can be explained in terms of personality structure. Our data are taken from the political continuum of personal ideology (Continuum I). The movement would be from the center loci (three and four) to a union with the moderate left locus (two). Student's *t* tests were applied to the dogmatism means of the various combinations.[f] There exists no statistically significant difference between loci three and four. A *t*-value of 2.654 was obtained between loci two and four (those of the right center opposing the movement). This indicates a statistically significant difference at the .02 level. But no such difference was found between loci two and three (those of the left center advocating the movement). These findings plainly show that significant differences in personality structure exist between the PSI and only those Christian Democrats who are opposed to *l'apertura à sinistra*. Those favoring the political maneuver apparently "perceive" the PSI as simi-

[f] These data may be inspected in Appendix E (Table 31).

lar to themselves. There are no significant differences in personality structure between these two categories.[g]

Objections to this coalition government continue from the right wing of the DC as well as from the left wing of the PSI. It was this very issue of the coalition government that led to the reorganization of the PSIUP by the dissident left-wing Socialists in 1964. The maintenance of the current government would seem to be contingent upon the dominant strength of factions within the respective parties *and* the degree of similarity in personality structure which thereby exists between these parties.[h] This situation substantiates the explanation given in the preceding chapter in reference to personality structures as a basis for factions within political parties. It would seem that were the findings of the PSI to be broken down into factions, even greater similarity in personality structure would result between its left wing and the right wing of the DC.

In this same connection we may mention that no statistically significant differences were found between positions one and two on either of the two continua. None likewise exists between the respective parties so represented, the PCI and the PSI. This is in line with theoretical expectancy in view of the fact that these two parties previously had been in political alliance on the national level, and continue in coalition in several municipal governments.[i]

[g] In regard to the other rejected party both loci three and four (Continuum I) are statistically significantly different from locus one. Thus a coalition with the PCI seems most improbable.

[h] This center-left coalition has been continued to the present day through three successive governments of the DC—all under the premiership of Aldo Moro, who was one of its original proponents. The Second Moro Government collapsed in January 1966 because of an alleged lack of support for the government program by the conservative faction of the DC.

[i] The PSI and the PCI were united by pact in 1934 and 1936. These two parties offered joint electoral lists in 1953. More recently, Luigi Longo, the

This evidence shows that government coalitions are formed along the lines of personality structure. Yet our data suggest that personality is not the sole determinant upon which political alliances are formed by virtue of the fact that some parties revealing no significant differences in personality structure either were excluded or excluded themselves from any political alignment with the ruling party. This specifically was the case with the conservative PLI. Even though it showed no statistically significant difference from the PSI, the PLI was not retained in the Fourth Fanfani Government that shifted toward the more liberal orientation; nor has it participated in any successive DC governments—each of which has continued the orientation to the political left. Factors other than personality structure, presumably that of ideological content in particular, are also important.[2]

The formation of an alliance usually involves compromises of one type or another on the part of all parties concerned. Nonetheless, while political ideology, as well as the specific platforms, of individual parties may differ, those that do unite into coalitions generally share a basic similarity in personality structure. Thus, political alliances are, to an extent at least, a function of perceived similarity in the structure of belief

current leader of the PCI, at its Eleventh Congress in Rome in January 1966, presented a proposal for a new majority alliance (*una nuova maggioranza*) that would unite the PCI, the PSI, and the left-wing Christian Democrats. None of the other parties (least of all those on the left wing) appears to be very interested in Longo's offer. Such reaction is consistent with the potentials predictable on the basis of our data (see Table 12), which show that such a "new leftist unity" would be possible only with the PSI. The same improbability is true for the similar plan offered by Giorgio Amendola, another PCI leader, to form the Italian Labor party by uniting the PCI, PSI, and PSDI. These latter two parties have agreed in recent national congresses to seek unity once again. Our data—speaking without consideration of factions, which in these parties is a very significant element—do not permit the tenability of such an alliance. The extreme left-wing group of dissident Socialists who reorganized the PSIUP still want to restore the former alliance with the PCI.

systems of the respective parties and the personality structure of their followers.

CHANGES IN POLITICAL PARTY AFFILIATIONS

Another specific political issue to which the personality structure approach may be applied is that of changes in political party affiliation. The basic elements which are involved are the same as those discussed above concerning government coalitions. We propose that when an individual changes his political allegiance, he does so on the basis of perceived similarity in the structure of a belief system with that of his own personal political ideology, and perhaps as well with that of the particular party which he is relinquishing.[3] Party changes, in other words, are more likely to take place between those parties which reveal similarities in the personality structure of their followers.

This study gathered some data on changes in political party affiliations. These comprise, however, only a very limited number of cases from which no generalizations are possible. Our consideration here perforce will be more in the nature of predictions. The probable order of political changes from each party has been determined on the basis of t-values obtained by testing for statistically significant differences between the mean dogmatism scores of the two parties in question. These data are given in Table 12. No such differences were found between the parties which are mentioned, and thus they are considered not to be dissimilar in terms of the personality structure of their followers.

One of the factors that precludes precise predictions is that of the party faction. These data and predictions refer to the respective parties as a whole and not to particular individuals who would be doing the actual changing of political party

TABLE 12

PROBABILITY DIRECTIONS OF CHANGES
IN POLITICAL PARTY AFFILIATIONS

DC to		MSI to		PCI to		PDI to	
PRI	.010	PDI	.085	PSI	.660	MSI	.085
PDI	.345	PSDI	.335	PLI	1.552	PSDI	.118
PSDI	.424	PRI	.769			DC	.345
MSI	.925	DC	.925			PRI	.397
PLI	1.782					PLI	1.469
						PSI	1.488

PLI to		PRI to		PSDI to		PSI to	
PSI	.657	DC	.010	PDI	.118	PLI	.657
PRI	1.443	PDI	.397	MSI	.335	PCI	.660
PDI	1.469	PSDI	.469	DC	.424	PDI	1.488
PCI	1.522	MSI	.769	PRI	.469	PRI	1.567
DC	1.782	PLI	1.443				
		PSI	1.567				

affiliation.[j] Accordingly, they should be thought of more in
the nature of "party line" changes. That is to say, given the
probable basis of party factions in terms of personality structure, individuals from the liberal faction of a particular party
would show a different pattern of potential change in contrast
to their colleagues from the conservative faction. Thus, for
more accurate predictions in these terms, those inevitable

[j] These probable party changes, in terms of our procedures, may be viewed
also as potential political alliances for any one of the respective parties. One
interesting aspect of these probability directions based on similarities in personality structure is that they are quite inconsistent with the perceived order of
ideological affinity among the parties. These perceptions of ideological affinity,
moreover, are not always mutual ones on the part of any two parties. For
relevant data see Table 39 in Appendix F.

questions which must be answered beforehand are, Which Christian Democracy? Which Communist party? Which Socialist party? and so forth.

Most individuals have multiple ideological potentials, and thus are capable of some ideological change. Party changes or defections, however, are more likely to be the product of open-minded people. Theoretically, the closed-minded individual is more apt to remain loyal to his political party and/or ideological convictions. He characteristically exhibits, in fact, greater resistance to the formation of new belief systems.[4] The relatively open systems, as Rokeach suggests, are likely to have a narrow latitude of isolation for belief systems as compared to the more closed systems.[5] Thus, the less dogmatic political parties would be expected to have a greater range of acceptability for other belief systems. It follows that changes in political party affiliations are more apt to occur when political ideologies are not deeply imbedded in the personality. Accordingly, in one sense the stability of political parties is reflected in the degree of dogmatism manifested by their followers *and* the relation of this to other "competing" ideologies. The greater the similarity in dogmatism (regardless of its degree), the more likely is an "exchange" between two parties.[k]

On this general question Levinson speaks of the role of two somewhat related postulates that are at work in the selection of political party affiliation:

> This general formulation implies a postulate of *receptivity:* the individual will be most receptive to those available political forms that have the greatest functional value in meeting the requirements of the personality as a system. He will prefer those ways of dealing with external political issues that best gear in with his preferred way of

[k] This element of party stability is closely related to the issue of factions. The more homogeneous the party in terms of personality structure, the more stable it is apt to be; the more heterogeneous, the more likely it is to split into factions, or to experience defections in the nature of party changes.

dealing with internal issues of impulse control, maintenance of self-esteem, fulfillment of esthetic urges, and the like. This approach involves, in addition, a postulate of *immanence:* many of the personality characteristics that influence the individual's political participation are directly reflected (immanent) within it. It is possible through psychological analysis of an individual's political thought and action to derive many of the personality features that have helped to establish and to maintain it.[6]

Each individual, therefore, is receptive to only a limited number of the total range of available political ideologies and/or parties. Accordingly, when the stimulus field is sufficiently diversified, political affiliations are a function of the individual's personality structure and, more specifically in this case, the dogmatism dimension of his personality.

We are not attempting to reduce all political behavior to a function of personality dynamics. Certainly, in some instances none would apply directly. Membership in the erstwhile *Partito Nazionale Fascista* may be mentioned as an example. Much of this was not the result of completely free choice for motives of political ideology. Rather, for many it was an expedient—even economically imperative—commitment. Consequently, when the party expired and its "followers" made more democratic selections of political parties, much theoretical inconsistency would have been expected between the two parties involved.[1] When a personally congenial mode of political participation is not readily available, and the individual cannot create one for himself, he may nominally accept an uncongenial affiliation without strong commitment or involvement. Another instance, as we have suggested, where personality structure is not apt to be a dominant element in party affiliation would be major American political parties. Political affiliations in these cases may be due more directly to histori-

[1] Our findings suggest that no such inconsistency should be true for the MSI sample, two-thirds of whom were former members of the PNF and whose dogmatism data are in theoretical harmony with fascist ideology.

cal, traditional, sociocultural, and even situational variables. Personality structure is apt to reveal greater distinction in terms of factions within these parties. Our proposition, to repeat, is that where the stimulus field is more complex and sufficiently diversified—that is, the greater the array of political parties and ideologies—the more likely will the individual make an affiliation in terms of personality structure.

Changes in political party affiliation, along with the formation of political alliances, appear to be a function of perceived similarity in belief systems. These two examples of political issues serve to illustrate the role which personality structure has in the major political consideration of consensus and cleavage. The crucial question in this issue concerns the degree of variation and difference which may be tolerated without consensus giving way to cleavage. At what degree of difference is a change in political ideology or party affiliation not likely to occur? What is the tolerable level of variation within political alliances and individual parties without risking cleavage in the form of factions or instability due to defections? Is statistical significance a valid criterion for making such predictive judgments? Obviously this question requires further research.

These considerations, hopefully, should serve to illustrate the practical application of the interpretations which have been given in preceding chapters, as well as to indicate some areas of sociological relevance for the personality structure approach. Political consensus and cleavage, manifestly or latently, appear to be a function of the composition of the total personality structures within the political system. Another question related to this context is whether or not particular forms of government are related to particular kinds of personalities. That is to say, do particular kinds of political systems or forms of government functionally require certain kinds of personalities? This issue, along with other practical implications, will be considered in the concluding chapter. The task

that remains is to relate our findings for dogmatic personality
structures to social background variables, our concern in the
next chapter.

Notes

[1] Milton Rokeach, *The Open and Closed Mind* (New York: Basic Books, 1960),
p. 328.

[2] See G. Poggi, "Studio dell'Ideologia nella Sociologia dei Partiti Politici,"
Rassegna Italiana di Sociologia, II (1961), 205–220.

[3] Our attempt is analogous to Rokeach's work involving changes of religious
affiliations. *Op. cit.,* Chapter 17.

[4] Rokeach, *op. cit.,* p. 193.

[5] *Ibid.,* p. 256.

[6] Daniel J. Levinson, "The Relevance of Personality for Political Participation," *Public Opinion Quarterly,* XXIII (1958), p. 7.

CHAPTER VIII

Personality Structures and Social Backgrounds

THE SOCIOLOGIST QUITE understandably is interested in exploring the relation of social backgrounds to personality, for as we have tried to point out, social factors are intimately related to personality. Personality is in fact fundamentally the product of the socialization process and a host of social situations to which the individual may be exposed. We already have suggested in this regard the influence of authoritarian social systems on national character as well as that of particular social structures and situations on the development of the dogmatic personality.

Evidence is ample that diverse social backgrounds have differential influences upon personality. The more crucial concern, however, is whether categorical variations in personality may be explained according to differential influences stemming from various social categories, such as religious, educational, occupational, and, more broadly, social class backgrounds.

We should like to pursue this general question with whatever pertinent data we have available.

A distinction which is most important for our consideration is that between sundry social background factors in general and the, more particular one of social class, which has been the focus of much research in this respect. We shall, therefore, discuss these two aspects separately, by treating first the former, and then continuing more specifically with the latter, element. These considerations will be limited to the political sample unless otherwise indicated.

SINGLE VARIABLES

Our data on social backgrounds which are applicable to cross-tabulation with the dogmatism findings include age, education, religion, parliamentary experience, and geographical region of constituency. For each of these factors the mean dogmatism score was computed by category within the respective question. Then an analysis of variance was applied to the means of all the categories for each factor. An F-ratio of statistical significance was found for only the factors of age and religion, both ratios being significant at the .01 level.[a] For those factors in which the F-ratio is not statistically significant, a more specific inspection was made for differences between the individual combinations of categorical means. By utilizing Student's t under these conditions statistical significance was acceptable only at the .001 level. None of the derived t-values, however, is statistically significant.[b]

The two factors that remain to be explained are age and

[a] The same procedures were followed for the nonpolitical control sample for only the factors of age, education, and religion. None of these social background elements indicated the presence of statistically significant differences.

[b] Data for the factors of parliamentary experience and geographical region of constituency may be inspected in Tables 33 and 34 given in Appendix F.

religion. Table 13 contains the dogmatism data for the age categories. The age factor was inspected on the basis of t tests to determine where the discrepancy might be. The dogmatism means of the following categories revealed statistically significant differences: 36–45 and 46–55 at the .001 level, and 46–55 and 56–65 at the .05 level.[c] Thus, of the five age categories the one with a mean and a standard deviation out of line is that of 46–55. This difference most likely reflects the fact that the representation in the low-scoring parties of the political left is considerably younger than that in the higher-scoring parties of the center and the political right.[d] It should be men-

TABLE 13

MEAN DOGMATISM SCORES OF POLITICAL SAMPLE BY AGE CATEGORY

Age Category	N	Mean	S.D.
31–35	7	5.00	4.59
36–45	45	2.35	6.29
46–55	44	8.68	5.42
56–65	28	5.50	7.58
66–75	5	7.00	5.36

$F = 4.952$	dfb, 4; dfw, 124	$p < .01$

tioned, however, that this category was at a particularly vulnerable age during the Fascist regime, and as such it shows perhaps more than the others the effect of socialization under

[c] The t-values are respectively 5.020 and 2.043.

[d] Data for age distributions may be inspected in Appendix B (Table 19).

such a system. Individuals in this age category were about eleven to twenty years old when Mussolini began his twenty-year tenure of Italian rule. Nonetheless, the result may be simply spurious, and we tend to favor this explanation given the fact that no statistically significant differences in terms of age were found for the nonpolitical control sample.

The more significant consideration in relation to dogmatism appears to be the factor of religion. These data are given in Table 14. Catholic respondents have the highest dogmatism means, while the lowest mean applies to nonbelievers. Student's t test inspections show that categorical combinations accounting for the statistically significant analysis of variance are the following: between the nonbelievers and Catholic categories, one, two, and four at the .001 level, and between Catholic categories two and five at the .05 level.[e] (The reference for these categories is given in the table that follows.)

It is interesting to point out that no statistically significant difference was found between nonbelievers and Catholics who never go to church (category five), and likewise none exists between Catholics who attend church regularly (category one) and those who never attend. The combined mean of all Catholic categories tested against that of the nonbelievers category yielded a t-value of 2.793, which is statistically significant at the .01 level.

The pattern of dogmatism is very evident. No significant differences exist between the various degrees of practicing Catholics. But between these and nonbelievers the differences are very significant. The more fervent the practice of Catholicism, the greater the difference and statistical significance. Or, the less fervent the practice of Catholicism, the greater the similarity with nonbelievers. We may illustrate with the following. The combined mean for the two more fervent categories of Catholic practice (one and two) was tested against

    [e] The t-values are respectively 3.922, 3.653, 3.583, and 2.091.

that for the two less fervent categories (four and five). The derived t-value equals .388, which is not statistically significant. However, the mean of nonbelievers tested against the combined mean of Catholic categories one and two yields a t-value of 2.757, which indicates statistical significance at the .01 level, while the difference between nonbelievers and Catholic categories four and five combined is significant at the .05 level ($t = 2.288$).

TABLE 14

MEAN DOGMATISM SCORES OF POLITICAL SAMPLE
BY RELIGION

Religion	N	Mean	S.D.
Nonbelievers	41	1.73	6.38
Catholic (1)*	38	7.55	6.64
Catholic (2)	11	9.18	3.48
Catholic (3)	5	6.80	4.87
Catholic (4)	17	8.35	6.07
Catholic (5)	13	4.76	5.88

$F = 4.510$ dfb, 5; dfw, 119 $p < .01$

* Catholic categories indicated here by number refer to the intensity of religious practice: one, attends church at least once a week; two, nearly every week; three, about once a month; four, only for major festivities; and five, never attends church.

The only elements we have to work with are the practice of Catholicism and nonbelievers. Nonetheless, the evidence clearly shows that there is a general correlation between religious practice and dogmatism.[f] These findings support those of other studies. Rokeach's research has shown that Catholics score relatively high on both the Dogmatism Scale and the F-scale.[1] The explanation offered is that the Catholic Church is essentially dogmatic in doctrine and authoritarian in its hierarchical structure. It is, moreover, strongly conservative in its Italian administration. Other evidence indicates that highly religious individuals tend to be the most intolerant politically.[2] It would seem that nonbelievers, possessing no religion and thus not having a definite system of beliefs, tend generally, as theoretically expected, to be more open-minded. (Of course, it is possible to be a closed-minded atheist.)

The significant aspect of these findings is that religious affiliation shows patterns of association with political party membership.[g] The political left is very heavily—even characteristically—represented by nonbelievers and Catholic nonchurchgoers. Only seventeen of the fifty-nine deputies representing parties of the political left are Catholics. Nine of these said that they never went to church. Accordingly, only thirteen percent in the leftist parties may be considered as practicing Catholics. This contrasts sharply with the fact that all of the members representing parties on the political right are Catholic, and only four out of these seventy individuals claimed never to go to church. More specifically, the DC had one of the highest dogmatism

[f] Our data on the religious factor are not consistent between the political and nonpolitical control sample. No statistical significance in terms of an F-ratio was found for the latter sample. Yet there is a pattern of response similar to that for the political sample. Nonbelievers account for one of the lowest dogmatism means (2.80), which is the same for those Catholics who never go to church. A basic explanation for this situation would seem to be that suggested in Chapter V. One would expect professional politicians to be more committed to their ideologies than political followers. For almost all Italian political parties the religious element is part and parcel of their political ideology. These findings lend themselves to a plausible interpretation in this perspective.

[g] See Table 22 in Appendix B for the religious distribution of respondents by political party affiliation.

means, and it too is the party in which thirty of its thirty-one representatives claimed to be Catholics of the most fervent variety. For the least dogmatic PCI, twenty-three out of twenty-five claimed to be nonbelievers, and many of these openly professed to be atheists.[h] As Lipset remarks:

> In such countries as France, Italy, Spain, and Austria, being Catholic has meant being allied with rightists or conservative groups in politics, while being anticlerical, or a member of a minority religion, has often meant alliance with the left. . . . For many secular intellectuals in contemporary Italy, opposition to the Church legitimizes alliance with Communists.[3]

Our findings, thus, show a parallel between religious affiliation, political ideology, and dogmatism. That is to say, the left-right political pattern of the religious factor parallels the dogmatism pattern in terms of liberal and conservative political ideologies.

These associated patterns raise the question of whether political ideology or religious beliefs may be the more dominant (actual) influence which accounts for the respective dogmatism scores observed for the several political parties. Are the DC and the PCI respectively high and low in dogmatism due to political convictions or to religious practice? Apparently the two kinds of ideologies are not structurally differentiated for each party. Thus this question is theoretically meaningless. Both the political and the religious ideologies are "contents." The syndrome of dogmatism concerns only the *structure* of an individual's beliefs—of whatever variety.[i]

---

[h] The most fervent Catholics in the nonpolitical sample give majority support to the DC (fifty-two percent), while the nonbelievers predominantly support the PCI (fifty-five percent), as do another twenty percent of the Catholics who "never go to church." Catholic practitioners of less fervent varieties are distributed among the other parties.

[i] As Rokeach states, the words *religious* and *political* do not represent psychological concepts, and thus it is unlikely that the mind, or the belief system, is so compartmentalized. Milton Rokeach, *The Open and Closed Mind* (New York: Basic Books, 1960), p. 34.

Moreover, the respective religious ideology is part and parcel of the political ideology in both cases. Atheism is a cardinal tenet of contemporary Communism, and Christian Democracy is founded upon Christian, or specifically, Catholic, principles. As such, therefore, similar structural elements should be characteristic of both the political and the religious aspects of these political organizations. Theoretically, then, a particular personality attracted to one ideology would more likely be attracted to the other. With the exception perhaps of the PSI, no religious tenet is implicit in any of the other political ideologies, although in platform these tend to be either anticlerical or quite respectful of the Church. The "pro-Church" parties—the more dogmatic ones—are found on the conservative right, while the "anti-Church" and less dogmatic ones are on the liberal left. This situation indicates theoretical compatibility between religious beliefs and political ideology.

Thus, the question of whether religion or political ideology may be the determinant factor of personality structure does not appear to be valid. Since the former is a component element of the latter, there is not a question of religion rather than political ideology accounting for the associations of dogmatism which have been observed for the various political parties. Moreover, the associated religious and political ideologies are similarly structured. Accordingly, both would appeal theoretically to the same type of personality; individuals drawn to one would likely be drawn to the other.

Nonetheless, religion as a social background factor seemingly could account for dogmatism given the situation of chronological development in the socialization process. Insofar as early religious influences mold a dogmatic personality, they would share the responsibility for its being drawn into a similarly structured political party. There is considerable tenability for the position that religion, as an initial factor in the social background of the individual, may be a potent force in the development of the dogmatic political personality. Yet, given the implicit religious tenets of political ideology, it is possible that one's religious beliefs may be a consequence of his political ideology. Our point is that religious and politi-cal ideology may be both influences and consequences of personality structure.

SOCIAL CLASS

We have already alluded to the attempts made to account for different political ideologies, parties, and factions in terms of differences in their social-class foundations. Were this explanation true, then it could be argued that the differences in dogmatism which we have observed for the various political parties and political loci follow from the social bases of these organizations. Within limitations, evidence does show that particular social strata may predominantly favor a certain political party. Leftist parties supposedly are traditionally sup-ported by the lower social strata, and those of the political right are sustained by the upper strata. As Bendix and Lipset point out:

> Every study of the social bases of political movements in the several countries of Western civilization indicates that the parties represent distinctive strata. Despite the great and complex diversity of historical conditions among the "Western" countries, three main political tend-encies stand out in all of them: the left based on the working class; the conservative right, based on the more privileged strata and insti-tutions; and the center, based on the middle classes, especially the self-employed.[4]

Unquestionably there is ample evidence for making the gen-eralization that there is a relationship between political ideol-ogy and social class. But it seems much too simple. Poll data show that the various social classes support all ideologies, even though admittedly the extreme political left is predominantly "lower class and working class" in its foundations, and some parties of the political right attract the nearly exclusive support of the upper classes. What needs to be pointed out here is that while the majority of the professional and managerial classes may be sustaining the political right, the majority of the political right—in terms of numbers—may be representing another social stratum. This consideration is most important for our purposes in the light of the broad lower-class base of Italian society.[j]

Given the diversity of social bases for political parties and ideologies, it seems unlikely that such factors would account for the significant differences in dogmatism and personality structure that characterize political parties. Nonetheless, we shall consider this alternative sociological explanation. As we mentioned previously, even if political parties are distinguished by social bases, there still remains the fact that these ideologies—and particularly the extremes—are significantly distinguishable in terms of personality structure. Thus, the obvious conclusion would be that different personality structures, acknowledging their developmental process, are a function of social strata. The implication here is the often-contended position that significant differences of dogmatism in political parties are explainable in terms of the varying social-class foundations of these parties.

Our measure of social class is limited to only one indicator, namely, education. Yet this should serve as a suitable index

---

[j] In the 1958 national elections, deputies from the "working class" constituted only twenty-four percent of the PCI representatives, and only four percent of those in the PSI. Respectively in these parties, "upper middle" class deputies accounted for twenty-four percent and thirty-seven percent. No "working class" representatives were found for parties of the political right. Giovanni Sartori, "Parliamentarians in Italy," *International Social Science Journal*, XIII (1961), 589. Clearly, then, there is in Italy today no "parliamentary class" in terms of a distinct social stratum, as was the case during the constitutional monarchy—and is the case still in the parliament of some other nations.

for our purposes, particularly in the light of the Italian situation wherein occupation and income would be somewhat deceiving due to extensive underemployment.[k] Moreover, education is the focal indicator which has been used in other research of this nature, as we shall show subsequently.

Already noted is the fact that no statistically significant differences were found between the dogmatism mean of the various educational levels of our political subjects.[l] We conclude for our purposes, therefore, that there is no evidence

TABLE 15

MEAN DOGMATISM SCORES OF POLITICAL SAMPLE BY EDUCATIONAL LEVEL

Level Completed	N	Mean	S.D.
Elementary	5	1.20	7.83
Lower Media	5	1.20	7.11
Upper Media	7	.28	6.04
University (nondegree)	12	7.08	4.95
University (degree)	100	6.13	6.57
$F = 2.391$	dfb, 4; dfw, 124	$p > .05$	

that the observed differences in dogmatism are related to the social-class foundations of our subjects. The data available, admittedly limited, may be inspected in Table 15.

The argument goes that both evidence and theory suggest

[k] Employed below the level of one's qualifications.

[l] This result may be due to the small N's in some categories. Nonetheless, the nonpolitical sample with much larger N's in all categories yields the same negative results. See Table 36 in Appendix F.

that the lower social strata traditionally are relatively more authoritarian than others and that these strata (other things being equal) are usually attracted to extremist movements, parties, and ideologies which as such are supposed to be authoritarian according to the usual conception of extremism.[5] Says Lipset, "Many of these studies suggest that the lower-class way of life produces individuals with rigid and intolerant approaches to politics."[6] Our data, however, as elaborated in Chapter VI, are contradictory to this position. Insofar as the lower classes are liberally oriented toward the political left, they would tend to be open-minded; and insofar as the upper classes are conservatively oriented toward the political right, they would tend to be closed-minded.

Authoritarianism has been attributed more extensively to the lower social classes due to, among other things, their lower levels of education.[7] Notwithstanding that we can find no evidence for significant differences among educational categories, our data in fact would suggest just the opposite implication to follow from this assertion. The parties in our study with the "lowest" levels of education, the PCI and the PSI, are respectively the least dogmatic.[m] The more dogmatic parties tend to be the "more" educated parties—categorically speaking.

Of course it should be remembered that we are dealing here with two "different" concepts and two different measures of personality. Much, if not all, of what has been stated above is based upon research focused theoretically on the authoritarian syndrome and its F-scale measure. In fact, in studies using this scale there are significant negative correlations with education in particular and with social class more generally.[8] That correlations may exist between degrees of such authoritarianism and social class, or even other kinds of

[m] See Appendix B, Table 20. Our findings on the distribution of educational levels within the several parties parallel those for the entire Chamber, as well as those for the four legislatures during the Republic. See Sartori, op. cit., p. 590.

social backgrounds, cannot be denied. They do not appear to be related to dogmatism—at least not in this study. Our own findings, furthermore, sustain previous research by Rokeach which has shown significant variations in the dogmatism syndrome even though the social-class foundations of his subjects were constant.[9]

The general preference of various social classes for a particular political party or ideology is well substantiated. But political parties are not homogeneous in this respect. As Lipset himself points out, a rule of democratic politics is that every party has to appeal to all strata to remain a major power.[10] Nevertheless, even within these individual parties substantial differences in terms of dogmatism may be discerned. Our findings would be more consistent with Lipset's statement that "each major social stratum has both democratic and extremist (authoritarian) political expressions" which manifest themselves in different parties and ideologies or varying forms thereof.[11] This explanation would imply that if there were a homogeneous social-class basis to political parties, factions within them could be discerned as different expressions (that is, "democratic and authoritarian") of these parties. Our findings would offer some support for this general interpretation. Similarly, parties based upon the same social class could be distinguished in terms of democratic and authoritarian expressions. This could be offered as an interpretation for the deviation from the dogmatism pattern on the political left and the political right by the PRI and the PLI respectively.

Thus, both personality and social class appear to be influential elements in the choice of political ideology and party, but in different dimensions, such that the role of each in this matter is somewhat complementary to that of the other. This view is presented in the following statement offered by Inkeles:

> The formal or explicit "content" of one's political orientation—left or right, conservative or radical, pro- or anti-labor—may be determined mainly by more "extrinsic" characteristics such as education and social

class; but the form or style of political expression—favoring force or persuasion, compromise or arbitrary dictation, being tolerant or narrowly prejudiced, flexible in policy or rigidly dogmatic—is apparently largely determined by personality. At least this seems clear with regard to the political extremes.[12]

Our position is that dogmatism may be found in any social-class milieu. Specifically in terms of education, the indicator used above for social class, we repeat that it is not so much the *amount* of education that may influence the formation of the dogmatic personality as it is the *kind* (contents); not *how much* is taught, but rather *how* it is taught that is more important. Our more illustrative example is that of religion, which cuts across all social strata. This is not to say, however, that it would not be possible for social classes to vary significantly in terms of dogmatic structure. In this study, nonetheless, there is no evidence that dogmatism is correlated with social class. It would follow that knowing the social-class bases of political parties would not give any clue to the "psychological basis" of these parties or, more specifically, to their personality-structure foundations. Similarly, knowing the psychological character or parties is no clue to their social bases.

These findings provide at least a built-in "control," so to speak, for social backgrounds which supports the contention that the observed similarities and differences in terms of political ideology, parties, and factions are not products of concomitantly varying social background categories, with the significant exception of religion, which appears to be intimately associated with dogmatism. Yet, this factor—while it may be instrumental in the formation of the dogmatic personality—is a component element of certain political ideologies. Nonetheless, social backgrounds, including social class in particular, are an important consideration in political behavior and the relationship of personality to this.

NOTES

[1] Milton Rokeach, *The Open and Closed Mind* (New York: Basic Books, 1960), p. 111 and p. 351.

[2] Seymour M. Lipset, *Political Man* (London: William Heineman, 1960), p. 40.

[3] *Ibid.*, p. 84.

[4] Reinhard Bendix and Seymour M. Lipset, "Political Sociology: An Essay and Bibliography," *Current Sociology*, VI (1957), 91.

[5] Lipset, *Political Man*, p. 101.

[6] *Ibid.*, p. 98.

[7] *Ibid.*, pp. 109–114.

[8] Richard Christie, "Authoritarianism Re-examined" in Richard Christie and Marie Jahoda (eds.), *Studies in the Scope and Method of "The Authoritarian Personality"* (Glencoe: The Free Press, 1954), p. 169 and pp. 193–196.

[9] Rokeach, *op. cit.*, p. 111.

[10] Lipset, *Political Man*, p. 34.

[11] *Ibid.*, p. 131. This position was stated earlier in a somewhat varied version: "Each of these three tendencies [political left, center, and right] in the modern world has two expressions, one democratic and the other extremist and authoritarian." Reinhard Bendix and Seymour M. Lipset, "Political Sociology: An Essay and Bibliography," *Current Sociology*, VI (1957), 91.

[12] Alex Inkeles, "National Character and Modern Political Systems" in Francis L. K. Hsu (ed.), *Psychological Anthropology* (Homewood: The Dorsey Press, 1961), p. 193. This quotation is taken somewhat out of context. Inkeles actually asserts that these psychological characteristics pertain to both political extremes and that they are probably the same in all nations and institutional settings. Our data, of course, have shown that the two extremes are significantly distinguishable in terms of personality structure.

CHAPTER IX

Personality and Social Systems

OUR ATTEMPT HAS BEEN to relate a general personality structure to specific social contexts—namely, an occupational structure and an organizational structure—by demonstrating the intimate relationship between personality and political behavior. We shall now review what has been elaborated in the preceding pages as well as consider the theoretical significance of the findings and some of their implications regarding particular questions in the sphere of political behavior.

REVIEW OF THE FINDINGS

The six research hypotheses considered in this study have been substantiated. Our findings in these respects may be summarized as follows.

Professional politicians are distinguished from nonpoliticians in terms of a dogmatic personality structure. The professional politician, as a modal type, is more closed-minded than the nonpolitician. Moreover, this distinctive political personality is characterized by an authoritarian orientation toward power.

The dogmatism personality syndrome varies in significant degree along the traditional political continuum such that distinctive personality structures are found in association with various political parties and diverse political ideologies. Significant variations of personality structure exist with regard to ideological positions of the political left and those of the political right. Concerning distinctions between political extremists and political moderates the following is found. Extreme liberals tend to be less dogmatic than moderate liberals. Yet extreme conservatives tend to be neither more nor less dogmatic than moderate conservatives. The political left tends to be more open-minded, while the political right tends to be more closed-minded.

Significant relationships are found between various degrees of religious practice and the dogmatic personality structure, that is, there is a positive correlation between religious practice and the degree of dogmatism. Moreover, our findings show a parallel between religious affiliation, political ideology, and dogmatism. A left-right political pattern in terms of religious affiliation and the intensity of its practice parallels the dogmatism pattern in terms of liberal and conservative political ideologies. No other associations were found between social backgrounds, including social class, and the dogmatic personality structure of professional politicians.

CONCLUDING OBSERVATIONS

On the basis of these findings, considered in the context of our interpretations and other relevant aspects, the following concluding observations may be made concerning the role of personality in political behavior.

Varying methods of political recruitment influence the type of personality structure that is "attracted" into the political system. Where relatively free self-recruitment is allowed to operate, the dogmatic and power-oriented authoritarian personality is attracted to the political profession. Under these conditions personal power may be a dominant value of the politician and, as such, a potent incentive for political activity. This type of individual appears to be a modal personality type for the political profession. Where, however, the recruitment process is controlled, there is a differential type of personality selection that is apt to be more consistent with the needs and the purposes of the organization.

Personality structure appears to be a determinant of political ideology and political party preference, a condition suggested by the compatible relationship between ideological content and ideological structure. Moreover, the findings suggest that the sociocultural, particularly the political, context of political ideologies influences the structure of an ideology and its methodology, which in turn affect the selection and the attraction of personalities into its political system. Factions within political parties may be a function of significant variations in personality structure. The parallel association of political ideology, religious ideology, and dogmatism indicates a theoretical consistency, since the religious ideologies are in most cases intertwined with the respective political ideology. These party differences observed in personality structure for political leaders, however, may not be similarly true for political followers. Precise relationships between personality and political behavior should not be expected unless individuals are substantially involved in politics or are considerably committed to specific ideologies. The greater is the degree of personal involvement in political activity, the greater is the part played by personality. The fact that some of the observed relationships between personality and political dynamics did not obtain for the nonpoliticians supports this contention.

Social backgrounds have an instrumental role in the development and formation of the individual dogmatic personality. Such factors, in fact, may reveal—although this is not the situation in this study—categorical variations of a significant degree, such as in the case of religion. This suggests, therefore, that the dogmatic personality is chiefly the product of the kind of social structures and experiences to which the individual is exposed. Political and religious ideologies, in this respect, may be both influences and consequences of this type of personality structure. Differences in dogmatism and personality structure in terms of political ideologies, parties, and factions however are not related to the social-class foundations of the respective subjects.

The more pertinent question regarding the relationship between personality structure and political ideology is the value which this has for action within the political system, and particularly within the decision-making process. Such practical significance of these findings and their implications for political behavior is exemplified in that the pivotal element of consensus-cleavage, specifically illustrated in the forms of political alliances and changes in political party affiliation, seems to be—at least partly—a function of significant similarity and differences in underlying personality structures. Accordingly, the question of stability in political systems, involving forms of disorganization such as party factions and defections, is related to the degree of variation among the personality structures that comprise these respective groups.

Thus, political behavior to some degree appears to be a function of personality structure. It facilitates the acceptance or creation of options that are personally meaningful, and the rejection of those options which are similarly incompatible.[1] Each personality, therefore, is receptive to only a limited number of the total range of available political ideologies (forms) and organizations, namely, those which have the greatest functional value in meeting its requirements. The precision of the relationship between personality and political behavior, however, is related to the degree of one's personal involvement and commitment to politics.

DIMENSIONS FOR FURTHER RESEARCH

Any research undertaking inevitably concludes with the need for further research as suggested in the implications of the findings and their interpretation. Our data suggest that consideration for future experiments should be given to the following questions.

A more precise delineation of the professional politician, in terms of such considerations as different levels and functions of political office within a particular political system, may indicate an association of differential personality structures. Greater precision along these lines may be applicable in the framework of various sociological classifications of professional politicians. Particularly desirable in this respect are more thorough analyses distinguishing between the personality structure of the elective (self-recruited) and the appointive (recruited) political functionary. These entire schemata, of course, hopefully may be related to other types of *homo politicus*, that is, to decision-makers functioning similarly in spheres other than the political.

As for the question of the relationship between personality structure and political ideologies and parties, future considerations should be given to the influence which the particular sociocultural—especially the political—context has on these ideologies, and the influence of these in turn on the kind of personality structures that are found within the respective political systems. Thus, more cross-cultural research is needed to ascertain the role of such differential elements as history, tradition, and national character.

Equally instrumental would be contrasts of political systems wherein the political party structure and the bureaucratic structure are significantly diversified, and wherein the political stimuli, such as parties, are more or less varied or constricted. For example, would differential political systems, such as a two-party structure, or various forms of government, such as a monarchy, reveal significant variations in personality from those which have been observed here for a multiparty structured parliamentary form of government? Then, too, our findings in these respects are limited to political leaders. It would be well to compare such data with similar findings for political followers, the *homo civicus*. Contrasting research in these dimensions should be particularly beneficial for greater theoretical precision.

These considerations suggested for future experiments are not meant to be exhaustive. They are offered, however, as dimensions which appear to need more immediate precisioning which should lead to a greater predictive potential for political behavior, particularly in relation to the crucial sociological elements of political consensus and political cleavage, and the stable functioning of political systems.

THEORETICAL IMPLICATIONS

What then is the relationship between personality and social systems? In the light of the above considerations it would seem to follow logically that social systems recruit and/or develop particular personality structures according to the functional requisites of the social system. As Fromm states, "In order for any society [social system] to function well, its members must acquire the kind of character which makes them want to act in the way that they have to act as members of society [social system]. . . . They have to desire what objectively is necessary for them to do."[2] The basic principle here would seem to be true of all types of social systems, that is, in order for social systems to function as they have been structured to function, the personality systems involved have to function in harmony with the social system. The theoretical significance of this issue is seen in that social systems may recruit personalities that by and large do not or cannot function effectively within particular social systems. This raises, then, the question of the congruence or the compatibility between personality structure and social system.

Cohen suggests that there are two different questions in this issue.[3] Some situations involve only a question of "fitness" between personality structures and social systems, that is, a compatibility which is beneficial to the effective functioning of both systems. On the other hand, some situations may involve more specifically a question of "dependency" between particular personality structures and social systems, such that certain personality systems are strategically necessary to the functioning of specific social systems.[a] Then, too, some situations may involve both "fitness" and "dependency."

Now what happens, as Inkeles asks, to a social system that is marked by the substantial lack of congruence (which is always only a matter of degree) between the requirements of the personality system and the requisites of the social system?[4] The results would seem to be some degree of dysfunction and/or change in either or both of the systems. Inkeles and Levinson delineate four kinds of congruent situations: ideal, unstable (incongruous systems), institutionally generated incongruence (changes within the social system), and characterologically induced noncongruence (the introduction of personality structures into functionally inappropriate social systems).[5] Congruence (fitness and dependency) would seem to be mutually beneficial—that is, for the effective and efficient function of the social system and the psychological gratifica-

---

[a] Perhaps this relationship is more strategic for particular roles within the system.

tion (function) of the personality system—such that both are capable of achieving their respective goals with minimum "effort." Any situation, however, which brings about incongruence or noncongruence is apt to result in dysfunctional consequences for either or both systems, that is, change within either system is apt to disrupt the "fitness" or "dependency" between the two. Briefly, a substantial change in one system will mean a substantial change in the other. Similarly, to perpetuate one is to perpetuate the other.[b] Thus, the stability and the change in social systems and social organization are to an extent a function of incongruity which they share with the personality systems involved therein. The greater the congruity—the more perfect the "fit"—the more stable the organization and the more minimal is social change.[c]

The question now is what evidence can be given that particular kinds of political structures or forms of government require certain kinds of personalities to function therein. Does a democratic state or system require democratic (open-minded) personalities, and does an authoritarian state or system require authoritarian (closed-minded) personalities? The dogmatic and authoritarian personality contains those psychological elements which are considered to be pathological to such an extent that they inhibit one's contribution to the democratic process.[6] Yet, dogmatic and authoritarian personalities can and do function within democratic structures. Dogmatism and authoritarianism

---

[b] As Levinson points out, "an individual's political role may not be entirely congenial to him; the fit between role and dynamics is seldom perfect. An incongruent role has the effect of perpetuating and perhaps intensifying inner conflicts and anxieties. In addition, change in a political ideology or affiliation may have consequences for the personality." Daniel J. Levinson, "The Relevance of Personality for Political Participation," *Public Opinion Quarterly*, XXIII (1958), 8.

[c] This relates specifically to the issue of consensus-cleavage as discussed above, as well as to the question of defections involving the lack of compatibility between ideological structure and ideological content.

are each continuous rather than discrete variables. The democratic and the authoritarian personalities represent, not distinct
psychological syndromes, but rather two ideal types that characterize the polar extremes of a unidimensional syndrome.[7]
Accordingly, every individual possesses, in varying proportions,
characteristics of both the democratic and the authoritarian
personality. Seen in this respect, congruence between personality structure and any social structure, such as the political,
is always a matter of degree, as is the functionality of the
system, which is a consequence of this congruence.

The position has been stated often that the forms and structures of political organization (particularly democracy or
totalitarianism) depend upon the modal personality or national
character of the particular nation. Recall our mention in Chapter I of Aristotle's remark (*Politics*) about the necessity of
fitting the constitution of a city to the character of the people.
DeTocqueville stated: "The manners [character] of the Americans of the United States are the *real* cause which renders it
the only one of the American nations that is able to support a
democratic government."[8] Modern students of national character are convinced that societies with long histories of democracy are peopled by a majority of individuals who possess a
personality structure that is conducive to democracy, and that
those societies which have experienced prolonged or recurrent
forms of authoritarian, totalitarian, or dictatorial government
are inhabited by a proportionally large number of individuals
with respectively congruent personality structures.[9] Unfortunately, lacking in this respect is the empirical evidence from
nationwide studies of national character.

Nevertheless, this does not mean that all members of a particular nation are either democratic or authoritarian as the
case may be, but only that the active co-operation of a sufficient number of the respective type is required for the system
to function in either a democratic or an authoritarian manner.

The system must be supported—functionally supported. Dicks, for example, has shown that German prisoners of war who were fanatic about Nazi ideology possessed a personality structure that differed significantly from the norm of German national character.[10] This importance of the functional congruence between personality structure and social structure for the preservation of a particular type of political system is shown also in a similar study of the Soviet sociopolitical system and its citizens.[11] Speaking specifically of democratic societies, Berelson states that one requirement of the electorate is the possession of a suitable personality structure:

> Certain kinds of personality structure are not congenial to a democratic society, could not operate successfully within it, and would be destructive of democratic values. Others are more compatible with or even disposed toward the effective performance of the various roles which make up the democratic political system.[12]

Yet it does not follow necessarily that there is a completely incongruous relationship between democratic political *activity* and the dogmatic-authoritarian personality structure. Democracy as a form of government is based upon different political positions—or, if one may say so, upon open and closed orientations, high and low dogmatism, high and low authoritarianism. As a functional system, democracy may need both democratic and authoritarian "types" of personality structure. As Shils states:

> a liberal democratic society itself could probably not function satisfactorily with only "democratic liberal personalities" to fill all its roles. The tasks of a liberal democratic society are many and many different kinds of personality structures are compatible with and necessary for its well being. Even authoritarian personalities are especially useful in some roles in democratic societies and in many other roles where they are not indispensable, they are at least harmless.[13]

It is possible that all decision-making cannot be—and perhaps, from a functional perspective, should not be—the result of the democratic process. Certain roles may need more closed-minded and authoritarian personalities, just as others may need more open-minded and democratic personalities. Similarly, authoritarian structures may be functionally dependent to some extent upon more open-minded and democratic personalities. The crucial factor in either situation is the modality of the personality structure that characterizes the system.

The question is to what extent are particular societies or political systems prone—more or less—to authoritarian rule. It would seem that any society containing predominantly authoritarian social structures and personalities would be more susceptible to nondemocratic forms of government. It is, as we have stated, a commonplace statement that authoritarian and democratic political structures produce respective types of national character. But the reverse of this position may be advanced just as logically, namely, that the form of government is related to the kind of people that are recruited into the political structure or who are potential recruits for the system. As Ebenstein states, "The traditional analysis of political dictatorship has been centered on the motivation of dictatorial leaders, driven by lust for power and sadistic cravings for domination. The followers and subjects of a dictatorship are viewed exclusively as 'victims' who just happen to fall into the misfortune of oppressive rule."[14] But, certain types of political behavior just do not happen simply. Some people and some nations, we suggest, are more "dictatorship prone" than others. Any political system, of whatever form, needs the active support of a sufficient number of people. The system, to repeat, must be functionally supported.

A FINAL WORD

We have attempted to show the role, and consequently the analytical value, that personality has in social situations. The

personality approach, as used here in combination with sociological elements, offers another theoretical dimension for the
analysis of the decision-making process and other forms of
social action.

While personality is a central element in social behavior, it
is not the only one. Our presentation and perspective, however, would challenge the more strictly sociological approaches
that consider personality as simply secondary, derivative, and
noncausal.[15] Personality is essentially the result, a product, of
the process of socialization and other social experiences. But
it acquires through this formation a dynamic element and, as
such, becomes actively instrumental and even causal in the
social process. Personality thus does hold the answer to some
of the questions which are presented in sociological analysis.

On the other hand, neither is this meant to imply that political structures and political behavior—or any form of social
structure and social behavior—are totally or simply the passive
result of personality structures involved therein. Political behavior, including the structures which present the framework
within which it takes place, is also a question of more strictly
sociological elements, such as parties, pressure groups, socioeconomic strata, history, given social situations, and so forth.
And in specific instances such factors as these may be more
significant—perhaps even primary. It would be erroneous to
give the impression that political behavior is a mere epiphe-
nomenon of personality dynamics. Yet, these constitute one
element that appears instrumental in the organization and
direction of political behavior.

The relevance of personality in social organization remains
a largely neglected problem in contemporary sociological research and theory, although of late there has developed some
interest in this area.[16] Still it has been a common tendency to
introduce personality and psychological explanations only when
deviation is involved; little use of these has been made to

explain regularity or "normality" of social processes, behavior, and organization.[17] Yet, even in this respect the concern for personality has been confined by and large to cultural studies, such as "national character studies," in which the sociologists have not played a major role. It seems evident that the personality approach need not be so restricted but that more comprehensive sociological analysis in the same dimension can be applied quite fruitfully to particular types of social systems such as the political.

Both sociological and psychological elements—particularly considered in their dynamic relationship—offer a more thorough assessment of social behavior as well as of individual behavior. To place exclusive or undue stress on one at the expense of the other is to yield an incomplete explanation of human behavior and social organization that at its best is distorted.

Notes

[1] Daniel J. Levinson, "The Relevance of Personality for Political Participation," *Public Opinion Quarterly,* XXIII (1958), 7–8.

[2] Erich Fromm, "Individual and Social Origins of Neurosis," *American Sociological Review,* IX (1944), 380–384.

[3] Yehudi A. Cohen, *Social Structure and Personality* (New York: Holt, Rinehart & Winston, 1961), p. 225.

[4] Alex Inkeles, "Personality and Social Structure" in Robert K. Merton *et al.* (eds.), *Sociology Today* (New York: Basic Books, 1959), p. 267.

[5] Alex Inkeles and Daniel J. Levinson, "National Character" in Gardner Lindzey, *Handbook of Social Psychology* (Reading, Mass.: Addison-Wesley, 1954), pp. 977–1020.

[6] For a treatment of this question see Robert Lane's "Notes on a Theory of Democratic Personality" in *Political Ideology* (Glencoe: The Free Press, 1962), pp. 401–412.

[7] Martin and Westie, while agreeing with this position, speak of a "tolerant personality" which is described as a syndrome distinct from the "authoritarian personality." James G. Martin and Frank R. Westie, "The Tolerant Personality," *American Sociological Review,* XXIV (1959), 521–528. See a more elaborate treatment of this thesis in James G. Martin, *The Tolerant Personality* (Detroit: Wayne State University Press, 1964). See also for a consideration of this question

Ronald Taft, "Is the Tolerant Personality Type the Opposite of the Intolerant?" *Journal of Social Psychology*, XLVII (1958), 397–405.

[8] Alexis DeTocqueville, *Democracy in America* (New York: Oxford University Press, 1947), p. 213.

[9] Alex Inkeles, "National Character and Modern Political Systems" in Francis L. K. Hsu (ed.), *Psychological Anthropology* (Homewood: The Dorsey Press, 1961), pp. 193–194.

[10] Henry V. Dicks, "Personality Traits and National Socialist Ideology," *Human Relations*, III (1950), 111–153.

[11] Alex Inkeles, Eugenia Hanfmann, and Helen Beier, "Modal Personality and Adjustment to the Soviet Socio-Political System," *Human Relations*, XI (1958), 3–22.

[12] Bernard Berelson, "Democratic Theory and Public Opinion," *Public Opinion Quarterly*, XVI (1952), 313–316.

[13] Edward A. Shils, "Authoritarianism: 'Right' and 'Left' " in Richard Christie and Marie Jahoda (eds.), *Studies in the Scope and Method of "The Authoritarian Personality"* (Glencoe: The Free Press, 1954), pp. 48–49.

[14] William Ebenstein, *Today's Isms* (Englewood Cliffs: Prentice-Hall, 1961), p. 101.

[15] For an elaboration of this theoretical perspective, see Alex Inkeles and Daniel J. Levinson, "The Personal System and Social Structure in Large Scale Organizations," *Sociometry*, XXVI (1963), 217–230.

[16] Daniel J. Levinson, "Role, Personality, and Social Structure in the Organizational Setting," *Journal of Social and Abnormal Psychology*, LVIII (1959), 170–180; Yehudi A. Cohen, *Social Structure and Personality* (New York: Holt, Rinehart & Winston, 1961); Robert Presthus, *The Organizational Society* (New York: Alfred A. Knopf, 1962); Alex Inkeles and Daniel J. Levinson, "The Personal System and Social Structure in Large Scale Organizations," *Sociometry*, XXVI (1963), 217–230; and Daniel J. Levinson, "Toward a New Social Psychology: The Convergence of Sociology and Psychology," *Merrill-Palmer Quarterly of Behavior and Development*, X (1964), 77–88.

[17] Daniel J. Levinson, "The Relevance of Personality for Political Participation," *Public Opinion Quarterly*, XXIII (1958), 4–5.

Appendices

APPENDIX A

The Rokeach Dogmatism Scale

(Form D-10)

1. The worst crime a person can commit is to attack publicly the people who believe in the same thing he does.
2. It is often desirable to reserve judgment about what's going on until one has a chance to hear the opinions of those one respects.
3. Fundamentally, the world we live in is a pretty lonely place.
4. In the history of mankind there have probably been just a handful of really great thinkers.
5. In the long run the best way to live is to pick friends and associates whose tastes and beliefs are the same as one's own.
6. Most people just don't know what's good for them.
7. Once I get wound up in a heated discussion I just can't stop.
8. In this complicated world of ours the only way we can know what is going on is to rely upon leaders or experts who can be trusted.
9. A person who thinks primarily of his own happiness is beneath contempt.
10. While I don't like to admit this even to myself, I sometimes have the ambition to become a great man.

APPENDIX B

Social Background Characteristics of Political Sample

TABLE 16

PARLIAMENTARY EXPERIENCE OF POLITICAL SAMPLE

Party	Legislature III		Legislatures I and II		Legislatures I, II, and III		Legislatures I, III, and Constituent Assembly		Total	
DC	13	41.9	7	22.5	9	29.0	2	6.4	31	99.8
MSI	7	38.8	7	38.8	2	11.1	2	11.1	18	99.8
PCI	12	48.0	5b	20.0	6	24.0	2	8.0	25	100.0
PDI			1	33.3			2	66.6	3	99.9
PLI	3	27.2	5c	45.3			2	18.1	10d	90.6
PRI	1	20.0					4b	80.0	5	100.0
PSDI	4	50.0			1	12.5	3	37.5	8	100.0
PSI	9a	42.8	8	38.0	2	9.5	2	9.5	21	99.8
MISTO	3	42.8	2	28.5	1	14.2	1	14.2	7	99.7
Totals	52	40.6(%)	35	27.3	21	16.4	20	15.6	128	99.9

aOne had served in Constituent Assembly.
bOne had served in pre-Republic legislatures.
cTwo had served in Constituent Assembly.
dMinus one Liberal that had served in Legislatures I and III.

TABLE 17

GEOGRAPHICAL DISTRIBUTION OF POLITICAL SAMPLE
FOR CONSTITUENCIES REPRESENTED

Party	North		Central		South		Total	
DC	13	41.9	2	6.4	16	51.6	31	99.9
MSI	5	27.7	3	16.6	10	55.5	18	99.8
PCI	10	40.0	3	12.0	12	48.0	25	100.0
PDI					3	100.0	3	100.0
PLI	6	54.5	1	9.0	4	36.3	11	99.8
PRI	2	40.0	2	40.0	1	20.0	5	100.0
PSDI	6	75.0	1	12.5	1	12.5	8	100.0
PSI	11	52.3	2	9.5	8	38.0	21	99.8
MISTO	2	28.5			5	71.4	7	99.9
Totals	55	42.6(%)	14	10.8	60	46.5	129	99.9

TABLE 18

REGIONAL DISTRIBUTION OF POLITICAL SAMPLE
FOR CONSTITUENCIES REPRESENTED

North		Central		South	
Piedmont	6	Tuscany	3	Abruzzi and Molise	7
Aosta Valley	1	Umbria	4	Campania	13
Lombardy	15	The Marches	2	Apulia	10
Trentino-Alto Adige	1	Latium	5	Basilicata	2
Veneto	6		14 (11%)	Calabria	11
Friuli-Venezia Giulia	7			Sicily	16
Liguria	5			Sardinia	1
Emilia-Romagna	14				60 (47%)
	55 (43%)				

TABLE 19

AGE DISTRIBUTION OF POLITICAL SAMPLE

Party	31 - 35		36 - 45		46 - 55		56 - 65		66 - 75		Total		Mean
DC	2	6.4	10	32.2	13	41.9	5	16.1	1	3.2	31	99.8	48.4
MSI	1	5.5	6	33.3	6	33.3	3	16.6	2	11.1	18	99.8	50.8
PCI	2	8.0	13	52.0	4	16.0	6	24.0			25	100.0	46.3
PDI					2	66.6	1	33.3			3	99.9	53.8
PLI			1	9.0	6	54.5	4	36.3			11	99.5	53.2
PRI					1	20.0	3	60.0	1	20.0	5	100.0	60.5
PSDI			4	50.0	3	37.5	1	12.5			8	100.0	46.7
PSI	2	9.5	9	42.8	6	28.5	4	19.0			21	99.8	46.4
MISTO			2	28.5	3	42.8	1	14.2	1	14.2	7	99.7	51.9
Totals	7	5.4(%)	45	34.8	44	34.1	28	21.7	5	3.8	129	99.8	49.0

TABLE 20

EDUCATIONAL BACKGROUNDS OF POLITICAL SAMPLE

Level Completed	DC	MSI	PCI	PDI	PLI	PRI	PSDI	PSI	MISTO	TOTAL	%
Elementary	1		2					2		5	3.8
Lower Media	1		2		1			1		5	3.8
Upper Media		1	2	1				3		7	5.4
University (nondegree)	2	3	5				1	1		12	9.3
University (degree)	27	14	14	2	10	5	7	14	7	100	77.5
Totals	31	18	25	3	11	5	8	21	7	129	99.8

TABLE 21

FIELDS OF UNIVERSITY EDUCATION OF POLITICAL SAMPLE

Educational Field	DC	MSI	PCI	PDI	PLI	PRI	PSDI	PSI	MISTO	TOTAL	%
Jurisprudence	12[a][b]	8[a]	7	2[c]	7[a]	3	3	10[a]	5[a]	57	44.1
Engineering			2		1	1	2			6	4.6
Letters and philosophy	7	2	4				1	3		17[d]	13.1
Medicine	2	2			1		1		2	8	6.2
Education	1							1		2	1.5
Economic sciences	5		3							8	6.2
Natural sciences	1		1							2	1.5
Political sciences	1	4	2			1	1	1		10[e]	7.7
Other		1			1					2	1.5
None	2	1	6	1	1			6		17	13.1
Totals	31	18	25	3	11	5	8	21	7	129	99.5

a One has degree also in political science.
b One has degree also in letters and philosophy.
c One has degree also in political science and one in philosophy.
d Total, considering multiple degree holders, should be 19 and 14.7 percent.
e Total, considering multiple degree holders, should be 16 and 12.4 percent.

TABLE 22

RELIGIOUS BACKGROUNDS OF POLITICAL SAMPLE

Party	Catholic		Nonbelievers		Other		Total	
DC	31						31	100.0
MSI	18						18	100.0
PCI	2	8.0	23	92.0			25	100.0
PDI	3						3	100.0
PLI	11						11	100.0
PRI	3	60.0	2	40.0			5	100.0
PSDI	5	62.5	3	37.5			8	100.0
PSI	7	33.3	13	61.9	1	4.7	21	99.9
MISTO	6	85.7			1	14.2	7	99.9
Totals	86	66.5(%)	41	31.7	2	1.5	129	100.0

TABLE 23

OCCUPATIONAL BACKGROUNDS OF POLITICAL SAMPLE

	DC	MSI	PCI	PDI	PLI	PRI	PSDI	PSI	MISTO	Total	%
Lawyer	9	5	4	1	3	3		8	2	35	27.1
Lawyer and university professor	3	1			1		2			7	5.4
Functionary	2		1							3	2.3
Journalist	1	5	5		1		1	2		15	11.6
Clerk-accountant		1						1		2	1.5
Industrialist				1	2				1	4	3.1
Elementary school teacher	1	1								2	1.5
Secondary school teacher	7	1	2					4		14	10.8
Physician							1	1		2	1.5
Physician and university professor	2				1		1		1	5	3.8
Laborer or farmer	1		3						1	5	3.8
Publicist		2	3	1			1	1		8	6.2
Syndicalist	1	1	2					1	2	7	5.4
Engineer					1	1		2		4	3.1
Merchant	2						2			4	3.1
Chemist	1		1							2	1.5
Other		1a	2b		2c	1d		1e		7	5.4
None	1		2							3	2.3
Totals	31	18	25	3	11	5	8	21	7	129	99.4

aLanguage teacher.
bOne artist; one architect.
cOne magistrate; one banker.
dPractical economist.
eCultural writer.

APPENDIX C

Social Background Characteristics of Nonpolitical Control Sample

TABLE 24

POLITICAL PARTY PREFERENCES
OF CONTROL SAMPLE

Party	N	%
DC	139	31.8
MSI	60	13.7
PCI	35	8.0
PDI	28	6.4
PLI	44	10.0
PRI	28	6.4
PSDI	37	8.4
PSI	40	9.1
Other	3	.6
Unknown	22	5.0
Totals	436	99.4

TABLE 25

AGE DISTRIBUTION OF CONTROL SAMPLE

Age Category	N	%
31 - 35	122	27.9
36 - 45	137	31.4
46 - 55	113	25.9
56 - 65	51	11.6
66 - 75	10	2.2
76 - plus	2	.4
Totals	435	99.4

TABLE 26

EDUCATIONAL BACKGROUNDS OF CONTROL SAMPLE

Level Completed	N	%
Elementary	41	9.4
Lower Media	52	11.9
Upper Media	110	25.2
University (nondegree)	40	9.2
University (degree)	193	44.2
Totals	436	99.9

TABLE 27

RELIGIOUS BACKGROUNDS OF CONTROL SAMPLE
BY POLITICAL PARTY PREFERENCE

Party	Catholic		Protestant		Nonbelievers		Other		Total	
DC	139	100.0							139	100.0
MSI	58	96.6	1	1.6			1	1.6	60	99.8
PCI	22	61.1			11	30.5	3	8.3	36	99.9
PDI	28	100.0							28	100.0
PLI	39	88.6	1	2.2	2	4.5	2	4.5	44	99.8
PRI	26	92.8			2	7.1			28	99.9
PSDI	36	100.0							36	100.0
PSI	34	85.0	3	7.5	3	7.5			40	100.0
Other	2	66.6			1	33.3			3	99.9
Unknown	20	90.9	1	4.5	1	33.3			22	99.9
Totals	404	92.6 (%)	6	1.3	20	4.5	6	1.3	436	

TABLE 28

OCCUPATIONAL BACKGROUNDS
OF CONTROL SAMPLE

Occupation	N	%
Lawyer	36	8.2
Lawyer and university professor	3	.6
University professor	9	2.0
Functionary	24	5.5
Journalist	25	5.7
Clerk-accountant-expert	92	21.1
Industrialist	19	4.3
Elementary school teacher	25	5.7
Secondary school teacher	32	7.3
Physician	49	11.2
Physician and university professor	1	.2
Laborer or farmer	37	8.4
Publicist	6	1.3
Syndicalist	5	1.1
Engineer	33	7.5
Merchant	9	2.0
Military officer	3	.6
Other (nonprofessional)	13	2.9
Other (professional)	9	2.0
None	6	1.3
Totals	436	98.9

APPENDIX D

Mean Political Party Responses to Individual Items of Dogmatism Scale

TABLE 29

MEAN PARTY RESPONSES TO INDIVIDUAL ITEMS OF DOGMATISM SCALE

Scale Item*	POLITICAL SAMPLE									NON-POLITICAL SAMPLE TOTAL
	DC	MSI	PCI	PDI	PLI	PRI	PSDI	PSI	TOTAL	
1. Worse crime is to attack those of similar beliefs.	1.35	1.50	1.32	2.00	.81	1.80	1.62	1.00	1.26	.60
2. Reserve judgment until you hear other opinions.	1.61	1.38	1.48	-.33	1.72	1.60	1.50	.81	1.38	.49
3. World we live in is a pretty lonely place.	.41	.22	-1.56	.66	-.63	.80	.37	-.14	-.14	.33
4. There is just a handful of really great thinkers.	.61	1.16	-.64	1.00	.63	1.00	1.12	-.04	.39	.12
5. Pick friends with beliefs similar to one's own.	.83	.88	.36	1.66	.27	.40	1.75	.61	.73	.10
6. Most people don't know what's good for them.	1.45	1.50	-.48	1.33	1.27	1.20	1.25	.38	.85	.43
7. Once I get wound up, I just can't stop.	.41	.44	-.56	.00	-.27	-.20	-.50	.14	.00	.14
8. To know what is going on, rely upon leaders.	.03	.16	-1.12	.33	-.81	-1.20	-.12	-1.09	-.48	.23
9. A person who thinks of his own happiness is beneath contempt.	1.54	1.83	1.72	2.00	1.00	2.00	1.25	1.47	1.52	.75
10. Ambition to become a great man.	-.32	.44	.00	.66	.00	.60	.75	-.90	-.09	.45

*Abbreviated form.

APPENDIX E

Values Derived Fort in Tests of Significance Between Mean Dogmatism Scores for Political Parties and Political Ideologies

TABLE 30

VALUES DERIVED FOR t IN TESTS OF SIGNIFICANCE* BETWEEN
MEAN DOGMATISM SCORES FOR PARTIES IN POLITICAL SAMPLE

Party	MSI	PCI	PDI	PLI	PRI	PSDI	PSI
DC	.925	4.246[a]	.345	1.782	.010	.424	2.839[b]
MSI		5.573[a]	.085	3.125[b]	.769	.335	3.552[b]
PCI			2.451[d]	1.522	2.674[c]	3.803[a]	.660
PDI				1.469	.397	.118	1.488
PLI					1.443	2.218[d]	.657
PRI						.469	1.567
PSDI							2.311[d]

*Key for level of statistical significance:

a = .001   c = .02
b = .01   d = .05

TABLE 31

VALUES DERIVED FOR t IN TESTS OF SIGNIFICANCE*
BETWEEN MEAN DOGMATISM SCORES OF LOCI OF
POLITICAL CONTINUUM FOR PERSONAL IDEOLOGY

Locus	2	3	4	5	6
1	1.326	3.404^b	4.239^a	.110	4.76
2		1.778^e	2.654^c	.475	2.97
3			1.398	1.333	1.60
4				2.499^d	.07
5					3.13

TABLE 32

VALUES DERIVED FOR t IN TESTS OF SIGNIFICANCE*
BETWEEN MEAN DOGMATISM SCORES OF LOCI OF
POLITICAL CONTINUUM FOR PARTY IDEOLOGY

Locus	2	3	4	5
1	2.139^d	4.313^a	2.294^d	5.44
2		1.607	.779	2.50
3			.142	1.52
4				.94

*Key for level of statistical significance:

a = .001   c = .02
b = .01   d = .05

APPENDIX F

Supplementary Data on Dogmatism Scores and
rho Values for Ideological Affinities

TABLE 33

MEAN DOGMATISM SCORES OF POLITICAL SAMPLE
BY PARLIAMENTARY EXPERIENCE

Legislatures	N	Mean	S.D
III	51	4.52	6.5
II and III	32	5.65	8.1
I, II, III	21	7.14	5.9
I, II, III, and C	17	6.05	5.4

F = .768 dfb, 3; dfw, 117 $p > .05$

TABLE 34

MEAN DOGMATISM SCORES OF POLITICAL SAMPLE
BY GEOGRAPHICAL REGION OF REPRESENTED CONSTITUENCI

Region	N	Mean	S.D.
North	55	4.25	7.18
Central	14	7.07	5.36
South	60	6.31	6.42

F = 1.736 dfb, 2; dfw, 126 $p > .05$

TABLE 35

MEAN DOGMATISM SCORES OF CONTROL SAMPLE
BY AGE CATEGORY

Age Category	N	Mean	S.D.
31 - 35	122	3.86	5.67
36 - 45	137	3.48	4.98
46 - 55	113	3.56	5.10
56 - 65	51	3.94	6.12
66 - 75	10	4.60	4.73
76 plus	2	1.50	5.50

F = 219   dfb, 5; dfw, 429 p > .05

TABLE 36

MEAN DOGMATISM SCORES OF CONTROL SAMPLE
BY EDUCATIONAL LEVEL

Level Completed	N	Mean	S.D.
Elementary	41	3.14	4.23
Lower Media	52	4.21	6.64
Upper Media	110	4.24	4.64
University (nondegree)	40	2.72	6.79
University (degree)	193	3.49	5.19

F = .889   dfb, 4; dfw, 431 p > .05

TABLE 37

MEAN DOGMATISM SCORES OF CONTROL SAMPLE
BY RELIGION

Religion	N	Mean	S.D
Catholic	14	1.14	3.2
Protestant	6	7.33	4.9
Other	6	2.16	4.8
None	20	2.80	5.3
Catholic (1)*	144	3.82	6.0
Catholic (2)	95	4.18	4.9
Catholic (3)	66	3.39	4.8
Catholic (4)	64	3.75	4.8
Catholic (5)	20	2.80	6.1

$F = 1.37$ dfb, 8;   dfw, 426 $p > .05$

* Catholic categories indicated here refer to the intensity of religious practice: one, attends church at least once a week; two, nearly every week; three, about once a month; four, only for the major festivities; and five, never attends church.

TABLE 38

MEAN RESPONSES OF INDIVIDUAL PARTIES
FOR MACHIAVELLIAN QUESTION

Party	N	Mean	S.D.
DC	31	.74	2.31
MSI	18	1.22	1.31
PCI	25	.28	2.37
PDI	3	.33	2.62
PLI	11	.09	2.53
PRI	5	1.00	1.67
PSDI	8	-.75	3.26
PSI	21	.71	1.97

$\underline{F}$ = .733 $\underline{dfb}$, 7; $\underline{dfw}$, 114 $\underline{p}$ > .05

TABLE 39

VALUES DERIVED FOR rho IN RANK CORRELATIONS
OF PERCEIVED IDEOLOGICAL AFFINITY AMONG POLITICAL PARTIES

Party	MSI	PCI	PDI	PLI	PRI	PSDI	PSI
DC	.809*	.798*	.881*	.952**	.976**	.917*	.452
MSI		.523	.821*	.940**	.833*	.548	.321
PCI			.702	.786*	.774	.881*	.976**
PDI				.881*	.952**	.714	.286
PLI					.929**	.702	.381
PRI						.905*	.548
PSDI							.631

$*p \leq .05$
$**p \leq .01$

APPENDIX G

The Election of Deputies

A Note on the Italian Electoral System[1]

The method of voting in Italy is known as the *scrutinio di lista* (list vote). Although there are many variants of this method which has been adopted by several countries on the European continent, the basic principle is that the elector votes, not for an individual candidate or candidates, but rather for a party list of candidates. Strictly speaking, therefore, the competition is not among individual candidates but rather among the political parties. Yet every election under this method involves an intraparty as well as an interparty cleavage.

Each of the parties participating in the election submits for each constituency a list of candidates numbering not less than three nor more than the number of deputies to be elected.[2] In addition to this a party list of candidates is drawn up for the *Collegio Unico*

[1] Much of the following is taken from the Laws for the Election of the Chamber of Deputies, dated February 5, 1948.
[2] Special provisions in many of these matters are made for the region of Valle d'Aosta, the smallest of the nineteen regions.

Nazionale (National Single College) for the sole purpose of the utilization of residual votes. This latter list must be presented by not less than twenty active candidates of the same party-list. Each single list declares itself joined to a National Single College list, generally that of the same party. These party lists are printed on the ballot separately from each other.[3] The voter has only one list vote which he casts by marking an "X" over the party symbol on the ballot.[4]

The electoral-list figure (the sum of valid votes obtained by each list in the individual constituencies) serves as a basis for assigning the number of deputies to each list, according to the Hondt system.[5] To do this, the total number of valid votes is divided by the number of deputies to be elected plus three, to obtain thus the electoral quotient. Each list then is awarded as many representatives as the number of times the electoral quotient is contained in the electoral figures on each list. After the number of deputies assigned to each list has been established, the district central office determines the graduated list of the candidates of each list according to the respective individual figures. Where individual figures are equal, the order of presentation on the list prevails.

The number of parliamentary seats not attributable to any list due to the insufficiency of quotients or of candidates, as well as the number of residual votes of each list, are forwarded to the Court of Cassation to be attributed to the National Single College lists to which they have declared themselves joined. The sum of the residual votes of all the lists is divided by the number of seats to be attributed. The resulting quotient constitutes the electoral quotient for the National Single College. The sum of the residual votes given to each list is divided by this quotient. The result represents the number of parliamentary seats to be assigned to

[3] Between March 18, 1951, and March 27, 1956, it was possible for different parties to unite in one electoral list.

[4] For the 32 constituencies in the 1958 national elections there were 327 lists of candidates representing a total of 5,980 candidates for the Chamber of Deputies. This is an average of ten candidates per parliamentary seat. *Annuario Statistico Italiano* (Rome: Istituto Centrale di Statistica, 1960), p. 144.

[5] For reference see Robert G. Neumann, *European and Comparative Government* (New York: McGraw-Hill, 1951), pp. 630–631.

each list. The remaining posts are attributed respectively to the lists for which these last divisions have given greater remainders and, in case of equality of remainders, to the list which received more residual votes in the National Single College. The candidates then are proclaimed elected according to the order on the list.

Each party's share of the parliamentary seats corresponds roughly to its share of the total number of votes polled. Under this method the seats are awarded generally to the candidates in the order in which they appear on the party list.[6] No by-elections (special or off-term) are held. A seat that becomes vacant for whatever reason is attributed to the candidate who, on the same list, immediately follows the last one elected in the order verified by the controlling body. Under the list-vote method these individuals are as duly elected as the original officeholders.[7]

As we can see from this description, the voting system and the electoral procedure attempt to allow every vote the possibility of being given successful acknowledgment. This method, however, gives the party organization a great deal of power and correspondingly limits the rights of the voter in selecting the candidates for office. The order of the names on the party list is determined by the party organization before the election. Thus, although the electors choose between parties, the parties may decide for themselves—and generally do—who shall occupy whichever seats they win.[8]

The *scrutinio di lista* scheme purports to give the voter some voice in the selection of individuals by allowing him to indicate his preferences for candidates, but in practice this provision seldom proves effective, since experience shows that only very rarely has the personal popularity of a candidate succeeded in upsetting the

[6] J. F. S. Ross, *Elections and Electors* (London: Eyre and Spottiswoode, 1955), pp. 64–65.

[7] Of the total of 596 deputies elected in the 1958 national elections 490 were named from results within the constituency, 67 on the basis of residual votes, and 39 in the Chamber of Deputies as substitutions declared for those elected also as senators and for those making a selection between more than one constituency. *I Deputati e Senatori del Terzo Parlamento Repubblicano* (Rome: La Navicella, 1960), p. 618.

[8] Ross, *op. cit.*, pp. 64–65.

printed order.[9] Voluntary preferences from one to four, depending upon the number of parliamentary seats in the electoral district, may be expressed. Since no names appear on the ballot, the voter must write in his preferences. Accordingly, only the literate have the privilege of preferential voting, and this is all the more significant in the light of the high rate of illiteracy in Italy. Only about one-third of the voters in fact take advantage of this right.[10]

Moreover, it is well known that some parties have sufficient control of their voters that they can predict the outcome of the election as far as their own list is concerned, even though this may "upset" the order of the list. Prominent leaders are placed at the head of electoral lists, and these individuals usually receive the majority of the preferential vote. There are many other methods by which the party can exercise control in the election of parliamentary representatives. For example, it is possible for candidacies to be placed simultaneously for the Chamber and the Senate (not more than one list), and for a candidate to be listed on as many as three electoral lists for the Chamber, that is, in three electoral districts.[11] Individuals successful on more than one list simply take their preference—or, more likely, that of the party organization.[12] Thus, the electors determine how many parliamentary seats each party shall receive, but it is the party organization that decides who shall occupy them.

[9] *Ibid.*, p. 165.

[10] See Luigi D'Amato, "Il Voto di Preferenza," *Rassegna Italiana di Sociologia,* III (1962), 205–258.

[11] Instances of these two procedures are by no means rare. In the 1958 national elections twenty-five deputies were elected to both houses, and twenty-one deputies were elected in more than one constituency. (*I Deputati e Senatori del Terzo Parlamento Repubblicano,* p. 618.) As we may deduce from this procedure, it is not necessary that the candidate reside legally in the constituency in which he seeks election. In the samples drawn for this study twelve percent of the political subjects were not residents of the constituency that they represented. Nearly three-fourths of these were living in the city of Rome.

[12] The candidate placed on the list for the National Single College, if successful, is required to accept that seat.

Selected Bibliography

Adams, John C. and Barile, Paolo. *The Government of Republican Italy*. Boston: Houghton Mifflin, 1961.

Adler, Alfred. *Practice and Theory of Individual Psychology*. New York: Harcourt, Brace, & World, 1924.

Adorno, T. W.; Frenkel-Brunswik, Else; Levinson, Daniel J.; and Sanford, R. Nevitt. *The Authoritarian Personality*. New York: Harper & Row, 1950.

Alexander, Franz. *Our Age of Reason*. Philadelphia: J. P. Lippincott, 1951.

Almond, Gabriel A. *The Appeals of Communism*. Princeton: Princeton University Press, 1954.

Almond, Gabriel A. and Verba, Sidney. *The Civic Culture*. Princeton: Princeton University Press, 1963.

Barber, James D. *The Lawmakers*. New Haven: Yale University Press, 1965.

Barker, Edwin N. "Authoritarianism of the Political Right, Center, and Left." *Journal of Social Issues*, (1963), 19:63–74.

Barzini, Luigi. *The Italians*. New York: The Atheneum Press, 1964.

Bell, Wendell; Hill, Richard J.; and Wright, Charles R. *Public Leadership*. San Francisco: Chandler, 1961.

Bendix, Reinhard and Lipset, Seymour M. "Political Sociology: An Essay and Bibliography." *Current Sociology*, (1957), 6:79–169.

Berelson, Bernard. "Democratic Theory and Public Opinion." *Public Opinion Quarterly*, (1952), 16:313–30.

Bonnard, Augusta. "On Political Creed and Character." *Psychoanalysis*, (1954), 2:55–59.

Brim, Orville G.; Glass, David C.; Lavin, David E.; and Goodman, Norman. *Personality and Decision Processes*. Stanford: Stanford University Press, 1962.

Browning, Rufus P. and Jacob, Herbert. "Power Motivation and the Political Personality." *Public Opinion Quarterly*, (1964), 28:75–90.

Cassinelli, C. W. "The Totalitarian Party." *Journal of Politics*, (1962), 24:111–141.

Christie, Richard. "Authoritarianism Re-examined" in Richard Christie and Marie Jahoda (eds.), *Studies in the Scope and Method of "The Authoritarian Personality."* Glencoe: The Free Press, 1954.

Christie, Richard. "Eysenck's Treatment of the Personality of Communists." *Psychological Bulletin*, (1956), 53:411–430.

Christie, Richard and Jahoda, Marie (eds.). *Studies in the Scope and Method of "The Authoritarian Personality."* Glencoe: The Free Press, 1954.

Christie, Richard and Cook, Peggy. "A Guide to Published Literature Relating to the Authoritarian Personality Through 1956." *Journal of Psychology*, (1958), 45:171–199.

Cohen, Yehudi A. *Social Structure and Personality*. New York: Holt, Rinehart & Winston, 1961.

Craig, Gordon A. *Europe Since 1815*. New York: Holt, Rinehart & Winston, 1961.

Dahl, Robert A. *Who Governs?* New Haven: Yale University Press, 1961.

D'Amato, Luigi. "Il Voto di Preferenza." *Rassegna Italiana di Sociologia*, (1962), 3:205–258.

D'Antonio, William V. and Ehrlich, Howard J. (eds.). *Power and Democracy in America.* Notre Dame: University of Notre Dame Press, 1961.

―――. "Democracy in America: Retrospect and Prospect" in William V. D'Antonio and Howard J. Ehrlich (eds.), *Power and Democracy in America.* Notre Dame: University of Notre Dame Press, 1961.

Davies, James C. *Human Nature in Politics.* New York: John Wiley & Sons, 1963.

Decter, Moshe. *The Profile of Communism.* New York: Collier Books, 1961.

Dicks, Henry V. "Personality Traits and National Socialist Ideology." *Human Relations,* (1950), 3:111–153.

DiRenzo, Gordon J. (ed.). *Concepts, Theory, and Explanation in the Behavioral Sciences.* New York: Random House, 1966.

Downs, Anthony. *An Economic Theory of Democracy.* New York: Harper & Row, 1957.

Drake, David. "A Psychoanalytic Interpretation of Social Ideology." *American Imago,* (1955), 12:193–196.

Ebenstein, William. *Today's Isms.* Englewood Cliffs: Prentice-Hall, 1961.

Einaudi, Mario and Goguel, Francois. *Christian Democracy in Italy and France.* Notre Dame: University of Notre Dame Press, 1952.

Eysenck, H. J. *Psychology of Politics.* London: Routledge & Kegan Paul, 1954.

―――. *Sense and Nonsense in Psychology.* Baltimore: Penguin Books, 1957.

―――. "The Psychology of Politics and the Personality Similarities Between Fascists and Communists." *Psychological Bulletin,* (1956), 53:431–438.

Farris, Charles D. "Authoritarianism As a Political Behavior Variable." *Journal of Politics,* (1956), 18:61–82.

Frenkel-Brunswik, Else. "Interaction of Psychological and Sociological Factors in Political Behavior." *American Political Science Review,* (1952), 46:44–65.

―――. "Further Reflections by a Contributor to 'The Authoritarian Personality'" in Richard Christie and Marie Jahoda (eds.),

Studies in the Scope and Method of "The Authoritarian Personality." Glencoe: The Free Press, 1954.

Frenkel-Brunswik, Else; Levinson, Daniel J.; and Sanford, R. Nevitt. "The Antidemocratic Personality" in Eleanor E. Maccoby, Theodore M. Newcomb, and Eugene L. Hartley (eds.), *Readings in Social Psychology.* New York: Holt, Rinehart & Winston, 1958.

Fromm, Erich. *Escape From Freedom.* New York: Holt, Rinehart & Winston, 1941.

Goldhamer, Herbert and Shils, Edward A. "Types of Power." *American Journal of Sociology,* (1939), 45:171–182.

Gross, Feliks. *The Seizure of Political Power.* New York: Philosophical Library, 1958.

Groth, Alexander J. "Isms in Totalitarianism." *American Political Science Review,* (1964), 58:888–901.

Hagen, Everett E. *On the Theory of Social Change.* Homewood, Illinois: The Dorsey Press, 1962.

Harned, Louise. "Authoritarian Attitudes and Party Activity." *The Public Opinion Quarterly,* (1961), 25:393–399.

Hennessy, Bernard. "Politicals and Apoliticals: Some Measurements of Personality Traits." *Midwest Journal of Political Science,* (1959), 3:336–355.

Hughes, Everett C. "Personality Types and the Division of Labor." *American Journal of Sociology,* (1928), 33:754–768.

Hyman, Herbert H. *Political Socialization.* Glencoe: The Free Press, 1959.

Hyman, Herbert H. and Sheatsley, Paul B. "The Authoritarian Personality—A Methodological Critique" in Richard Christie and Marie Jahoda (eds.), *Studies in the Scope and Method of "The Authoritarian Personality."* Glencoe: The Free Press, 1954.

Inkeles, Alex. "Some Sociological Observations on Culture and Personality Studies" in Clyde Kluckhohn and Henry A. Murray (eds.), *Personality in Nature, Culture, and Society.* New York: Alfred A. Knopf, 1956.

———. "Personality and Social Structure" in Robert K. Merton, Leonard Broom, and Leonard S. Cottrell (eds.), *Sociology Today.* New York: Basic Books, 1959.

———. "National Character and Modern Political Systems" in

Francis L. K. Hsu (ed.), *Psychological Anthropology*. Homewood, Illinois: The Dorsey Press, 1961.

Inkeles, Alex and Levinson, Daniel J. "National Character" in Gardner Lindzey (ed.), *Handbook of Social Psychology*. Cambridge: Addison-Wesley, 1954.

_____. "The Personal System and Social Structure in Large Scale Organizations." *Sociometry*, (1963), 26:217–230.

Inkeles, Alex; Hanfmann, Eugenia; and Beier, Helen. "Modal Personality and Adjustment to the Soviet Socio-Political System." *Human Relations*, (1958), 11:3–22.

Janowitz, Morris and Marvick, Dwaine. "Authoritarianism and Political Behavior." *Public Opinion Quarterly*, (1953), 17:185–201.

Kaplan, Bert (ed.), *Studying Personality Cross-Culturally*. New York: Harper and Row, 1961.

Kluckhohn, Clyde and Murray, Henry A. (eds.), *Personality in Nature, Culture, and Society*. New York: Alfred A. Knopf, 1956.

Kogan, Norman. *A Political History of Postwar Italy*. New York: Frederick A. Praeger, 1961.

_____. *The Politics of Italian Foreign Policy*. New York: Frederick A. Praeger, 1963.

_____. *The Government of Italy*. New York: Thomas Y. Crowell, 1964.

Laing, Lionel H., *et al. Source Book in European Government*. New York: William Sloane Associates, 1950.

Lane, Robert E. "Political Personality and Electoral Choice." *American Political Science Review*, (1955), 45:173–190.

_____. *Political Life*. Glencoe: The Free Press, 1959.

_____. *Political Ideology*. Glencoe: The Free Press, 1962.

LaPalombara, Joseph. *Interest Groups in Italian Politics*. Princeton: Princeton University Press, 1964.

Lasswell, Harold D. *Psychopathology and Politics*. New York: The Viking Press, 1960; original edition: Chicago: University of Chicago Press, 1930.

_____. *Power and Personality*. New York: W. W. Norton, 1948.

_____. "The Selective Effect of Personality on Political Participation" in Richard Christie and Marie Jahoda (eds.), *Studies in the*

Scope and Method of "The Authoritarian Personality." Glencoe: The Free Press, 1954.

Lasswell, Harold D. and Kaplan, Abraham. *Power and Society.* New Haven: Yale University Press, 1950.

Lasswell, Harold D.; Lerner, Daniel; and Rothwell, C. Easton. *The Comparative Study of Elites.* Stanford University Press: Hoover Institute Series, 1952.

Lee, Alfred McClung. *Multivalent Man.* New York: George C. Braziller, 1966.

Levinson, Daniel J. "Authoritarian Personality and Foreign Policy." *Journal of Conflict Resolution,* (1957), 1:37–47.

―――. "The Relevance of Personality for Political Participation." *Public Opinion Quarterly,* (1958), 23:3–10.

―――. "Role, Personality, and Social Structure in the Organizational Setting." *Journal of Abnormal and Social Psychology,* (1959), 58:170–180.

―――. "Idea Systems in the Individual and in Society" in George K. Zollschan and Walter Hirsch (eds.), *Explorations in Social Change.* Boston: Houghton Mifflin, 1964.

―――. "Toward a New Social Psychology: The Convergence of Sociology and Psychology." *Merrill-Palmer Quarterly of Behavior and Development,* (1964), 10:77–88.

Lindquist, John H. "Socioeconomic Status and Political Participation." *Western Political Quarterly,* (1964), 17:608–614.

Lindzey, Gardner (ed.), *Handbook of Social Psychology.* Cambridge: Addison-Wesley, 1954.

Linton, Ralph. "The Concept of National Character" in Alfred H. Stanton and Stewart E. Perry (eds.), *Personality and Political Crisis.* Glencoe: The Free Press, 1951.

Lipset, Seymour M. *Political Man.* London: William Heineman, 1960.

Mangone, Gerard J. "Part IV: Italy" in Taylor Cole (ed.), *European Political Systems.* New York: Alfred A. Knopf, 1959.

Manheim, Henry L. "Personality Differences of Members of Two Political Parties." *Journal of Social Psychology,* (1959), 50:261–268.

Martin, James G. *The Tolerant Personality.* Detroit: Wayne University Press, 1964.

Marvick, Dwaine (ed.). *Political Decision-Makers: Recruitment and Performance.* Glencoe: The Free Press, 1961.

————. "Political Decision-Makers in Contrasting Milieus" in Dwaine Marvick (ed.), *Political Decision-Makers: Recruitment and Performance.* Glencoe: The Free Press, 1961.

Maslow, A. H. "The Authoritarian Character Structure." *Journal of Social Psychology*, (1943), 18:401–411.

Matthews, Donald R. *The Social Background of Political Decision-Makers.* New York: Random House, 1954.

————. *U.S. Senators and Their World.* Chapel Hill: University of North Carolina Press, 1960.

McClosky, Herbert. "Conservatism and Personality." *American Political Science Review*, (1958), 52:27–45.

McConaughy, John B. "Certain Personality Factors of State Legislators in South Carolina." *American Political Science Review*, (1950), 44:897–903.

Merton, Robert K. "Bureaucratic Structure and Personality" in Clyde Kluckhohn and Henry A. Murray (eds.), *Personality in Nature, Culture, and Society.* New York: Alfred A. Knopf, 1956.

Metz, Harold W. and Thomson, Charles A. H. *Authoritarianism and the Individual.* Washington: The Brookings Institution, 1950.

Meyer, Alfred G. *Communism.* New York: Random House, 1960.

Meynaud, Jean. "General Study of Parliamentarians." *International Social Science Journal*, (1961), 13:513–543.

Michels, Robert. *Political Parties.* New York: Collier Books, 1962.

Milbrath, Lester W. *Political Participation.* Chicago: Rand McNally, 1965.

Milbrath, L. W. and Klein, W. W. "Personality Correlates of Political Participation." *Acta Sociologica*, (1962), 6:52–66.

Mitchell, William C. "The Ambivalent Social Status of the American Politician." *Western Political Quarterly*, (1959), 3:683–698.

————. "Occupational Role Strains: The American Elective Public Official." *Administrative Science Quarterly*, (1956), 1:210–288.

Money-Kyrle, R. E. *Psychoanalysis and Politics.* London: Gerald Duckworth, 1951.

Mosca, Gaetano. *The Ruling Class.* New York: McGraw-Hill, 1939.

Munro, William B. and Ayearst, Morley. *The Governments of Europe.* New York: Macmillan, 1954.

Mussen, Paul H. and Wyszynski, Anne B. "Personality and Political Participation." *Human Relations,* (1952), 5:65–82.

Poggi, G. "Studio dell'Ideologia nella Sociologia dei Partiti Politici." *Rassegna Italiana di Sociologia,* (1961), 2:205–220.

Presthus, Robert. *The Organizational Society.* New York: Alfred A. Knopf, 1962.

Reich, Wilhelm. *The Psychology of Fascism.* New York: Orgone Institute Press, 1946.

Roe, Anne. *Psychology of Occupations.* New York: John Wiley & Sons, 1956.

Rokeach, Milton. *The Open and Closed Mind.* New York: Basic Books, 1960.

———. "Political and Religious Dogmatism: An Alternative to the Authoritarian Personality." *Psychological Monographs,* #425, (1956), LXX, #18, Whole issue.

———. "The Nature and Meaning of Dogmatism." *Psychological Review,* (1954), 61:194–204.

Rokeach, Milton; McGovney, Warren C.; and Denny, M. Ray. "A Distinction Between Dogmatic and Rigid Thinking." *Journal of Abnormal and Social Psychology,* (1955), 51:87–93.

Rokeach, Milton and Fruchter, Benjamin. "A Factorial Study of Dogmatism and Related Concepts." *Journal of Abnormal and Social Psychology,* (1956), 53:356–360.

Rose, Arnold M. *Indagine sull'Integrazione Sociale in Due Quartieri di Roma.* Università di Roma, Centro Richerche di Sociologia Empirica, 1959.

———. "Prejudice, Anomie, and the Authoritarian Personality." *Sociology and Social Research,* (1966), 50:141–147.

Ross, J. F. S. *Elections and Electors.* London: Eyre and Spottiswoode, 1955.

Saenger, Gerhart. *The Social Psychology of Prejudice.* New York: Harper & Row, 1953.

Sanford, R. Nevitt. "The Approach to the Authoritarian Personality" in J. L. McCary (ed.), *Psychology of Personality*. New York: Logos Press, 1956.

Sartori, Giovanni. *Il Parlamento Italiano*. Naples: Edizioni Scientifiche Italiane, 1963.

————. "La Sociologia del Parlamento." *Studi Politici*, (1961), 8:352–382.

————. "Parliamentarians in Italy." *International Social Science Review*, (1961), 13:583–599.

Schulze, Rolf. "A Shortened Version of the Rokeach Dogmatism Scale." *Journal of Psychological Studies*, (1961), 13:93–97.

Schumpeter, Joseph A. *Capitalism, Socialism, and Democracy*. New York: Harper & Row, 1950.

Seligman, Lester G. "The Study of Political Leadership." *American Political Science Review*, (1950), 44:904–911.

Sforza, Carlo. *The Real Italians*. New York: Columbia University Press, 1942.

Shils, Edward A. "Authoritarianism: 'Right' and 'Left'" in Richard Christie and Marie Jahoda (eds.), *Studies in the Scope and Method of "The Authoritarian Personality."* Glencoe: The Free Press, 1954.

Smith, M. Brewster; Bruner, Jerome S.; and White, Robert W. *Opinions and Personality*. New York: John Wiley & Sons, 1956.

Spiro, Melford E. "Social Systems, Personality, and Functional Analysis" in Bert Kaplan (ed.), *Studying Personality Cross-Culturally*. New York: Harper & Row, 1961.

Spitz, David. *Democracy and the Challenge of Power*. New York: Columbia University Press, 1958.

————. "Power and Personality: The Appeal to the 'Right Man' in Democratic States." *American Political Science Review*, (1958), 52:84–97.

Spranger, Eduard. *Types of Men*. Halle: Max Niemeyer Verlag, 1928.

Stagner, Ross. "Attitude Toward Authority: An Exploratory Study." *Journal of Social Psychology*, (1954), 40:197–210.

Stanton, Alfred H. and Perry, Stewart E. *Personality and Political Crisis*. Glencoe: The Free Press, 1951.

Stewart, Don and Hoult, Thomas. "A Social-Psychological Theory of the Authoritarian Personality." *American Journal of Sociology,* (1959), 65:274–279.

Taylor, Irving A. "Similarities in the Structures of Extreme Social Attitudes." *Psychological Monographs,* (1960), LXXIV, #489, Whole issue.

Tomasic, Dinko. *Personality and Culture in Eastern European Politics.* New York: W. Stewart, 1948.

Wahlke, John C.; Eulau, Heinz; Buchanan, William; and Ferguson, Leroy C. "The Role of the Representative: Some Empirical Observations on the Theory of Edmund Burke." *American Political Science Review,* (1959), 55:742–756.

Weitman, Morris. "More Than One Kind of Authoritarian." *Journal of Personality,* (1962), 30:193–208.

Wrightman, Lawrence S.; Radloff, Roland W.; Horton, David L.; and Mecherikoff, Michael. "Authoritarian Attitudes and Presidential Voting Preference." *Psychological Reports,* (1961), 8:43–46.

Zariski, Raphael. "Party Factions and Comparative Politics: Some Preliminary Observations." *Midwest Journal of Political Science,* (1960), 4:27–51. Italian reference: "Partiti e Fazioni." *Studi Politici,* (1961), 8:383–403.

Index

257